AF513518

Enterprise Resource Management

Enterprise Resource Management

D. J. Syam

(Retd.) AGM, BHEL, Hardwar

Ex.-Prof. EMPI B-School, Chattarpur, New Delhi

Ane Books Pvt. Ltd.

New Delhi ♦ Chennai

Enterprise Resource Management
D.J. Syam

© Author, 2023

Price: Rs. 1495/-
Pages : 254 (HB)
Size: Crown (6.25" X 9.50")
Paper Quality (GSM):80

Published by

Ane Books Pvt. Ltd.
4821, Parwana Bhawan, 1st Floor, 24 Ansari Road, Darya Ganj,
New Delhi - 110 002, Tel.: +91(011) 23276843-44, Fax: +91(011) 23276863
e-mail: kapoor@anebooks.com, Website: www.anebooks.com

Branch Office:

- Avantika Niwas, 1st Floor, 19 Doraiswamy Road, T. Nagar,
  Chennai - 600 017, Tel.: +91(044) 28141554, 28141209
  e-mail: anebookschennai@gmail.com, rathinam@anebooks.com

Please be informed that the author and the publisher have put in their best efforts in producing this book. Every care has been taken to ensure the accuracy of the contents. However, we make no warranties for the same and therefore shall not be responsible or liable for any loss or any commercial damages accruing thereof. Please do consult a professional where appropriate.

ISBN: 978-81-8052-142-3

All rights reserved. No part of this book may be reproduced in any form including photocopying, microfilms, photoprints, storage in any retrieval system, transmission in any permanent or temporary form, without the prior written consent of the publisher.

Printed at : R.K. Offset Process, New Delhi.

Dedicated to

the professional managers
engaged in the management and administration
of Business and Industrial Enterprises.

के. रवि कुमार
अध्यक्ष एवं प्रबंध निदेशक

K. RAVI KUMAR
Chairman & Managing Director

भारत हेवी इलेक्ट्रिकल्स लिमिटेड
Bharat Heavy Electricals Limited

Foreword

Business Enterprises, both industrial and non-industrial, require different kinds of resources as vital inputs for their successful operation. These resources, some of which may be scarce, need regular attention of the enterprise management for their planned procurement, efficient depolyment and effective utilization for achieving viable operational sustenance and probable growths.

In today's globalized competitive business environment, it has become imperative that the resources are not only efficiently managed, but also sustained efforts are required to be made for optimal deployment and utilization of available resources across the board in the enterprise.

In this book titled 'Enterprise Resource Management', the author Sri D.J. Syam, has ably attempted to discuss various aspects of resource management in a structured and discernible presentation for due appreciation of the line managers whose roles and contributions are cirtical for the objectives of resource-focused business administration for successful operations.

In view of the above, I commend the author for his efforts in writing this book and recommend the same to business managers who have to efficiently deal with enterprise resources for achieving business excellence.

(K. Ravi Kumar)

"बीएचईएल हाउस" सिरी फोर्ट, नई दिल्ली-110049 दूरभाष : (का.) 26001001, 26001002, फैक्स : 011-26492043, 26493659
"BHEL HOUSE", Siri Fort, New Delhi-110049 Tel.: (O) 26001001, 26001002, Fax : 011-26492043, 26493659

Preface

All human endeavours whether they are for commercial or non-commercial purposes, require the deployment and utilization of resources of different kinds commensurate with the desired objectives. For business enterprises, particularly for industrial units, by the very nature of their operations, resources of the desired kinds are required as vital inputs for successful operation, viable sustenance and probable growth. Since business enterprises have to operate in a market driven competitive environment, there has to be adequate planning for the acquisition, deployment and eventual optimal utilization of the resources both in qualitative and quantitative terms, in conformity with the size of operation. Enterprise management as well as the line managers have to necessarily pay adequate attention to this aspect also besides other priorities relevant to the operations.

Since the business enterprises, especially the industrial units, operate with a multitude of variable conditions and constraints, line managers' roles and services are critical for successful operations. Therefore, adequate awareness and training in the matters of business management and administration become an imperative necessity for them to make positive result-oriented contributions; this is not only essential for successful sustenance of the enterprise, but also for their own career development and prospects. Enterprise Resource Management (ERM) will be one of the critical sets of activities that make big impacts on the operating results. Hence, managers posted in different functions and levels are to be made aware of these aspects regularly.

This book is an attempt to present certain operating aspects of Resource Management for the benefit of the practising corporate managers. While conceding that many of the corporate managers are already aware of many of these issues, nevertheless, an appreciation of the topics dealt with in this book may help managers in recapitulation and updating their knowledge base for enabling better preparedness professionally.

The author invites constructive criticism and suggestions for improvements in the coverage of this book.

Author

"Professional success cannot be achieved only through relevant education and training; it also requires a lot of work-experience and interaction with knowledgeable professionals; passive knowledge cannot replace work experience".

— Taken from a lecture given by a Management Educator.

THEMATIC REPRESENTATION OF RESOURCE DEPLOYMENT AND UTILIZATION IN AN INDUSTRIAL ENTERPRISE

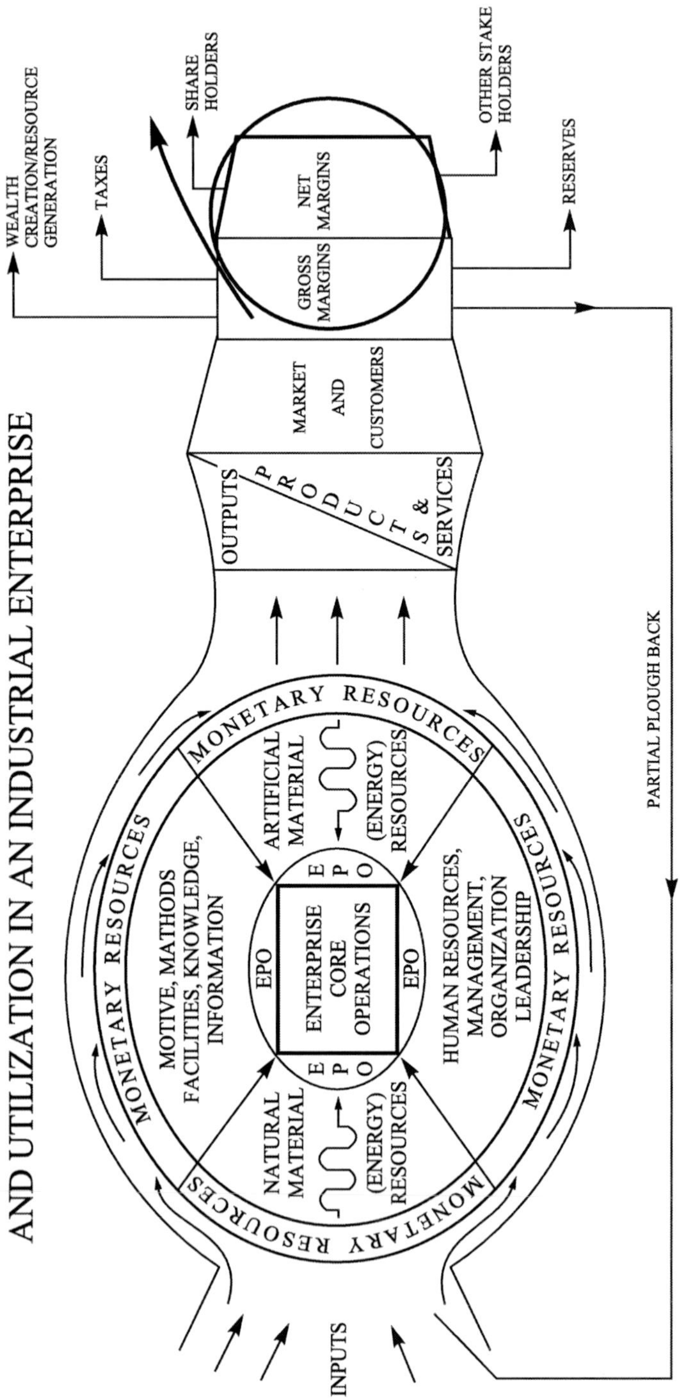

Acknowledgement

I express my sincere thanks to the friends and ex-colleagues from business and industry for their encouragement and valuable suggestions in articulating the various topics covered in this book.

I am also grateful to Sri K. Ravi Kumar, the respected CMD of BHEL, New Delhi, for agreeing to give a recommendatory 'FOREWORD' for this book and particularly indebted to Sri B. Kumar, SDGM of BHEL, Hardwar, for rendering his guidance and help in carrying out the resource-optimization exercises incorporated in Chapter-16 of this book.

Lastly, but not the least, I am thankful to Mr. Sunil Saxena and Mr. J.R. Kapoor of Ane Books Pvt. Ltd., New Delhi for their acceptance for printing and publishing of the book for the benefit of the practicing corporate business managers.

– D. J. Syam

Contents

Chapter-3 Commercial Exploitation of Natural Resources: Socio-Political and Environmental Issues 27-36

Chapter-4 Adopting Strategies for Optimal Deployment and Utilization of Resources in Business Enterprises 37-48

Chapter-5 Budgeting and Budgetary Controls for Resource Management in Business/Industrial Enterprises 49-60

Chapter-6 Asset Management in Industrial Enterprises 61-66

Chapter-9 Inventory Control: A Tool for Material Resource Optimization 81-90

Chapter-10 Management of Energy — A Vital Resource for Enterprise Operations 91-97

Chapter -11 Total Quality Management (TQM) Approach Helps in Resource Optimization for Business Excellence 99-112

CHAPTER-1

RESOURCES: VITAL INPUTS FOR BUSINESS ENTERPRISE OPERATIONS

"Resourcefulness is a key factor in entrepreneurial success."
—*A Business Management Educator*

1.1 Introduction

For successfully running any business enterprise, industrial or non-industrial, resources of different kinds are required to be mobilized and utilized after getting them from the available sources, or at times, even got to be created artificially to serve the purpose in mind. These resources can exist both in concrete physical forms, or may be in the invisible abstract forms as well. The abstract resources get manifested through knowledge based ideas and concepts, which in turn can be converted through appropriate efforts and processes, into concrete physical forms as desired so as to be able to utilize the same for productive purposes/end results in mind.

These resources, both concrete and abstract, when deployed judiciously with pre-conceived intentions, and in turn result in generation/regeneration of further resources, thus helping in creation of goods, services and wealth; and this cycle can go on and on, with creative and innovative ideas injected into the process.

1.2 Generalised Definition

Now confining our discussions here to the topic of resource acquisition, mobilization/deployment and utilization for business enterprises, the resources can generally be defined as:

"Physical items and conceptual ideas available from both natural as well as artificial sources, when gainfully exploited for creation of further resources in the form of products, services and resultant wealth of economic value, may be called resources for business endeavours."

Another definition often put forward goes like this:

"Resource is something physical or abstract, which can be converted into a product, process, or service of utility having an economic value."

Thus, from the above definitions, any resource which does not help in creation of further resources of any economic value, has no appreciable role to play in business endeavours, and therefore best be excluded from the scope of this discussion.

1.3 Resources for Business Enterprises

In the case of a composite industrial enterprise, incorporating a comprehensive set of activities encompassing product—engineering/design, product technology and manufacturing, testing, marketing, customer services and other related operational aspects, the need for resource mobilization and deployment also become rather wide-spread, and thus, all connected issues and aspects come with into play. Therefore, if we attempt to discuss resource management issues pertaining to such composite industrial enterprises, we can make a comprehensive treatment of the subject encompassing all aspects of resource management. This approach will enable grasping the basics as well as the practical aspects of **Enterprise Resource Management (ERM).**

1.3.1 Resource Categorization for Business Enterprises

For establishing and running a business-cum-industrial enterprise, the basic resources required, by traditional considerations are three type: **Man, Machine and Materials.** However, there are other supporting resources which also play important roles in the successful operations of the enterprise: namely- **Motive, Methods, Management and Money;** thus these **'7-Ms'** when deployed with proper discretion and in optimal proportions, the enterprise not only can attain successful sustenance but can also gain an impetus for perpetuality and growth.

1.3.1.1 The '7-Ms': the resources that play vital roles

Whether the enterprise is small or a large one, all the above seven resources will come into play in varying proportions depending on the size and complexity of the organization, technological processes involved and the products to be produced and the services to be rendered for commercial exploitation.

1.3.1.2 The concrete, abstract, semi-abstract resources, and the linking resource

While the first 3-Ms, *i.e.*, Man, Machine and Materials can be considered as 'Concrete Resource', the next 3Ms *i.e.*, Motive, Methods/Knowledge and Management can be considered as 'Abstract Resources and Semi-Abstract Resources', and the last, but not the least, Money is a 'Linking Resource' which pervades into all areas of industrial and business endeavours.

1.3.1.3 The behind the scene resource: energy

There is another 'Behind the Scene Resource': Energy — which is normally taken for granted, but it plays a vital role in running an enterprise, specially an industrial unit.

1.3.2 Resources: The Vital Inputs for Business Enterprise Operations

We shall discuss briefly, in the following paragraphs, the role and significance of all the above mentioned resources in a business/ industrial enterprise.

1.3.2.1 3Ms :The concrete resources (Man, Machine, Material)

(*i*) **Man (Human Resources):** All categories of people working for and in the organization, *i.e.*, owners/promoters, employees of different categories manning various functions, sub-contractors, associates who make direct and indirect productive contributions in running the enterprise.

However, human resources working in and for an industrial or a business enterprise will require proper skills, training and motivation for making positive contributions towards its operational goals.

Notes: (*i*) *Human beings not making positive contributions of economic value cannot be considered as a Resource in business operation.*

(*ii*) *Please refer to para 15.4.0 in chapter-15 for a brief on Human Aspects of Resource Management.*

(*ii*) **Machine:** The machine is a generic term here, it refers to all facilities including the machines, equipments, devices etc. which are to be used for generation of saleable products and services; these will be mainly fixed-asset type of items on which capital expenditures will have to be incurred. The monetary investments made on Fixed Assets are called 'Capital Investment' which is different from the investments on shares, bonds, fixed deposits etc. as well as other monetary instruments (propagated by Financial Institutions, Companies, Banks etc.).

Note: *Machines and facilities which cannot be utilized for productive contribution of economic value, cannot be considered as a resource for business operations.*

(*iii*) **Materials:** These includes raw materials, components, finished and semi-finished products, purchase-resold, spares, tools and tackles, various other direct and indirect materials.

Notes: (*i*) *More about Material Resources is described below in paras 1.3.5, (1.3.5.1, 1.3.5.2, 1.3.5.3)*

(*ii*) *Materials which are available but Not usable for the enterprise's business, cannot be considered as a Resource; rather continued holding of these in the inventory can become a liability and a drain on financial resources.*

1.3.2.2 3Ms : The abstract and semi-abstract resources

Abstract Resources

(*i*) **Motive:** Motive is a rather abstract but a vital one which culminates into a forceful positive thinking that kindles entrepreneurial urges in human endeavours. In fact, all the above resources become rather redundant unless there is a strong motive for putting them to use for entrepreneurial endeavours for gains and wealth creation. Motive is an integral manifestation of Human Resources but to emphasize its importance, it is worthwhile to earmark this (motive) as a separate resource. **When there is a high degree of tuning between 'Man' and 'Motive' the enterprise tends to achieve excellence in performance utilizing the other resources to an optimum level.**

(*ii*) **Methods and Knowledge:** This is again an Abstract Resource predominantly conceptual in nature. Every business or industrial enterprise must necessarily have to have certain relevant methods (*i.e.,* systems, procedures, working processes, etc.) in practice, some documented and some unwritten, following certain well-established conventions to enable the personnel working there to perform respective jobs and discharge the assigned responsibilities towards the objectives and goals set forth by the enterprise management; devoid of proper methods (*i.e.,* systems, procedures, etc.), the organization will be like a blind-folded traveller on a busy street.

Therefore, this is a tool to be used by the management for a result-oriented systematic work-culture.

Here again, the Methods to be successfully conceived and effectively used, certain levels of 'Knowledge' inputs are required matching with the specific needs of the enterprise. 'Knowledge-Management' therefore, also becomes crucial for a result-oriented organizational approach to business management. Lack of adequate knowledge on relevant subjects and absence of updation of the same may, in the long run, critically affect the operational viability since business enterprise cannot always totally or heavily depend on external agencies for knowledge inputs for its sustenance and growth. Therefore, 'Knowledge' is also to be treated at par with the Method as a resource (which need regular updation/upgradation in a competitive business environment).

(*iii*) **Management: The Semi-abstract Resource: (**)** This is a vital resource, in fact a crucial human-resource-oriented driving force which steers and supervises the various activities in the enterprise towards an

---

(* *) *Management is an organizational concept for managing operations, but at the same time, it is also the physical embodiment of the organization; therefore, it has a dual existence in the form of a semi-abstract resource providing conceptual as well as physical leadership for the enterprise.*

organized and focused efforts for achieving the set goals and targets. Without an appropriate management setup in place, the enterprise will become a ship without a rudder, and thus tend to become directionless.

1.3.2.3 Money: The link-resource

Money is an all pervading driving force for any business organization. Money is a powerful resource as without adequate monetary support no venture, whether commercial or non-commercial, can even start. Earning money through generation of reasonable margins in business ventures is a central issue which motivates man to go for such ventures. However, there is a difference of opinion exists on this as financial wizards differ as to whether money at all be identified as a separate 'resource' since money involved everywhere; but taking into consideration the present-day commerce and trade in a global context, the predominant view is that Money should be earmarked as a separate Resource, since it is not very readily available without rather stringent conditions attached to it.

1.3.3 Energy: The 'Behind the Scene Resource'

Besides the '7-M' Resources discussed above, there is another important resource in the form of Energy which is required for running the operations; specially in an industrial enterprise, continuous and dependable supply of energy is essential since without energy supply, almost all industrial activities may come to a standstill. In practice, while **'3 Ms—The Concrete Resources'** get the most preferred attention, the Energy Resource, in most cases, is rather taken for granted, and hence tend to remain a 'behind the scene' resource. However, energy is derived mostly from the natural resources like solar rays, water, wind, biomass, fossil fuels and uranium, etc.; a part of the energy supplies can also come from certain artificial sources such as storage battery and fuel cells, but the quantum of such energy supply is rather limited, and not suitable for large scale industrial use because of technological and economic limitations th at persist at present.

Note: *Please refer to Chapter-10 for more on the subject.*

1.3.4 Judicious and Efficient Usage of Resources

Industrial enterprises, depending on the type of operations, technological processes followed, the end products and associated services rendered, require the utilization of considerable amounts of resources of the above kind in varying proportion: An appropriate strategy for judicious and optimal deployment and utilization of the resources is one of the most critical factors effecting the successful running of the enterprise. Everyone working in and for the enterprise have to be made conscious about this to avoid wastages and inefficient working culture.

1.3.5 More about Material Resources

Material resources come in two broad categories:

(*a*) Naturally occurring, (*b*) Artificially created.

Both categories find use in business and industry in different forms and specifications in conformity with the type of business line, products generated/dealt with, and the technological processes and designs preferred/followed:

1.3.5.1 Naturally occurring materials

Minerals and stones, jewels and precious stones, wood/timber, hydrocarbons and fossil fuels; seeds and fruits and foliages of different kinds—animals and animal products, various types of naturally occurring metals and non-metals, various types of naturally occurring salts and ceramic compounds, natural gases, even air, water and ice, mineral-based as well as organic and inorganic chemical compounds and their derivatives, medicinal plants and herbs, their derivatives, roots of plants, various agricultural and horticultural produce: all these find usage in industrial products and associated services. Even sunlight/rays and wind find usage for business purposes (mainly as energy source both for power generation as well as for industrial and scientific resource purposes).

1.3.5.2 Artificially created materials

Such as plastics and polymer-based compounds of various grades, synthetic yams, synthetic chemicals and their compounds/derivatives, formulated/synthesized drugs and pharmaceuticals, composites/fibrous compounds/products, etc., find use in various industrial products. In fact, rapidly depleting natural resources/materials and scarcity due to continuous over-exploitation, the industrial enterprises are increasingly on the lookout for alternative artificially created materials for various applications; some of these artificially created materials (such as Teflon, certain special grade glasses, ceramics and composites) show better mechanical and chemical properties for rigorous anticorrosive and toughened duty cycles/applications. Presently, material science R&D to a considerable extent is focused towards developing and inventing such artificially created futuristic new materials which find high-tech applications in scientific and industrial products and processes, besides also being used in household appliances, healthcare and food processing devices and implements. In fact, this is a technologically energized field, which is opening up new possibilities almost everyday, somewhere in the world, including India. We may see many new revolutionary developments and happenings in the areas in the coming decades, particularly in the fields of nano-technology (nano-materials), bio-technology, pharmaceuticals, electronics, energy development and food processing to mention a few, to cope up with ever-increasing demands resulting from continuously increasing population throughout the globe, coupled with increasing aspirations for better standards of living in various emerging societies.

1.3.5.3 Material resources from the seas and oceans

(*i*) Already, quite a large number of marine life items namely, fish and other marine animals, sea weeds, corals etc., are being captured/ extracted to meet increasing demands of food products and pharmaceutical uses; this exploration will continue.

(*ii*) Undersea petroleum and gas fields are being explored in a big way to meet increasing energy demands.

(*iii*) Plans are being actively persued for exploration/extraction of ocean-bed materials like minerals/metallic nuggets, methane hydrate crystals etc. in order to meet increasing industrial and domestic demands for products and energy.

> ***" None of us are as smart as all of us."***

CHAPTER-2

PLANNING RESOURCES FOR BUSINESS ENTERPRISES

"If you keep your eyes and ears open, ready to read a lot on relevant topics and willing to interact with knowledgeable people, information and knowledge will be at your command."

—Taken from a Management Institute Brochure

Remarks: Before going into details of the topic mentioned above we would like to state the following to clarify/define scope of the discussions in the following pages:

(*i*) We are attempting to discuss the topic in its plain and simple meaning for easier understanding of the sundry readers many of whom may not be adequately conversant with various nuances of sophisticated business management and administrative affairs (but of course, interested in enterprise's development and operational efforts).

(*ii*) In the last one decade or so, 'Enterprise Resource Planning (ERP)' as a business operation management tool is being propagated by various Management Consultant Groups in the light of global competitive business scenario and impressing upon Indian Business houses, particularly Industrial Enterprises, the need to adopt ERP to be able to face global competition successfully not only for enabling viable sustenance, but also for growth prospects in a competitive environment, by aligning their operating systems with those practised in the arena of International Trade and Commerce.

(*iii*) These ERP concepts are more sophisticated as compared to the traditional organisational operations planning processes. ERP is heavily based on IT-enabled computerized working systems requiring application of rather sophisticated softwares such as SAP/SAP-R3/my-SAP, Prima-Vera, etc., which in turn require the services of highly trained and skilled IT-savvy personnel in various functional areas and almost at all levels to make ERP workable in a business enterprise. Till date, only a very few Indian compaines have opted to adopt ERP, but not all of them with a satisfactory level of success. Application of ERP requires very good IT-enabled intra and extra-enterprise networking of all and sundry activities and functions to be successful and to sustain. This is not to opine that ERP is no good but it is as good as its practical adoptability in the Indian context; experienced managers say it is rather a costly option, without any guarantee of successful implementation. In Indian context, very large multiproduct industrial corporations with complex organizations may find it rather difficult to practise ERP successfully. Inter-functional work-culture differences may further aggravate the situation. ERP requires almost 100% IT-enabled working in all core functions with near perfect networking amongst them, as well as with concerned external agencies, and also with dedicated peripheral supporting services.

(*iv*) Considering the high costs involved in adopting ERP at one go throughout the organization, certain medium and large enterprises are opting for selective implementation of ERP in certain priority functional areas like budgeting and budgetary control, material management (inventory control in particular), production planning and control, pay roll, customer contract management, supply chain management/ logististics, etc.

Notes: (*i*) *With the prospects of concerned Management Conslting Groups providing close guidance through expert supervision services, many medium size trading and industrial enterprises in India have now adopted ERP processes and the trend is catching on gradually with many more enterprises planning opting for the same as success stories trickle in.*

(*ii*) *More about ERM and ERP scopes of activities with respect to business enterprises is discussed in Chapter-13.*

Planning Resources for Business Enterprises

Normally, resources for business enterprises do not come by themselves; a lot of thinking, planning and efforts have to go into this aspect for their acquisition in line with the business objectives set out, as well as for their optimal deployment and utilization, because most of these resources, as described in Chapter-1, come with a lot of monetary commitments and investments. There should be some conscious and well thought-out strategies before going in for their procurement and deployment so as to avoid these later becoming infructuous and a burden on the enterprise's operational viability. Therefore, adequate planning efforts have to necessarily go into resource acquisition and deployment. Taking the example of an industrial enterprise, most of the resources (in fact, all) as mentioned in Chapter-l will required to be systematically planned for procurement and deployment. In the following paragraphs, we shall deal with each type of resources with respect to their planning and deployment in business enterprises.

2.1 Motive

This resource, though abstract in nature, is very important as without motive nothing really happens in business endeavours.

2.1.1 Planning

Motives for business ventures cannot really be planned; it comes from entrepreneurial urges in some individuals or a group of like-minded individuals who start thinking of undertaking a project or business venture for which stimulation and encouragement can come from:

(*i*) Ventures being put up or being run successfully by other entrepreneurs in the surrounding/vicinity areas setting examples for encouragement.

(*ii*) Inventions and creative achievements of the individual or the group, who may see an opportunity and like to capitalize on this.

(*iii*) New opportunities offered by emerging markets and expanding customer needs.

(*iv*) Entrepreneurs/promoters are normally guided, by and large, by the following motivations to go in for capital investments on setting up an enterprise:

- to earn adequate/higher returns on investments (ROI) on a sustainable basis.
- to create wealth that results in perpetual economic sustenance and growth.
- to acquire a place of pride in the community of business enterprises and in the society at large.
- to fulfil the urges of taking challenge and attaining higher successes.
- to expand operations for better/optimum utilization of available resources.

Note: *There can be additional motives depending on the investor's preferences and psyche as well as certain environmental aspects that contribute to investment motivations.*

2.1.2 Deployment

'Motive' is considered to be deployed when the entrepreneurs or the promoters, by themselves, or through their agents/employees put into shape the idea of the business venture thought of in the following manner:

(*i*) (*a*) Start feasibility studies for a New Greenfield Business venture/project.

(*b*) think of further expansion (qualitative and quantitative) of the enterprise.

(*c*) think of diversifying into new attractive business fields.

(*d*) think of divestment of some non-performing ventures/business lines, (getting rid of 'dead' or 'dying' horses) and redeploy resources elsewhere for a more lucrative proposition.

(*ii*) Carry out analysis of the proposals for a critical appraisal for a final decision (techno-commercial and techno-economic appraisals with quantified data).

(*iii*) Take concrete action for execution of the venture (new, expansion, diversification, etc.) including lining up of other relevant and related resources to support the venture.

2.2 Management (and the Organization)

There has to be a standing organization with management personnel in place to lead and give a directional thrust in order to carry forward the set objectives of the enterprise and deal with the affairs of running the venture.

2.2.1 Planning

Even at the initial stage of conceiving and setting up the enterprise, the issues relating to the organization and management set up have to be considered and decided/settled as best as possible. The roles of important personalities (partners, promoters, hired leading managerial persons) have to be defined and earmarked so that there is no confusion and ambiguity later when the results are expected for accrual of benefits. Even for a running enterprise, these issues may crop up from time-to-time and solution will have to be found out within the framework of the **'Articles of Association'** and as per the provisions of the relevant Company Laws.

2.2.2 Deployment

While the partners/owners and the promoters in most cases take leading roles in the management, they may also decide to hire the services of certain other persons on whom they may repose their confidence and appoint as key functionaries like Directors, President, Vice-President, General Managers, etc. Recruitment of certain key persons and functionaries may also be done through open advertisement and through a prescribed/declared selection process. For a Greenfield project some of these functionaries may have to be hired and deployed right at the initial stage to enable the venture to take off, get completed on schedule and go into result-oriented operational mode.

2.3 Money

Although this is a link resource, its role is all pervasive; nothing takes off unless there is matching fund available. Funds are required to be arranged at a cost-effective regime both for capital investment (for fixed assets) as well as for working capital to run the day-to-day affairs.

2.3.1 Planning

(A) For a New Greenfield Project

Unless or otherwise decided for certain valid reasons, for all the initial activities towards facility creation and putting matching organization in place, expenses may have to be covered under 'Capital Investment' fund. The quantum of fund and cash outflow requirements (daily, weekly, monthly, annually, etc.) have to be determined by proper analysis based on the project feasibility studies carried out and the resultant Project Reports (PPR, DPR) prepared for execution. Capital Structure (Debt-Equity Ratio) of the venture will have to be determined by experts in the field who will also advise the management personnel (owner, promoters, top project functionaries) about the quantum and the phasing of fund requirements; they have to then line up the funds from appropriate sources (promoter's fund/equity, loans from FIs/Banks, other funding sources); also the budgeting process has to be followed for controlling expenditure and enforcing budgetary control/financial discipline.

(B) For an Already Running Enterprise

(*a*) Funds requirements will be mainly for working capital to meet the expenditures for running the day-to-day operations of the enterprise.

(*b*) There may be requirements of some capital expenditure funds also for expansion and modernization projects for infrastructural facilities such as additional buildings, services equipment, plant and machinery, devices, etc. (including replacements).

Supply sources for such funds for the purposes at (A) and (B) above will have to be lined up, either from internal sources (from surplus/reserve funds), or by borrowing from external sources such as FIs/Banks, loans from other sources—including public borrowings or even by going to the capital market through issue of shares, debentures, bonds, etc.

2.3.2 Deployment

Deployment and utilization of the available funds/borrowed funds is a challenging and critical task, since money for such business ventures normally comes with lots of conditions and commitments attached to it. The cost of capital, whether for working capital or for capital expenditure, is a factor to be kept in mind constantly while borrowing and/or deploying the same for business operations which, in turn, are associated with a lot of uncertainities and risks. Casualness or mis-management of funds may result in lots of complications or even industrial sickness and ultimate collapse unless corrective measures including proper budgetary controls are exercised at the appropriate stages. Proper budgeting method and adequate budgetary controls right from the inception are imperative steps. Then there are the chances of fraudulent dealings by some persons posted in certain critical positions in the enterprise who may prefer personal gains above the overall welfare and sustenance of the enterprise and try to divert cash and other resources to greed-driven divergent avenues, which may bleed the venture to sickness and ultimate demise. There has to be some inbuilt security systems and regulatory checks to guard against-such eventualities. **However, in a business venture, right from the inception stage, there has to be deliberate efforts and determination to follow the ethical paths with integrity and fairplay.**

2.4 Man (Human Resources)

This is the most crucial resource in any human endeavour. Whether they are for industrial/business ventures, or for socio-religious or welfare purposes, there is one thing in common *i.e.,* people, and it is the people who conceive them, establish them and run them. Therefore, there will be a touch of human behaviour in all these efforts. Along with the main objectives set forth before the enterprise management, the management functionaries have to necessarily deal with human-relations aspects as well. In this respect, professionals working in business and industrial enterprises will have to perforce deal with these aspects rather satisfactorily, not only for smooth working of the enterprise where they are working/managing affairs, but also for their own career, well-being and images; whether one is the owner, or a manager or a lower level employee, image is very important for job satisfaction and status in the society around, as well as in the enterprise where one is working.

Note: *Please refer to para 15.4 in Chapter-15 for a brief on 'Human Aspects of Resource Management'.*

2.4.1 Planning

While conceding that human behavioural/relations aspects will be encountered everywhere in the society. Management in business enterprise will have to deal with such eventualities squarely and rather successfully.

All other conditions remaining more or less the same, human resources play a vital role in all entrepreneurial endeavours for its success or failure; this realization should be there with the owners/promoters and the managers at all levels.

The enterprise management authorities will be well-advised to take care of the following issues right from the beginning of the enterprise operation; hesitation or fumbling in taking well-considered and right decisions in right time may jeopardize the set objectives; nevertheless, the internal and external constraints that may come up as challenges, have to be tackled with determined positive actions:

(*i*) Choosing and deploying right people for right jobs and at the right time will be imperative, keeping in mind that a few so-called 'all rounder' or 'all fitting screws' may not always be the right solution in operating complex organizations and situations. Conceding that there may be a few cases of odd personal choices of the top-management executives, nevertheless, these 'picked ones' are to be fitted into the total organizational efforts and some one in the hierarchy may have to mentor them rather closely for getting some positive contributions from them. All said and done, the chosen ones will be a mixed bag of apples and we have to accept that fact.

(*ii*) People are human beings and therefore, are not infallible; they have inherent strengths and weaknesses and have to be treated and tackled that way. To harness their potential for positive contributions, the leadership skills of managers and supervisors will be very important.

(*iii*) Well-trained, experienced, motivated (well-meaning), challenge-taking business leaders (manager/supervisors) are assets to be cultivated, nurtured and supported by the enterprise management so long they work with ethics and integrity expected of them.

2.4.2 Deployment

(*i*) Deployment of skilled and motivated workforce will be important for good results, and sustainable operations.

(*ii*) Motivating factors such as employee welfare measures, incentive schemes (including career advancement prospects), congenial working atmosphere and environment, need adequate attention by the enterprise management.

(*iii*) Training/retraining and skill development opportunities and facilities be provided as required for all levels of employees, since some of these trained and motivated persons may have to be redeployed later for meeting the operational needs of the enterprise; a long-term perspective is called for in the greater interest of the organization.

(*iv*) Above all, a set of well-defined and practised personnel policies should be in place. These policies may undergo changes to keep pace with the changing requirements of the time, but not according only to the whims and fancies of persons in the top-management set-up.

(*v*) Public Relation aspects should be kept in mind and a suitable set-up is put in place wherever possible; for a large organization/enterprise, this is essential as the enterprise will have economic and social impacts in the surrounding areas. In a democratic society like ours, the business enterprise operations cannot be insulated from prevailing socio-economic and political environment; whether the enterprise is a private or a government venture hardly makes any difference; people are becoming increasingly conscious about their rights and welfare and that has to be appreciated.

(*vi*) Dealing with auditors properly and tactfully by managers to avoid controversial situations with respect to proper implementation of systems, methods, procedures, financial management aspects, relevant documents/records and tax-matters, assets, etc.

(*vii*) **Natural justice and fair play** should be the hallmark of personnel policies, otherwise the organization may loose credibility and momentum leading to organizational slow-down, staleness and disloyality, and these may be detrimental to the very existence of the enterprise, not to speak of successful operations. A shortcut truncated selfish approach may produce some immediate benefits/ dividends, but in the long-run, this can kill the golden-goose. In the present HR-environment, attrition rates amongst experienced professionals are rather high and this aspect may have to be kept in view while planning recruitment and deployment.

(*viii*) **Corporate Ethics and Organizational Integrity:** Whether the enterprise is small or big, it has to operate with an ethical corporate attitude and a sense of successful continuity. Corporate attitudes and culture very much influence the employees and the personnel managing the enterprise. Rather self-centric and inward looking policies of the owners/management in many family-owned business/ industrial houses have, to a large extent, contributed (besides other factors) to the closing down and disintegration of many such enterprises in the last three decades or so. Also, a large number of small scale industries have vanished from the industrial and business arena and many are rather in a bad shape, not always because of competitions and lack of opportunities, but because of un-ethical corporate governance and personal greed. The purpose of deliberating on this is that the promoters of the project may consider these aspects before venturing into the project.

(*ix*) In case there is a collaborator, while we expect him to be ethical and cooperative, the same is true for us (*i.e.,* the client enterprise) as well; both sides have to be rational and mature in approach for a successful long-term relationship.

(*x*) **The customer is supreme in business dealings** and his support is critical to the very survival of the enterprise; hence customer must be treated and cultivated properly and tactfully for a long-term relationship which may offer repeated benefits and opportunities.

(*xi*) Sufficient level of tact and resourcefulness is required in dealing with government and local-body agencies; by the very nature of their function, they tend to be regulatory and sometimes rather unsupportive; but they cannot be antagonized (for God's sake, if you mean business, don't ever do this). Therefore, people with good negotiating/persuasive (and a bit diplomatic) skills in the enterprise should be entrusted with such liaison jobs for better results.

(*xii*) Lastly, but not the least, managers and supervisors have to muster skills and tacts in dealing with labour unions; in fact in a open democratic society like ours, they will be there and we have to deal with them almost daily. It may be worthwhile to train and equip managers/executives to prepare them rather well as to how to deal with labour unions with tact and magnanimity (both warm and cool depending on situations, but avoid being hot as far as possible); in fact, it should be a part of Management Development Programmes for executives and supervisors. As a practical approach, discourage engagement at a junior supervisory and management levels, since lack of experience and maturity may aggravate an issue instead of solving it.

> ***"Hire for attitude, train for skill."***
>
> *—Rajiv Khurana,*
> *HR-Management Educator*

2.5 Machine

Machines of different kinds are used in industrial enterprises primarily for converting raw materials and semis into finished saleable products and components. Depending on the type of products and the technological processes followed, a variety of them, such as metal and non-metal cutting/working machine tools/equipment, devices for heating and thermal cutting, devices and instruments for measurement, quality control, assembly and testing, equipment for material handling, transportation, etc., will have to be procured and put into operation for production and related operations.

2.5.1 Planning

Planning for machines, both for manufacturing and supporting services, require adequate knowledge and skill on the part of the concerned engineers and technologist. Besides being conversant with the purpose and application of the machines, they are supposed to keep themselves aware of the latest technological advancements that are taking place in this field so that in case occasion arises, proper replacements (of old and obsolete) and modernization of the existing ones can be undertaken to keep these facilities in productive and healthy state. Supporting maintenance and repair facilities will have to be created and kept in working condition along with deployment of skilled personnel for such jobs. In fact, **Facility Planning** is a very important function for the production management authorities; dedicated technologists may have to be kept engaged, particularly in large and medium industries for Facility Planning function. As regards facility identification and planning in the small scale industries, services of external experts can be hired in case necessity arises since in-house expertise may not be available because of organizational limitations.

2.5.2 Deployment

Proper deployment and utilization of machines are also important for cost-effective operation of the enterprise. Skilled and experienced technologists are supposed to constantly engage themselves in selecting technological processes matching with the machines available and draw up programmes and schedules for appropriate deployment and utilization. Their responsibility will also include design, selection, procurement and in some cases, even in-house manufacture of various tools, tackles, jigs and fixtures that are required for productive usage of machines and equipment. Machine utilization for productive outputs is one of the most critical operational aspects of a manufacturing enterprise, since machine utilization process consume other resources, *viz.*, man (skilled labour), money, energy and material in substantial quantum.

2.6 Materials

Referring to paras 1.3.5, 1.3.5.1, 1.3.5.2 and 1.3.5.3 in **Chapter-I,** raw materials, semi-finished components, bought out items and other sundry items are to be arranged and made available to the manufacturing and other supporting operational areas so that saleable products get produced in cost-effective regimes (so that these can be competitive in the prices in the market place).

2.6.1 Planning

(*i*) **Material Planning and Inventory Control (MPIC)** is an important function in an industrial enterprise to enable procurement of materials in time, in a cost-effective regime and in optimal quantities in conformity with the prescribed specifications/characteristics so as to avoid locking up money in dead inventory or slow-moving inventory since such a situation may have a detrimental effect on the operational viability of the enterprise: Wrong planning on the material front has a direct effect on the working capital management since cost of such capital (interest burden, etc.) may go out of control because the cost of material is a major portion of the product manufacturing costs (material cost may be anything between 30% to 65% of the cost of product depending on the kind of product and the technological processes involved). A constant watch on material stock/inventory is imperative and concerned functionaries in Materials Management department have to be alert all the time about maintaining optimal inventory level.

(*ii*) **Vendor Development for dependable sources:** For any industrial enterprise, dependable and continuous supply of raw materials, bought out components and other sundry items is essential for trouble free successful and sustained operations. Vendors play a vital role in this respect. In fact, as per the latest business strategy, vendors/suppliers are considered as parteners in business endeavours and conscious efforts are made (from both sides) to develop and cultivate a mutually beneficial and supportive relationship. Organizational efforts and systems are put in place to identify and develop vendors who can meet the requirements-both in quantity and quality, at a competitive pricing regime. This approach is giving a very good result for some successful industrial enterprises.

2.6.2 Deployment

From the usage point of view, there are broadly two categories of materials required in industrial enterprises:

(*a*) **Direct Materials:** Materials which directly go into the construction of the products and product-related components, parts, etc., *i.e.,* raw materials, semi-finished items and bought out components *i.e.,* items which form parts of the end products.

(*b*) **Indirect Materials:** These are sundry items which are not forming the parts of the main products, but are also required, some of them rather essentially, to support various operations and associated services (including administrative and welfare related) in realizing the end products; such indirect materials may comprise of items of office equipment and stationeries, consumables and equipment/implements for medical/canteen/security services; various consumables, tools, tackles, implements required for plant maintenance and repair services, and such other sundry items which do not go into products, but are required for supporting operations.

2.6.3 Both the above Categories of Materials Need Judicious Procurement and Usage to Avoid

- Unwanted inventory build up beyond permissible limits, (thus blocking working capital funds).
- Wastages and expenses towards storage and handling of excess materials in stock.
- Cost escalation on product-costs and prices, rendering the product-price un-competitive and thereby losing/depleting market share.

2.7 Methods and Knowledge

Methods are developed from knowledge and experience; both together help in drawing up processes and procedures for cost-effective, efficient and result-oriented working-regimes to achieve the set objectives and results. Methods and knowledge have an all pervasive role in all areas of enterprise operations.

2.7.1 Planning

Worthwhile planning for usage of Methods and Knowledge will come from creative thinking and innovative work-culture. Therefore, enterprise management should encourage employees at various levels for increasing their skill and knowledge base, and actively think in terms of creativity and innovative work-culture, if needed, by introducing appropriate reward and incentive schemes. Methods planned for adoption must be relevant to the business operations undertaken and there should be matching procedures in place enabling periodical reviews and updation to keep pace with the changing circumstances and market preferences.

2.7.2 Deployment

2.7.2.1 Harnessing employee knowledge and experience

It has been the experience in many successful business/industrial corporations that given the environment, encouragement and support, knowledgeable employees rise to the occasion, and develop new ideas which lead to creative outcomes and innovations that bring considerable commercial benefits to the enterprise. Harnessing their knowledge and experience as well as their enthusiasm can be rewarding not only to the concerned employees, but also to the enterprise itself.

2.7.2.2 What is knowledge management in a business enterprise?

- A systematic and integrated coordination of organization-wide activities of acquiring, creating, storing, sharing, disseminating, developing and deploying knowledge by individuals and groups in pursuit of organizational goals.
- Knowledge management is taking to ‘digging for gold in ones’s own backyard’. Knowledge management is all about management of intangibles to deliver tangible results.
- Knowledge, by definition, resides within people. To derive competitive advantage, the organization should be able to harness this individual knowledge through its systems and procedures hereby institutionalizing it into, (Organizational Knowledge) and use this organizational knowledge into adding value in its business propositions (activities).

2.7.2.3 Types of Knowledge

Tacit or Embodied or Informal	Personal beliefs, Perspectives and values (self-conceived or inherited)	People's head/brain refers to undocumented information, intuition, empathy and experience
Explicit or Formal or Represented	Can be stored in a piece of paper, computer, etc.	Refers to documented information and should be basis of decision making

2.7.2.4 Focus on knowledge

- The strategic use of knowledge will differentiate better-run firms from the rest. Knowledge base serves as the hub of the organization wheel.
- Organizations that have world-class ambitions will need to nurture knowledge workers.
- The only thing that sets apart one enterprise from another is the quality of people (Knowledge Workers) employed there in.

2.7.2.5 Methods are derived from knowledge

(*i*) Succeeding in the competitive market and following methods that supports such efforts:

- In a competitive situation, strategic decision-making is incumbent on predicting competitors' intentions both in operation and time or knowing something better than that. The ability to predict market developments and assimilate new ideas is one of the basis of innovation in business operations.
- Superior insight into customer needs and behaviours provides an edge in marketing and in making efficiency gains. The ability to price and configure products and offers, and to design appealing new services depend on forecasting customers' tendency to buy at perceived value. Understanding customer behaviour may be the basis of initiatives in bridging cost/specification gaps.

(*ii*) Combating internal inefficiencies and revamp/update methods and procedures and related documentation for regular usage.

(*iii*) Organization is concerned with how experience can be transferred more effectively, quickly and how to capture and document valuable insight so that it can be used in a better way.

2.7.2.6 What do we need in organizational knowledge management?

- Creating and populating a repository of in-house knowledge.
- Valuation of knowledge with respect to business objectives.

- Facilitating the transfer of knowledge and active dissemination. Creating a knowledge sharing environment.
- Building an organizational culture focused on innovation and knowledge creation.

2.7.2.7 Need for introduction of knowledge management

- For actualization of organizational vision, there is need to build **Intellectual Assets (IA);** Fig. 2.1 below represents knowledge creation and utilization cycle:

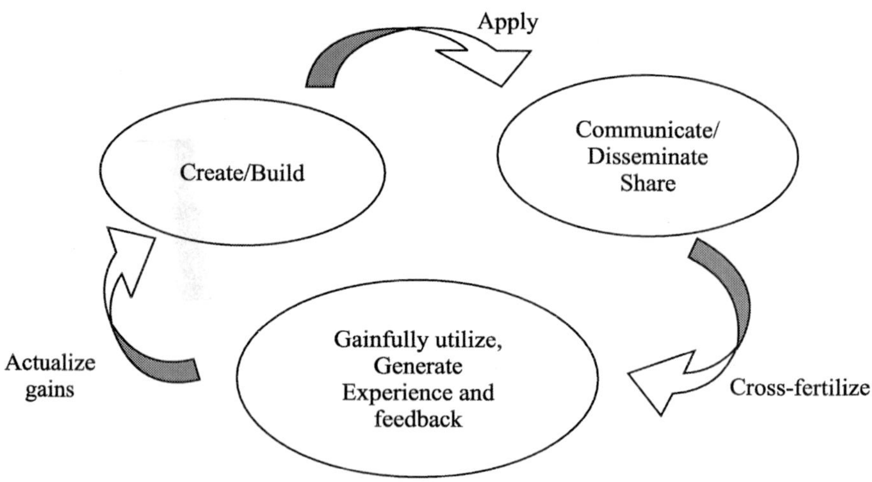

Fig. 2.1 Knowledge creation and utilization cycle.

2.7.2.8 Integrated approach to methods and knowledge

Build Databases	Establish: Infrastructure	
	Mental	Physical
• Organizational yellow pages • Best practices system that captures lessons learnt • Competitive intelligence (environmental scanning)	• Learning Attitude • Recording & Sharing Culture • Discipline • Dedication • Innovation • Creativity	• Resources, Men, Tools • Systems Organization • Documentation and other recording media

2.7.2.9 A learning organization

- Is an active philosophy of work-culture, not merely an organizational system.
- Believes that its only competitive advantage is learning.
- Encourages people to learn to produce the results they desire.
- Nurtures creative and innovative patterns of collective learning.
- Develops fresh organizational capabilities continuously.

2.7.2.10 Why knowledge management?

- Good decisions are rare but mistakes keep on repeating.
- Our earning and business are from knowledge. Do we know how to revive our business in case of major unforeseen disasters?
- Knowledge inspired contingency plans help develop in-house competence and capabilities to weather uncertainties and upheavals.

2.7.2.11 Learning organization can be created

- Keeping the enterprise in a state of constant flux: seek newer strategies, knowledge, challenge.
- Cultivating diversities in the function of the organization (updation/revamping/re-orientation).
- Creating mechanisms to abandon old and obsolete knowledge (divestment/re-organization).
- Building settings where people collectively learn and take decisions.
- Disseminating learning throughout the organization systematically through appropriate communication media.

2.7.2.12 People are crucial for knowledge resources

- The exclusive source of knowledge for organization is people.
- Individual knowledge is the starting point for organizational knowledge.
- The knowledge pool of each individual cannot be replicated, but can be transferred and shared.
- Only people can spread knowledge across the enterprise.
- It is only people who can convert knowledge into efficient action.

2.7.2.13 Organizational knowledge management depends upon acceptance and effective utilization of technologies/methods

Buying a computer does not make one a better programmer. Similarly, just acquiring new technologies does not make an organization better at Managing Knowledge. What is critical is acceptance and effective utilization of the technologies; and this can happen through the process of facilitating a culture of information sharing, relationship building and trust, and above all, the commonality of purpose.

2.7.2.14 Organizational knowledge development: A structural representation

Figure. 2.2 seeks to present a structural representation of knowledge development in a business organization.

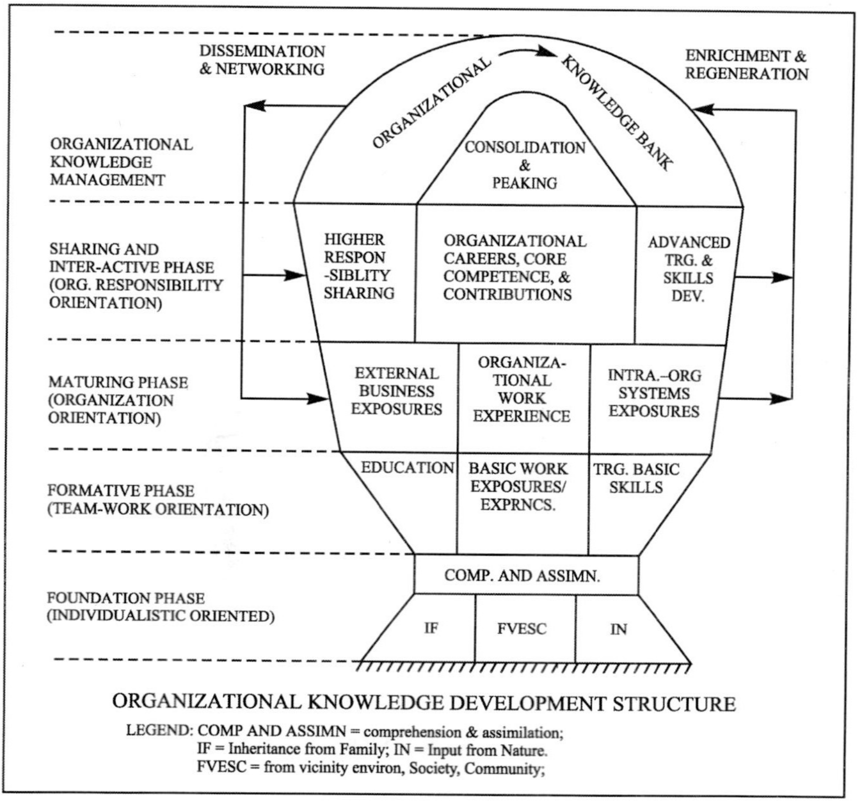

Fig. 2.2 Knowledge development in a business organization.

2.8 Energy

Taking the case of industrial units, where energy consumption is much more than those in the non-industrial sectors, the energy is mostly obtained in two forms: heat/thermal and electricity for running the operations.

Note: *Use of other form of energy viz.Solar and wind find very limited use in industry.*

2.8.1 Planning

The Thermal Energy as required is normally derived from solar rays, by burning fossil fuels like coal/oil/gas, etc., as well as in some cases by burning combustible bio-mass and wood in case the same are available in adequate quantity in a reliable and cost-effective supply regime. Thermal energy is also obtained from electricity through appropriate conversion devices, provided sufficient electrical power supply at a cost-effective regime is available.

• **Electrical Energy:** In today's business operations, electricity is the most preferred form of energy inputs because of its many advantages. Electricity can be obtained, depending on the scale of requirements, from the following sources:

(*i*) From the grid-system of the electric supply company/agency; this is the most cost-effective method of energy supply.

(*ii*) From inhouse Diesel Generator sets, in case the supply from the grid system/electric supply network is intermittent/unreliable, or, quantum of supply is inadequate.

(*iii*) From captive thermal generating station (steam-turbine driven or gas turbine driven generators).*

Note: **This is a rather costly option and normally only the large industrial houses may consider going into this to ensure dependable power supply.*

2.8.2 Deployment

2.8.2.1 Thermal energy for heating

(*i*) Heating required for industrial production processes (baking, curing, melting, heat treatment, etc.).

(*ii*) Heating required for drying and moisture control.

(*iii*) Heating required for comfort (air-conditioning in offices/rooms).

(*iv*) The heat based mechanical drives (heat engines, steam engines, I/C engines).

2.8.2.2 Electrical energy

(*i*) For lighting and fan cooling in office, factory premises.

(*ii*) For Airconditioning (winter, summer).

(*iii*) For industrial drives and controls.

(*iv*) Telecommunication and EDP/computer operations.

(*v*) Entertainment devices and systems.

(*vi*) For generation of heat (through appropriate devices) for the purposes mentioned at 2.8.2.1 (*i*, *ii*) above.

> ***"It is a mistake to try to look too far ahead. The chain of destiny can only be grasped one link at a time".***
>
> — *Sir Winston Churchill*

❍❍❍

CHAPTER-3

COMMERCIAL EXPLOITATION OF NATURAL RESOURCES: SOCIO-POLITICAL AND ENVIRONMENTAL ISSUES

> *"Wealth acquired with proper means will yield virtues and happiness."*
>
> — *Thiruvallavar*

Business and industrial enterprises are basically entities with primary objectives of earning a return/profit on capital employed and generation of surpluses in terms of money and wealth creation; other related aspects of business operations are rather incidental to the main entrepreneurial urges for financial gains.

Business enterprises, particularly the industrial units heavily depend on various types of resources, some directly and some indirectly, as inputs to sustain their operations. In fact, without resources, no venture can ever take off, not to speak of continued operations.

As we have already mentioned about various resources in Chapters-l and 2, we shall now discuss the various ways these resources, both natural and artificial, are used for commercial exploitation.

3.1 Exploiting Natural Resources

From time immemorial, human beings are exploiting natural resources for their very survival and economic development. In the following paragraphs, we are discussing a few of the most commonly used natural resources which are being widely exploited by business enterprises for commercial gains:

Note: *The listing is not exhaustive, only the most commonly used ones are mentioned below.*

3.1.1 Air

Various commercial uses are:

(*i*) Compressed air for industrial devices and process applications.

(*ii*) Deriving Oxygen and Nitrogen gases for various industrial, medical and other scientific uses.

(*iii*) For cooling applications, both for industrial and domestic (air blasting, refrigeration, summer air conditioning, etc.).

(*iv*) For air-transport facilities/aviation-civilian, aviation-defence.

(*v*) For use as heating and drying media (winter air-conditioning, hot air drying, etc.).

(*vi*) Air medium (air-wave) is used for radio, television and satellite communication/transmission systems.

(*vii*) Wind energy is used for running mechanical drives and electric power generators.

3.1.2 Water

Various industrial uses are listed below:

(*i*) Cooling/removal of heat: Industrial, domestic applications.

(*ii*) Formation of ice for both industrial and domestic usages.

(*iii*) Hydro power generation by harnessing the kinetic energy of falling waters.

(*iv*) Agricultural irrigation.

(*v*) Generation of steam for heating as well as for thermal power generation, driving of steam engines/steam turbines.

(*vi*) Washing - both industrial and domestic applications.

(*vii*) Fire-fighting, hydroblasting, hydro-jet machining, etc.

(*viii*) Hot water supply - both industrial and domestic usages.

3.1.3 Sunrays/Solar Energy

Sunrays are not only being used for heating and drying, but nowadays, solar energy from sun rays are being exploited for electrical power generation through the use of solar photo-voltaic panels. Sunrays charged solar batteries are also being used as electrical power source in a limited quantum.

3.1.4 Minerals

Both ferrous and non-ferrous minerals of different kinds and their compounds find wide usage in industrial products, pharmaceuticals and drugs, construction projects (iron, steel, stones, sand, shingles, etc.); Mineral derivatives from silica, naturally occurring salts, organic and inorganic mineral compounds, Kaolin (for ceramics), soil based nitrates and nitrites etc., are being used for a large variety of industrial products for commercial exploitation. The list can be endless, since R&D in material science are developing more and more new materials based on minerals and their derivatives and compounds, for use in structurals, electrical and electronic components, chemical products, etc.

3.1.5 Fossil Fuels/Hydrocarbons (including Natural Gases)

Petroleum derivatives like petrol, diesel, naptha, furnace oils, aviation fuels, lubricants, sulphur, waxes, etc., are extracted from crude petroleum and processed for a miryad of usages. Hydrocarbon based natural gases and coal-bed based methane gases are also being explored and used for thermal power generation. Methane hydrate crystals available in deep sea beds in some areas are being considered for alternative source of fuels to be used for thermal power generation.

Natural gas extracted from underground sources (mostly associated with petroleum sources) are being used in large scales for heat energy, industrial processes and electricity generation.

3.1.6 Timber

Forest-products like timber, wood and wood-derivatives (like ethanol, charcoals, etc.) are being widely used for commercial exploitation; rather over-exploitation over the centuries causing rapid depletion and also causing ecological degradation and adverse environmental impacts.

3.1.7 Stones

Commonly available silicate stones, sand stones, marvel, granite and various other types of stones are being used on a large scale for construction purposes (roads, buildings, bridges, etc.); in some locations over-exploitation is again causing ecological degradation. Granite slabs are also being used as beds for certain special purpose machines.

Certain varieties of precious and semi-precious stones such as diamonds, garnets, topaz, ruby, emerald, etc., not only find uses in jewellery items but are also being used for certain kinds of industrial products and components (watches, tracers, laser-ray devices, cutting tools, etc.). Lime stones are being mined for manufacture of cement and other industrial products like calcium and its derivatives; also used as construction material for buildings, etc.

3.1.8 Sand

This is an abundantly available natural material, used not only for construction/building purposes, but also being used in a variety of ways for a variety of industrial products; silicon extracted from monasite sand is further refined and used in electronics/electrical industries for manufacturing different kinds of semiconductor elements, micro-chips, etc. Silica is also used to prepare a certain type of special purpose durable coating compounds and varnishes. Sand is also used in the manufacture of glass materials and ceramic items.

3.1.9 Tree Leaves, Seeds, Foliages

Leaves, seeds and foliages (even flowers), latex, resins from trees, shrubs, etc., found in forests and grown in social forestry and agri-farms also find variety of use in medicines /pharmaceuticals and cosmetic products. Natural Rubber made from latex of rubber plants are very widely being used both as industrial products as well as items of household use.

3.1.10 Sea Weeds

Extracts from certain varieties of sea weeds are being used for preparation of mosquito-repellants, medicinal formulations, and some varieties are also used for food products.

3.1.11 Paper and Paper Boards

Prepared from bamboos, weeds, grass, trees, leaves, etc., are in daily use both in industry as well as for domestic office-work, and educational (books, note-books, etc.) purposes.

3.1.12 Animals and Animal Products

Meat products derived from animals and a variety of fishes are popular food items in various parts of the world, and supports thousands of food-processing units in different countries. Milk and milk-products derived from cows and buffaloes, are widely used as nourishing food-drinks and food products all over the world; milk from camels and yaks are also being consumed as food items in some countries. Animal skins are used in large quantities for shoe-making and other leather-based products.

3.1.13 Wool

Wool taken from Sheeps, Yaks, Alpacas, Chirus, etc., are being processed for preparation of wool of various grades which are being used in making garments, blankets and shawls, both by cottage as well as by larger industrial units.

3.1.14 Cotton

Natural cotton is widely used for preparation of clothing materials. BT (Biologically Terminating) cotton is the recently propogated variety which has high yield per hectare and having long fibre advantage **(but there are controversial issues on BT Cotton seed availability and seed source control).**

3.2 Using Artificial Material Resources

A few major items are being discussed ahead.

Note: *With the advancement in material sciences, more and more artificial materials are being developed and put to industrial use.*

3.2.1 Synthetic Yarns/Fibres

Synthetic yarns-fibres are derived from hydro-carbons (brand name Terelene, Nylon, Teflon, Viscose) processed with certain organic and inorganic chemicals. These are now present everywhere particularly for clothing and garments; besides, these are also being used for preparation of ropes of different grades and sizes, for fishing nets, parachutes, for use on ships and boats, also for industrial and domestic purposes.

3.2.2 Other Synthetic Materials

Hydrocarbon based and polymer based new toughened compounds, both heat and corrosion resistant, and also with di-electric properties are being developed to be used as materials for various industrial uses as well as for making household goods such as utensils, door-window frames, lubrication-free bearings for food processing gadgets; some such materials such as fibre-glass and metallic glass, exhibiting every high-strengths but light in weight, are even being considered for constructing bodies of engines, ships, cars, building superstructures, etc., besides making other wear resistant machine parts like gears, pinions, bearings, supporting brackets, etc.

3.2.3 Plastics and Resins

Plastics and resins are derived from hydro-carbons and other synthetic chemicals are so widely being used that they now find usage everywhere: both for domestic and industrial usages. Today, life without plastic and plastic material is rather un-imaginable. Resins are being used for various industrial products for coating, bonding, preservatives, etc.

3.2.4 Glass

Glass manufactured from compounds of naturally occurring ingredients like silica, potassium, sodium and other non-synthetic and synthetic chemicals, has wide variety of use in industry and domestic appliances. Optical Fibre glass and Metallic glasses are revolutionizing in the fields of construction, communication, lighting and household appliances.

3.3 Entrepreneurial Usage of Other Relevant Resources

The following two other relevant resources also play very important and sometimes crucial roles in the success (and failure) of business enterprises, and we shall discuss the commercial implications of these in the paragraphs that follow:

(*i*) Management and Organization

(*ii*) Methods and Knowledge

3.3.1 Management and Organization

(*i*) Management and Organization together are the physical embodiment of an enterprise without which business entities are only ideas and objectives floating in the air. Unless personified through appropriate functionaries, these by themselves are incapable of converting ideas and motives into concrete human endeavours. Persons occupying the management positions and forming the organizational structure are supposed to take lead roles. Qualified and capable persons with requisite experience and background have to be selected and hired with due compensation packages and perks so as to encourage/motivate them for making positive and result oriented contributions which are crucial for success and sustenance of the business enterprises. The organization structure put in place must be compatible with the nature and size of the business enterprise; both over-sizing and under-sizing have to be avoided to make it effective and efficient.

(*ii*) **Organizational Development (OD):** It is a continuous endeavour on the part of the management to keep the enterprise tonned up and motivated at all levels for deriving sustained positive contributions from its people. Commercially speaking, commitments, better productivity and higher efficiency. Therefore, employees have to be motivated not only to get involved in the development and work-culture improvement processes, but also to be motivated through appropriate incentives and rewards, mostly in the form of extra money and extra benefits (welfare schemes, etc.). OD ideas cannot only preach, but have to be a down-to-earth approach to propagate and motivate to improve work-culture and commitment.

3.3.2 Methods and Knowledge

For the organized activities that take place in business enterprises, there has to be a set of methods, to be followed at all levels for logical, sequential, and disciplined work culture tuned towards achieving the set goals. Methods are to be further broken down to processes, procedures and work-instructions to avoid confusion, overlapping of works and infructuous duplication. Proper procedures can also help avoiding multitude of agencies doing the same process over and over again wasting time and resources. In order to draw up relevant methods and related procedures, knowledge and work-experience play a vital role. Therefore, methods are to be considered along with knowledge as a vital resource; **methods shorn of knowledge will be like "Madness in Method", rather than "Method for Logical Endeavours".**

For business enterprises, both method and knowledge have great commercial implications, particularly where original processes are developed through R&D and innovations resulting in development of saleable products, processes and services.

Enterprise management, therefore, have to encourage knowledge-culture and give due recognition to this aspect. A 'Knowledge Organization' has a much higher chances of success even in a highly competitive situation.

Note: *Please refer to paras 2.7.2.2 to 2-7.2.14 in Chapter-2 to read more about knowledge as a resource.*

3.4 Environmental and Social Impacts of Commercial Exploitation of Natural Resources

3.4.1 Conflict of Interests between Commerce and Socio-Political Aspirations

Through the ages, there has always been some degree of conflict of interests between commerce and socio-political aspirations, of the communities, emerging societies and countries.

Speaking of human instincts, commerce always aim at generation of monetary benefits/profits and creation of wealth; and in the pursuit of such goals, there were scant regards for environmental and ecological aspects of business operations. Besides environmental issues, drastic impacts were also there over the centuries and still occurring, with respect to changes in life styles of people hankering after higher standards of living, in various parts of the world, though in varying degrees. Such impacts were both positive and negative. Positive effects resulted in emergence of affluent societies who aspired for achieving higher and higher standards of living; whereas the negative impacts resulted not only in the over-exploitation of resources, particularly the natural resources, there are also the ever increasing environmental/ecological degradations: for example, ozone depletion, polluted rivers and seas, deforestation, emission of green house gases causing climate change/global warming, etc. The share of benefits and bounties arising out of the usages of these resources are also causing world-wide socio-political-economic tensions and conflicts (trade blocks at logger-heads, WTO-negotiations failures, war breaking out for control of energy/hydrocarbon resources, etc.). In today's world, societies and nations, while preaching enlightened self-interest and global cooperation on the one hand, on the other hand many of them are showing signs of selfish trends, ignoring the sufferings of the have-not-societies in certain zones; the international and inter-society conflicts on resource sharing (and non-sharing) have become common occurrance, and there is a tendency to settle scores by force/military means, reminding us of the pre-World-War I and II eras. There are ominous signs that future World War (WW III) as and when it occurs, will be fought, not for grabbing of Land, Gold and Jewels, but on Energy-resources (oil and gas fields, etc.) and food supply sources, unless the UNO plays moderating roles and could persuade nations concerned to be more rational and considerate in their attitudes. 'Live and Let-live' must prevail over 'We want it first - no matter what'. Besides the world scenarios, there are inter-zone/inter-society/inter-community conflicts on resources sharing within a Nation itself (*e.g.,* in India, river-water sharing between states, tribal land usurping by others). With increasing pressure of global population growth (already crossing 6.5 billion in 2007), such conflicts are bound to increase. In India, with around 113 crore population (2007), which increases by at least 2% (net) annually, resource crunch and resultant conflicts are likely to grow. While there are over-exploitation of natural resources, the level of agricultural produce is not keeping pace with the population growth; same is the case with energy availability. There is an average 30% shortfall on peak-demand *vis-a-vis* the availability of electric power in India at present, and there is very remote chance of this gap narrowing down during next 20 years unless huge amount of capital invested (average Rs. 4.5 crore per MW) with determined efforts to increase the generation capacity. It is estimated that at least an additional generation capacity of around 2 lakhs MWs (over and above the present 1.45 lakhs MWs in 2007) will be required by 2025; (population in India is estimated to be at around 130 crore by 2025 at present rate of growth).

3.4.2 Issues to be Considered in Indian Context

Keeping the above in view, the issues that need serious consideration can be summarized as under:

3.4.2.1 Issues in the government domain

(*i*) Governments both at the centre and the states must give more priority for long-term policy formulation and bring in legislation for strict and justified regulation of exploitation of natural resources like hydrocarbons, forest produces, water usage, and of minerals.

(*ii*) Take steps for generation of higher level of public awareness and industry awareness towards depleting natural resources and ecological and environmental degradation caused by careless and over exploitation of such resources.

(*iii*) Encourage industrial enterprises to increasingly resort to R&D for reducing usage of natural resources and opt for alternatives, renewable sources of material and energy supply.

(*iv*) Educate public about these issues and encourage articulation of public opinion for drawing up/updating national policies and follow up action plans, regulatory legislations, etc.

3.4.2.2 Issues in industry domain

It has been the experience in India as well as in other countries that most business/industrial houses give more priority to earning rather than caring much for ecological/environmental issues, unless they are compelled by national and international regulations to comply with certain rules and control regimes. However, the trend is changing in various industrially developed countries due to public pressure, thereby forcing the industrial houses to take more balanced and socially responsible posture and take adequate preventive and corrective measures with respect to ecological and environment impacts of their business operations. Introduction of ISO-9001-QMS, TQM, EMS-14001, and OHSAS-18001 concepts of work-culture in many countries are helping in articulating the action plans towards balancing socio-political aspirations and commercial interests. However, in Indian context, industry need to do much more than what has so far been done/achieved with respect to exploiting natural and national resources *vis-a-vis* discharging of social obligations. A few salient issues may be mentioned below for serious considerations of the industrial houses/associations, chambers of commerce (like CII, Assocham, FICCI, PHDCCI, etc.):

(*i*) Reduce dependence on natural resources by resorting to alternate sources through R&D and Technological advancements/innovations.

(*ii*) Be serious about ecological and environmental issues while exploiting natural and other national resources.

(*iii*) Give preference to green-technologies (environmental friendly processes).

(*iv*) Cooperate with government agencies and responsible NGOs in implementing national policies and regulatory programmes.

(*v*) Keep the stakeholder's interest in consideration, with an eye on national well-being.

(*vi*) Earmark a part of your annual budget allocations towards implementation of such programmes.

(*vii*) Constitute committees/task groups on a permanent basis to monitor implementation of programmes aiming at reducing over-exploitation of resources/wastage of resources and in identifying viable alternative solutions.

(*viii*) Be cautious while borrowing resources and technologies from abroad with respect to their ecological and environmental impacts and socio-political implications.

3.4.2.3 Issues in the public domain

As citizens of a democratic welfare country like India, public at large, particularly educated sections have to think and act keeping in view aspects like the following:

(*i*) greater consciousness about the impacts of over-exploitation/wastage of natural and other national resources, and support national programmes drawn up for corrective measures and balancing commerce with social issues.

(*ii*) Help form public opinion so as to influence government and local bodies' policies towards environmental and socio-economic Issues.

(*iii*) While forming opinions, stakeholders interest be kept in mind.

(*iv*) Conduct lifestyles (individual, community, state levels) to make positive contributions towards national programmes for wise usage and conservation of resources.

(*v*) Form public opinion for influencing government policies for adopting **'development programmes without tears';** development programmes need not create upheaval in public life and cause uprooting of citizens without considering alternative socio-economically viable/justified measures to mitigate the sufferings forced on them due to economic development programmes/projects.

(*vi*) Help keeping your own vicinity free of pollution and filth; individually and collectively render voluntary services towards these objectives and efforts.

> ***"Govern by doing nothing that goes against nature."***
>
> — *A Chinese Proverb*

❍❍❍

CHAPTER-4

ADOPTING STRATEGIES FOR OPTIMAL DEPLOYMENT AND UTILIZATION OF RESOURCES IN BUSINESS ENTERPRISES

> *"Obstacles are those frightful things you see when you take your eyes off your goal."*
>
> — *Henry Ford*

Resources for business operations do not come by easily and without sufficient efforts. Resources are also made available at a cost and in most cases are associated with lots of conditions. Enterprise owners/management are supposed to be sufficiently aware of these aspects, right from the beginning, so that there is no illusion about this. Therefore, adequate thinking and analysis have to go into the connected issues relating their cost-effective availability and wise deployment. These aspects need careful consideration so that the enterprise remain viable and can sustain operations on a long-term basis, and also aspire for a growth if opportunity comes by. Wise enterprise management would, therefore, like to adopt a set of strategies for optimal deployment and utilization of various resources available at its command. We will now discuss, in the following paragraphs, what these strategies can be and how these can be implemented for operational sustenance at a reasonable viability level.

4.1 In the Case of Naturally Occurring Resources: (Acquisition and Deployment)

(*i*) Adopt compatible policies to balance resource needs through optimal usage (avoiding excess consumptions and wastages beyond permissible limits), adopt reasonable conservation efforts and also confirm to the National policies and programmes.

(*ii*) Select such sources of natural resources where there are less chances of public controversy regarding over-exploitation and ecological impacts; enterprise management cannot be oblivious of and insulated from such implications.

(*iii*) Select green technology which will have minimal adverse impacts on environment and the people living in the vicinity areas.

(*iv*) Avoid, by all means, violation of National and International standards and regulations; ethical approach pays off in the long run.

(*v*) Always think of contingencies and plan accordingly.

(*vi*) Avoid self-centric policies ignoring the welfare of the society at large.

4.2 In the Case of Artificial and Conceptual Resources (Acquisition and Deployment)

(*i*) Points mentioned above at 4.1 (*i*) to (*vi*) also apply here to a large extent, but the degree may vary depending on the kind of resource being used.

(*ii*) Encourage R&D and innovations so as to derive optional benefits; reward good innovations and creativity to motivate concerned employees.

(*iii*) Keep knowledge updated continually for such resource applications and if need arises (due to competition and other valid reasons), do not hesitate to change over to new resources and sources to keep abreast with latest developments but in a cost effective manner; change over should be compatible with the organizational objectives and the core-strength.

4.3 In Case of Borrowed Resources from External Sources (Mainly for Methods/Knowledge/Technology/Monetary Support and Management)

(*i*) Weigh all pros and cons before jumping into a new option; it may not be always compatible with your kind of operational regimes, work-culture and the organizational core-competency.

(*ii*) Evaluate reliability and usefulness of the offered resource before deciding adoption: in-house capability to absorb and utilize the same will be a critical issue with respect to the operational resilience and viability.

(*iii*) Take a long-term perspective in such cases, particularly in case of technology and monetary dependence.

(*iv*) All legal aspects be kept in view regarding success as well as failures and their implications: contractual arrangements require deft handling by experienced functionaries.

4.4 Resource Utilization-Management Strategies

Even if the required resources are available at a cost-effective regime without stringent conditions, that do not mean that their proper utilization can also be taken for granted and treated rather casually. Careless and casual utilization process adopted by one or a few enterprises may deprive other needy ones of their vital needs, since most resources are not abundant enough to be frittered away, and there is a necessity for sharing for optimal utilization by all concerned. A few strategic approach may help achieving optimal level of utilization:

(*i*) A strict control on inventory build up and levels: follow the prescribed norms.

(*ii*) A close watch on Input-Output Relationship, *i.e.,* productivity within the permissible limits of variations; corrective measures have to be taken in case of appreciable deviations from the prescribed norms occur.

(*iii*) Constant watch on wastages, pilferages and abuse; corrective action for deviations from norms must be effective; take matching organizational steps to prevent/minimise.

(*iv*) Constant efforts for improvement in processes to reduce consumptions beyond the prescribed norms and also to improve system efficiency.

(*v*) Maintain strict budgetary controls on resources acquisition, deployment and usage: appropriate monitoring mechanism should be in place to enable corrective steps at the appropriate time.

(*vi*) Training and skill development and updation of process knowledge should be adopted as a regular feature.

(*vii*) Have in place appropriate reward and incentive schemes to encourage resource savings, higher productivity and higher efficiency at all levels of employees.

(*viii*) Energy savings and periodical energy audits should be a regular feature of operational strategy. Wastage avoidance should be a regular periority.

(*ix*) Introduce suggestion scheme and encourage innovative ideas and working methods.

(*x*) Avoid self-centric policies and recognize other's needs as well: practise enlightened cooperative approaches in resource utilization particularly where sharing is imperative for joint survival and progress.

(*xi*) Adoption of ISO-9001 QMS, TQM and EMS may greatly help in creating organizational work-culture towards optimization of resources.

(*xii*) Capitalize on organizational knowledge pool available/generated and encourage intra-group, inter-group, inter-departmental/inter-functional knowledge sharing and exchange of ideas and experiences.

(*xiii*) Take a mature and patient approach to resolve intra-group, inter-group and inter-functional conflicts/difference of opinion with the overall objectives of unity of organizational purpose.

(*xiv*) Give due importance to Industrial Relation and Public Relation (image building) aspects.

(*xv*) Keep stakeholders' legitimate interests also in view.

4.5 Resource Regeneration Strategies

This is an important aspect but often ignored. Proper strategy adopted may be rewarding in terms of economic gains and better resourcefulness. A few strategies that can be adopted, may be mentioned as under: (Suggestive listing only, not exhaustive):

(*i*) Recycle scraps/rejects and retrieve economic value out of the same.

(*ii*) Encourage and accordingly train and give proper incentives for multi-skilled multi-tasking working force; this may help reduce manpower drastically and improve productivity.

(*iii*) Adopt group-technology and multi-functional machines and equipment to the extent feasible to reduce capital investments and operating costs.

(*iv*) Adopt policies for quicker disposal of scraps, old/obsolete machines, and dead inventories-prolonged holding of these Non-Performing Assets will only be a burden on financial and other resources.

(*v*) Adopt action plans for reconditioning and retrofitting/life-extension programmes for older machine-tools and other production equipment, to the extent they are compatible with the ongoing products and technological processes; however, the economics of total replacement by a new advanced technology machine **Versus** the cost of reconditioning/retrofitting of the old one have to be carefully analysed before a decision is taken.

Note: *New is New and Old is Old, and the Economics of operation is an important issue.*

(*vi*) Adopt appropriate separation schemes (VRS, etc.) for non-performing employees/surplus manpower.

(*vii*) Adopt appropriate re-training and re-deployment programmes for skill-wise redundant employees to increase/improve their performance and productivity.

(*viii*) Adopt conscious policies and workable steps for energy saving and avoidance of energy wastages; energy saving lead to more energy being made available to more consumers/ needy people. Periodical Energy Audit can help re-casting energy needs and economise on consumptions.

(*ix*) R&D efforts for developing technologies and process for recycling and re-usage of material and machine, developing technologies and process for recycling and re-usage of material and machine resources can be rewarding.

(*x*) As regards re-generation of monetary resources:

- Adopt careful strategies for deployment of surplus funds (fixed deposits, inter-corporate deposits, investment in capital markets, etc.).
- Keep a very close watch on working capital management (cost of capital (interest burdens, levels of inventory, levels of current assets and liabilities, etc.).

4.6 Critical Factors for Successful Mobilization and Utilization of Resources in an Industrial Enterprise

In an industrial enterprise optimal management of Resources and Assets require rather constant focus on certain critical operational aspects. The related critical factors are needed to be identified and action-oriented organizational efforts directed towards these to ensure the desired results. While initial identification may help in articulating the objectives, regular monitoring of activities as well as updation/course correction will be imperative for successful implementation on a sustainable basis. It is also to be ensured that any mid-course abandonment or drastic revision in targets should best be avoided unless such changes are justified after a critical analysis of the prevailing circumstances and the constraints being encountered.

Right from the inception of such optimization exercises, the period of implementation or the 'Action-cycle' for each critical factors be determined and responsibilities enmarked, even if the implementation period extends beyond the initially scheduled time-frame. Therefore, while drawing up action plans and the matching responsibility matrix, the objective continuity should also be kept in view.

While there can be wide variations in the identified critical factors from enterprise to enterprise (depending on the kind of business operations), an attempt is being made in the Table 4.6.1, to present a Representative Chart of Critical Success Factor with respect to an industrial corporation dealing with high-tech products and processes.

4.6.1 Critical Success Factors (Period: Say 2007-2008); (Selective Focus), (Table: 4.6.1)

Sl. No.	Critical Activity (Selective Focus Areas)	Resources Linkage	Nodal Agency(ies) (Note: *Please see Legend below)*
1.0	**FOCUS ON HUMAN RESOURCE MANAGEMENT:**		
1.1	Recruitment strategy: • Hire for Attitude, Train for Skill. • Regular employment only for core-activity area, rest on non-permanent engagement. • Off-load/Out-source non-core-area services/activities.	Man, Management, Methods/knowledge	HRM/HRD
1.2	Training/Re-training and skills development	Man, Management, Methods	HRM/FM
1.3	Industrial Relation and Employee welfare	Man, Money, Management, Methods	HRM
1.4	Incentive and Reward Schemes	Man, Methods/Knowledge, Machine, Material	HRM, IE/PS/FM
2.0	**FOCUS ON OPERATIONS MANAGEMENT:**		
2.1	Production/Manufacturing • Technology and process development/improvement	Man, Methods/Knowledge, Machine, Material	PM/Mfg/PT/QM/PMS/FM

(Contd...)

Sl. No.	Critical Activity (Selective Focus Areas)	Resources Linkage	Nodal Agency(ies) (Note: *Please see Legend below)*
	• Machine and Labour deployment and utilization	Man, Machine, Management	PM/PT/Mfg./PPC
	• Sub-contracting/Off loading	Materials, Machine, Management	PM/MM/Mfg./FM
	• Stream-lining shop floor up-keep through 5-S system	Man, Material, Management, Methods	PM/Mfg./PMS/PS
2.2	Plant Maintenance and Repair Services • Preventive Maintenance and Down-time reduction	Man, Machine, Methods/Knowledge, Management	PM/PMS/PT
	• Retrofitting/Reconditioning	Man, Machine, Methods/Knowledge, Management	PMS/FE
	• Adopting 'Jishu-Hoizen' (Autonomous Maintenance)	Man, Machine, Methods/Knowledge, Management	PMS/Mfg./PT/PS/FE
2.3	Quality Management: • Quality Plans	Man, Machine, Methods/Knowledge, Management, Material	PM/QM/QA/EM/PT
	• SQC/QTM	Methods/Knowledge	QM/QA

(Contd...)

Sl. No.	Critical Activity (Selective Focus Areas)	Resources Linkage	Nodal Agency(ies) (Note: *Please see Legend below)*
	• ISO-9001 QMS	Man, Machine, Methods/Knowledge, Management, Material	All functions related to Production and Support Services
2.4	Materials Management: • Inventory Control	Materials, Methods, Knowledge, Money, Management	MM/MPI & C/FM
	• Vendor Development	Materials/Knowledge/Management	M M
	• Disposal of Surplus/scraps, etc.	Material, Methods	M M
	• Supply Chain Management and Logistics (Internal and External)	Material, Methods, Knowledge, Management	MM/CM/Shipping (Inward and Outward)
2.5	Security and Safety • Accident control/avoidance	Man, Machine, Material, Methods, Management	SS/GA/SM/PMS
	• Pilferage/Sabotage avoidance/control	Methods, Management	SS/GA/SM
2.6	Energy Management • Energy Audits (periodical)	Man, Machine, Methods/Knowledge	PM/PMS/PS

(Contd...)

Sl. No.	Critical Activity (Selective Focus Areas)	Resources Linkage	Nodal Agency(ies) (Note: *Please see Legend below*)
	• Energy Conservation/economizing	Man, Machine, Methods	PM/PMS/PS
	• Fuel supply, storage and distribution/utilization	Man, Materials, Machine, Methods	MM/PM/PMS
3.0	**FOCUS ON CUSTOMER SERVICES:**		
	• Marketing Strategy	Man, Methods, Management	CM/MKM/PM
	• After Sales Services	-do-	-do-
	• Contract Management	-do-	-do- /FM
4.0	**FOCUS ON FINANCIAL RESOURCES:**		
	• Funding Strategy and Cash/Treasury Management	Money, Methods/Knowledge, Management	FM
	• Working Capital Management	-do-	FM
	• Effective Budgetary Controls	-do-	-do-
	• Effective Internal Auditing	-do-	-do-

(Contd...)

Sl. No.	Critical Activity (Selective Focus Areas)	Resources Linkage	Nodal Agency(ies) (Note: *Please see Legend below)*
5.0	**FOCUS ON GENERAL ADMINISTRATIVE MANAGEMENT:**		
5.1	Special-purpose Tasks • TQM work culture	Man, Machine, Materials, Methods, Motive, Management	All functional Heads/ BEA
	• Environmental Management System (EMS)	Man, Methods/Knowledge, Management	-do-
5.2	• Public Relation and Social Responsibility	-do-	All concerned agencies
5.3	• Business Ethics and Corporate Governance	Man, Methods, Management	All Functional Heads, CEO, BEA.

(Contd...)

Notes :

(i) Scope of coverage can be expanded depending on the organizational priorities and type of operation.

(ii) LEGEND:

PM	=	*Production Management;*
PT	=	*Production Technology;*
PMS	=	*Plant Maintenance and Services;*
PS	=	*Productivity Services;*
IE	=	*Industrial Engineering;*
FE	=	*Facility Engineering;*
MM	=	*Materials Management;*
CM	=	*Commercial Management;*
MKM	=	*Marketing Management;*
Mfg	=	*Manufacturing;*
QM	=	*Quality Management;*
SQC	=	*Statistical Quality Control;*
QTM	=	*Quality Through Measurement;*
HRM	=	*Human Resource Management;*
HRD	=	*Human Resource Development;*
PPC	=	*Production Planning and Control;*
MPIC	=	*Material Planning and Inventory Control;*
QA	=	*Quality Assurance;*
QC	=	*Quality Control;*
SS	=	*Security System;*
GA	=	*General Administration;*
SM	=	*Safety Management;*
TQM	=	*Total Quality Management;*
EM	=	*Engineering and Design Management;*
BEA	=	*Business Excellence (Nodal) Agency;*
CEO	=	*Chief Executive Officer.*

> ***"Shoot for the moon and if you miss, you will still be among the stars."***
>
> — *Les Brown*

❍❍❍

CHAPTER-5

BUDGETING AND BUDGETARY CONTROLS FOR RESOURCE MANAGEMENT IN BUSINESS/ INDUSTRIAL ENTERPRISES

> *"The right people are those who have innate ability to integrate themselves into the company and work with others whether it is sales, production, finance, technology, IT, R&D, or even Formula one."*
>
> *— Gunther Fleig, Global HR Director, Daimler-Chrysler*

For all business enterprises, industrial or non-industrial, the process of budgeting and budgetary controls is a very important tool for a rational management strategy. Appropriate budgeting method and budgetary control processes keep the enterprise tonned up all the time, keeping its functionaries alert towards focused and result-oriented management of operations at all levels and in all the functional areas.

It is also to be appreciated that the budgeting and budgetary control process have a direct bearing on the acquisition, deployment and utilization of various resources that contribute to the economic value of enterprise operations.

From the point of view of budgeting and budgetary control for resource, there are basically two types of budgeting; one for Capital Investment towards acquisition of Fixed Assets, called the 'Capital Budget' and the other is for operations-called the 'Revenue or Operations Budget'. In the following paragraphs, we shall elaborate on both.

5.1 Capital Budget

Capital budgeting relates to expenditures incurred/to be incurred on acquisition and deployment of capital asset, also called the 'Fixed Assets' comprising of Plant & Machinery (for production lines), Building/Sheds, Services plants and Services lines for supporting operational areas, offices and office equipment, equipment/machinery and facilities for the purposes of material handling and storage, facilities for assembly and testing, facilities for medical and canteen services, equipment and facilities for safety, security and fire-fighting, etc. These capital/fixed assets have long life (may range from 5 to 30 years or beyond) and give productive outputs for generation of saleable products and services over a period of years, depending on their normal/prescribed life span which also depends on, to a considerable extent on (*a*) the degree of usage, (*b*) technological obsolescence.

The Annual Action Plan drawn up for expenditures to be incurred on such fixed assets (cash outflow basis) is called the annual Capital Budget (or annual capital expenditure programme).

All the fixed Assets are concrete resources which go on contributing towards successful operation of the enterprise for generation of saleable products and services as long as these fixed asses remain productive and healthy for smooth functioning and also till the related technological processes remain commercially viable, and marketable.

Note: *Besides the concrete resources in the form of Fixed Assets as mentioned above, capital expenditure is also incurred, at the inception of the capital project, for certain abstract resources like technological process knowledge inputs form external sources (consultants/collaborators), project execution,supervision-assistance from consultants/collaborators, initial training and skills development expenses, etc., which normally get charged to capital expenditure programmes, and hence covered by the Capital Budget.*

5.1.1 Capital Budget Scope

It is an annual exercise necessarily to be undertaken in conformity with the project planning and execution schedules drawn up for execution and installation of fixed asset type facilities which may be:

(*i*) Part of a Capital Investment Project (Greenfield or expansion).

(*ii*) Part of Technological Modernization programme for the capital/ fixed asset type facilities (including replacements) for the production lines as well as for the supporting services functions like plant maintenance and repairs, quality control, material handling, transportation and other such infrastructural facilities.

(*iii*) Part of a Welfare schemes like Hospital, Canteen, Housing for employees, Recreation centre, etc.

5.1.2 The Structural Approach to Capital Budget Formulation

Notes: (*i*) *The approach towards structuring of Capital budgeting (having long-term implications) may vary from organization to organization depending on the work-culture followed, but the basics will be the same or similar.*

(*ii*) *For more details about Capital budgeting process, readers may please read the book titled "Capital Investment*

Projects: Concept to Commissioning", written by the same author (also refer to books listed under Group-C of Annexure 9 attached to this book).

From the experiences gained in some large successful corporations, the annual capital budget can be drawn up in three distinct parts for clarity of follow up action and budgetary control and monitoring; these are mentioned below:

(*a*) Capital Budget Estimates (BE) for the ensuing year (year starting 1st day of the next financial year);

(*b*) Revised Capital Budget Estimates (RE) for the current year;

(*c*) Preliminary Capital Budget Estimates (PBE) for the 3rd year (year following the ensuring year, *i.e.,* next year):

5.1.2.1 BE for the ensuing year

The **Budget Estimates (BE)** for the ensuing year have to be prepared well before the year starts so that all executing agencies can plan their activities in advance and work out the estimated expenditures (and incomes if any) for respective functional areas. In most Indian business enterprises, budget year (financial year) starts on 1st April and ends on 31st March next year (in line with governmental system for certain advantages in accounting and corporate tax matters). For convenience of articulation, compilation and finalization, the budget exercise starts around six months ahead of the start of the budget year, *i.e.,* sometimes in June-July of the current year. Capital expenditure programme has to be necessarily dovetailed with the physical execution programmes/schedules of the capital investment projects and schemes either already in progress or are being planned for execution during the next two financial years or so, in line with the short-term and long-term operational and growth objectives drawn up for the enterprise. The expenditure figures are estimated in prescribed methods for fixed asset-type facilities to be procured and installed (civil works, plant and machinery, services lines and related infrastructural facilities, etc). According to the Project Reports (PPR/DPR) already approved or under consideration for approval, cost estimates, cash outflows required during the budget year are known based on the physical execution schedules broken down to weekly, monthly, quarterly action plans. A collated compilation of these cash outflows, item-wise and project/scheme wise, forms the basis of the budget estimates; these data are then presented in the prescribed budget formats for the ensuing year. After due scrutiny and evaluation followed by recommendation by the concerned agencies, the budget proposals are approved and funds sanctioned by the competent authorities for execution as per budgeted action plans for the budget year.

The budget formats may be developed as per the needs and work-culture of the enterprise, keeping in view, of course, certain statutory requirements as per the provisions of the Company Laws and Income Tax/ Corporate Tax Laws applicable.

5.1.2.2 RE for the current year

A mid-year review of BE drawn up last financial year for the current (under current execution) throws up more realistic situation needing certain corrections and adjustments to be incorporated in the budgeted programme and resultant cash-outflow requirements. These corrections and adjustments are reflected in the **Revised Estimates (RE)** (of expenditure) for the current year. These are debated, scrutinized and evaluated by the concerned knowledgeable agencies/functionaries who recommend the proposed expenditure programmes to the competent authorities for due approval. With appropriate monitoring and budgetary control mechanism in place, achievements of the RE programme can be near or even more than 100% (of course, within the permissible limits of variations). In fact, in today's competitive environment, to avoid time and cost over-runs, budgetary performance is one of the critical measurement criteria for judging the achievements of the enterprise as well as the competency of its management.

5.1.2.3 PBE for 2nd financial year

For certain long-lead time projects and items, some cashflow requirements may to be projected for the third year (*i.e.*, next to the ensuing year). These cash outflow requirements are reflected in the capital budget proposals as **Preliminary Budget Estimates (PBE).** PBE is not a complete budget proposal; this is drawn up to help advance planning for continued (approved) projects as well as for new projects planned for execution, fully or partly, during the third year as well.

5.1.2.4 Need for a long-term perspective for perfecting budgetary processes

From the above paragraphs it becomes evident that for a business enterprise, particularly an industrial organization, short-term and long-term company objectives (for sustenance and growth) are required to be drawn up and updated from time-to-time (may be in a cycle of 2-3-5 years period) to be more realistic about the requirement of capital investments matching with the drawn up company broad objectives and action programmes.

Capital investments on resources (mainly Fixed Assets) must have a long-term perspective since money is locked up for a number of years and not retrievable readily in liquid cash like the current assets.

5.1.2.5 Implication of capital expenditure on enterprise resources

As a result of capital expenditure, certain new resources get created in the form of Fixed Assets (machines, structures/buildings, etc.) which are essential for generation of saleable products and services and hence sustenance of business operations. These fixed assets after installation and duly valued (at the installed cost) get entered into the Company's Asset

Books as 'Capitalized Fixed Assets' on which depreciation is charged at the end of every financial years. The total Capitalized Gross-value of Fixed Assets is termed as 'Gross-Block (GB)' and the written down value, after deduction of applicable depreciation amount, is termed as 'Net-Block (NB)'. The values of GB and NB are important factors to be considered for the preparation of the company's Balance Sheets as well as for determination of the company's asset base.

Note: *All capital expenditure programmes/projects are to be duly appraised and analyzed by experts for determining the cost-benefits (ROI, IRR, ARR, etc.) of such investments; and before execution, approval of the competent authorities must be obtained; deciding on expenditure/ investments must be based on adequate techno-commercial and financial justifications.*

5.2 Operations Budget (Revenue Budget) for Resources Used in Running the Enterprise

This is an all encompassing budgeting exercise to cover all aspects and all areas of operations in a business/industrial enterprise. This annual exercise may even include a part of capital investment related items like depreciation, interest on borrowed capital, and cash-flow trends for capital expenditure. This annual exercise aims at drawing up action plans for incomes and expenditures arising out of various physical and conceptual work programmes scheduled for execution during the budget year for generation of saleable products and services. Here also, the exercise is done in two steps first for drawing up annual budgeted programmes for the next financial year, at least 2-3 months ahead of the start of the financial year; and the second part is for the drawing up of the revised estimates (RE) for the current year after a mid-year review around August-September every year, assuming that the budget year start on 1st April and ends on 31st March.

The Operations Budget is also called the 'Revenue Budget', since the main purpose of this budget is to draw up action plans for utilization of resources predominantly in monetary terms to facilitate generating revenues out of the operations in the form of returns/profits on capital employed. Therefore, all aspects of operations have to be dovetailed and tuned to this objective. The operation budgeting process aims at working out targets for all functional areas at macro and micro levels and enables quantitative measurement of performance *vis-a-vis* the set targets, at the end of desired periods.

The Operations Budget is also in a way closely associated with acquisition, deployment and utilization of various resources; some in concrete physical shape, like Man, Material, Machines, as well as others in abstract/ conceptual form such as Motive, Method/Knowledge, etc., besides making use of the link resource 'Money' which has a role everywhere; also 'Energy', the 'behind the scene' resource vital for operational activities, and finally, 'Management' providing the leadership and directional thrusts.

5.2.1 The Operation/Revenue Budgeting for Physically Visible Resources

5.2.1.1 HR-budget

Human Resources (HR) related activities like recruitment and posting of manpower, establishment matters including salary and compensation packages, welfare matters, disciplinary matters, etc., physical targets and financial implications/cash flows for these are to be reflected in the budget including the expenditures to be incurred towards labour and supervision costs involved in various functional activities. Besides the related expenditures on the above, the HR budget will also include the following:

*(*i*) Identification and quantification of wastages (transfer out, resignations, retrenchments, severence, deaths, etc.): and reflecting these in the budgeted programmes;

(*ii*) Drawing up programmes for training re-training, skill development and updation of knowledge for employees at different levels, and necessary re-deployment.

* *Based on past trends and intelligent guestimates.*

5.2.1.2 Materials budget

In an industrial enterprise, as we have already stated in Chapter-2, materials comprise of a major chunk of product costs, varying from 30% to 65% depending on the kind of product and the technological processes followed. Therefore, Material Resource budgeting has to find a very important place in the Operations Budget, in the form of the following budgetary processes:

(*i*) Procurement/Purchase budget and cashflows thereon, based on the production plans/physical turnover level drawn up, and other related functional programmes being undertaken for the year, including the provisions for Accretion and Decretion to WIP build-up programmes. Materials will comprise of Direct Materials (raw materials, components, bought out items, etc., which form the parts of the product), and Indirect Materials like tools, tackles and consumables for the supporting services such as shop auxiliary activities, plant maintenance and repair services, other infrastructrual services including offices and administrative/ establishment matters; other sundry materials and consumables, etc.

(*iii*) Materials budget may also include the activities as well as the related expenses and incomes generated from disposal of old/ obsolete machines and equipments, scraps, rejects, surpluses in stock/inventory.

5.2.1.3 Machine related budget

(*i*) Procurement/purchase as well as installation of Plant and Machinery (including provisions for Labour, Consumables, supporting services, etc.) are normally covered under (Capital Budget as discussed above under paras 5.1.1 and 5.1.2 and therefore, these activities are not covered by Operations Budget (Revenue Budget).

(*ii*) **Expenses to be incurred towards their upkeep, maintenance, repair, disposal, etc., normally get covered in Operations Budget (towards the cost of operations).

Notes:**(*i*) *Depending on the policies on accounting and asset management followed in the company, and also subject to permissibility under the relevant statutory provisions,incomes accruing from the disposal of surplus and obsolete/old Capital Machinery (Fixed Asset Type) may either be kept separately in a 'Reserve Fund', or get absorbed in the incomes generated out of the operations.*

(*ii*) *The 'Reserve fund' mentioned above, may be later utilized, like the 'Depreciation fund' for future Capital expenditures in case such occasion arises.*

5.2.2 Operation/Revenue Budgeting for Other Important Resources

5.2.2.1 Motive

This invisible but forceful resource, although present in every human endeavour, cannot be quantified and hence not as such reflected in the budgeted programme.

Note: *Budgeting exercise itself is driven by certain business motives.*

5.2.2.2 Management

This is the physical embodiment of the organization and is the driving and leading force behind all operational activities of the enterprise, but at the same time cannot the quantified in a way so as to be reflected in financial terms in the budgeted programmes. However, salaries and perks of the management level persons are reflected partly in the salary budget and partly in the administrative overheads as a percentage of cost of production. It is difficult to evaluate executive contributions fully in monetary terms as a percentage of turnover, unless the information and cost data can be maintained specifically for this purpose and appropriate identifiable systems could be put in operation. Unlike 'Value Added' , 'Executive Value Addition (EVA)' is rather difficult to quantify, since Executive/ Managerial efforts get reflected in the overall performance of the enterprise, both in tangible and intangible form.

5.2.2.3 Methods and knowledge

Here again, although these are present in every sphere of activities, it is difficult to quantify their contributions to the overall turnover value, but their impacts can be felt. However, a part of such contributions can be reflected through the productivity gains arising out of innovative and creative ideas and suggestions from the employees executed through specific projects. Such gains when converted into financial terms may get quantified and highlighted in the value of production/turn over, and therefore, a percentage *vis-a-vis* turnover value can be worked out provided the data are maintained separately for this purpose.

Technological process knowledge and expert-guidance borrowed from external sources can be financially quantified since certain fees are to be paid and expenses are to be incurred for the purpose. Here again, the data have to be maintained properly at all the stages, and these should be retrievable on demand.

5.2.2.4 Money: The link resource

Being omnipresent, money is reflected everywhere in the budgeted programmes; all operational results are finally interpreted in monetary terms, and different performance indices (ratios) are worked out to evaluate overall achievements as well as drawbacks if any. Cost of capital (interest rates, etc.) is an important factor, both in Capital expenditure as well as in Working Capital Management. Funding and Cash flow programmes have to find a prominent place in the Operation Budget.

5.2.2.5 Budgeting for energy

There is supposed to be a continuous assessment and control on energy consumptions in various forms: lighting, cooling, heating, air-conditioning and refrigeration and for industrial drives and controls as well as for other infrastructural and operational activities. Budget estimates for fuels (oil, coal, gas, etc.) and for electricity usages have to be based on prevailing costs and tariffs and the quantitative consumption levels forecast for the budget year. Various agencies involved, consuming agencies and the internal supplying/controlling agencies, have to play their respective roles responsibly and effectively so that consumptions are controlled within the prescribed norms and that wastages, pilferages, abuses, etc., are kept at the minimum, if not totally avoided.

An analysis of consumptions/connected loads at various load/consuming centres must precede the working out of the budget estimates on protracted expenditure and all the data and information thus generated, must be recorded and records maintained properly for enabling future use/ analysis: with PCs/ Computer Networking in place everywhere nowadays, this should not be a difficult task anymore. Most manufacturers of plant and machinery and equipment, these days, indicate energy consumptions (mostly in KWhrs units and KWs) at various levels of machine loading. Such data can be compared with actuals for enabling monitoring and control of energy consumption. Periodical (at least once a year) **Energy Audits** may be very useful tool in the hands of enterprise management for enabling energy efficient operations.

5.3 Budgetary Control

A discussion on budgeting process is rather incomplete without a discussion on budgetary control processes. Budgetary control is primarily exercised by the finance department, but it is the duty of all sanctioning authorities/agencies as well as the execution agencies to conform to budgetary discipline and avoid excesses over budgeted sanctions/provisions for various heads and sub-heads of expenditure. While excess income over budgeted income is welcome, on the other hand excess expenditure without adequate justification is unwelcome and best be avoided unless there is compelling reasons like unforeseen circumstances pushing costs upwards, or inadvertent under-estimation of expenditure due to lack of adequate information/data input at the time of budget formulation. Since it is difficult to prepare cost/expenditure estimates absolutely correctly at the time of budget preparation, certain flexibility is allowed to the executing agencies by approved **Delegation of Power (DOP)** for excess-over-sanction (normally ranging from 5% to 10%); beyond the prescribed permissible limits, re-approval of the competent authorities has to be obtained with due justification prior to entering into excess commitments and incurring excess expenditure. Budgetary discipline has to be practised at all levels in various functions. Designated controlling agencies like finance department, internal audit, budget allocating agencies etc., have to regularly monitor and exercise control through periodic reviews and scrutiny of expenditure trends and presenting the findings to the concerned agencies and regulatory authorities for enabling corrective actions which may include amongst other things, stopping further release of fund unless revised sanctions (with due justification) are obtained from the appropriate authority. Appropriate MIRs are to be put into practice for such evaluation, monitoring and regulatory controls.

5.3.1 Elements of Budgetary Control

Budgetary control refers to controlling expenses, commitments, cash outflows and inflows, resource mobilization and utilization *vis-a-vis* the set budgetary targets/allocations and monitoring the implementation results/progress in physical and financial terms, at various stages of execution under different heads of activities and accounting.

5.3.1.1 MIRs (Management Information Reporting Systems)

For the purpose of budgetary control and monitoring, it is essential to have a system of periodical feedbacks to the controlling agencies/management for enabling status appreciation and corrective measures if required. Management Information Reporting System (MIRs) is one of the most effective feedback system tools for the Management control.

These MIRs periodically (weekly, monthly, quarterly, etc.) brought out in the appropriate formats presenting meaningful data, reflects status of performance in various areas of operation. An analysis of these reveal, amongst other things, weak areas/deficiencies which need immediate attention for corrective measures.

5.3.1.2 Specific objects of MIRs

The elements of budgetary control that these MIRs, together with periodical reviews, help identify, are broadly as under:

(*i*) Cash flow (inflow-outflow) pattern/trends.

(*ii*) Materials inflow and consumptions patterns, inventory level/trends.

(*iii*) Production progress/output trends *vis-a-vis* targets and customer commitments.

(*iv*) Machine utilization levels/trends.

(*v*) Labour utilization levels, productivity, shop/work-centre efficiency.

(*vi*) Sales and dispatches trends, sales proceeds realization trends, (dispatches as per customer commitments).

(*vii*) WIP build-up trends.

(*viii*) Expenditure and Income trends.

(*ix*) Profitability indicators.

(*x*) Order book trends.

(*xi*) Other relevant aspects not mentioned above.

For the practising Corporate Managers, it is necessary to understand the significance of these elements and the occurrence patterns for the same, since such knowledge inputs help in increasing managerial competency and control.

5.4 Performance Budgeting

(*i*) This is a non-traditional budgeting concept where both financial and physical targets and action plans go hand in hand maintaining a more realistic relationship between the two.

(*ii*) In olden days, till around late 1960s, in general, budgeting exercise in industry and business as well as in the government establishments used to be a routine annual ritual mostly based on the premise of assumed and guestimated financial figures drawn up partly from past experiences/performances, and partly based on hunches/wisdom of those managers preparing the budget. The results in most cases used to be large scale deviations from the budgeted programmes and mismatching between the physical progress and financial expenditure targets.

(*iii*) The Performance Budgeting technique, introduced first time in the USA in early 1950s, and in India in .mid 1970s (mainly in

Govt. Sector Corporations and Govt. Departments), attempts to synchronise physical progress and financial expenditure progress as an unified working strategy to achieve the budgeted/planned goals. Performance budgeting system presents the budget in terms of functions, functional quantified programmes and activities, correlating the financial and physical aspects to establish a relationship between inputs and outputs.

(*iv*) Performance Budgeting system incorporates three important aspects:

Structural:	Relating to organizational and functional broad objectives.
Analytical:	Relates to macro and micro level detailing about all related activities, resources, performance, etc.
Informational:	Information needed for budget formulation. Information needed for implementation monitoring. Information needed for control. Information needed for evaluation of progress/results and for corrective actions.

(*v*) Performance Budgeting: exercise with respect to resources will entail more or less the same elemental aspects as mentioned above under Capital and Operations budgeting processes (Paras 5.1 & 5.2).

5.5 Information Sharing with Stakeholders (Employees Shareholders, Suppliers, Customers, Statutory Agencies, FIs, etc.)

Information on the budgeted programmes and operational results should be shared with the stakeholders; this is a pious duty of the enterprise management, to maintain transparency in operations, and building up a respectable image. This is generally done by bringing out Annual Reports (which includes Balance Sheets also).

> ***"If all economists were laid end to end, they would not reach a conclusion."***
>
> — *George Bernard Shaw*

❍❍❍

CHAPTER-6

ASSET MANAGEMENT IN INDUSTRIAL ENTERPRISES

> *"Good business leader creates a vision, articulate the vision, and relentlessly drive it to conclusion."*
>
> — *Jack F. Welch*

Industrial enterprises, by the very nature of their operations in the normal circumstances, shall posses a variety of assets generated over a period of time through deployment and utilization of different kinds of resources. The high level of Performing Assets (PA) holdings in an industrial enterprise actually reflects its ability to manage its resources quite well, proving that the resources are being put to productive usage effectively. Similarly, when an enterprise generates good operating results, it can be assumed that the enterprise is able to optimally use its assets as well.

However, the asset holdings almost invariably will be a mix of PA (Performing Assets) and NPA (Non-Performing Assets). In a successful enterprise, earning a good return on capital employed, the ratio PA/NPA will be quite high, but there are always chances of this ratio changing, both upwards and downwards, in the course of regular operations, depending on the quality and quantum of asset usage.

Assets may be in the form of physically visible ones, as well as conceptual ones, and a mix of both exists in most enterprises. We shall discuss in the following paragraphs, the three basic categories of assets generally available to enterprises for their operations: Physically Visible Assets, Conceptual (abstract) Assets, and Monetary Assets.

6.1 Physically Visible Assets

These generally comprise of the following:

6.1.1 Fixed Assets

Fixed Assets in the form of facilities like buildings, structures, plant and machinery, services plants, services lines, other infrastructural facilities created by capital investments.

6.1.2 Current Assets

Current Assets in the form of:

(*i*) Inventory holdings of raw materials, components, spare parts, other sundry materials, etc.

(*ii*) Finished goods in stock; Finished goods with customer on which sales proceeds yet to be realized.

(*iii*) WIP on shop floors.

(*iv*) Cash holdings: in hand, in banks.

(*v*) Receivables due from debtors.

(*vi*) Jewellery and other such costly items in possession/in banks.

(*vii*) Bonds and Fixed Deposits with FIs/Banks.

(*viii*) Shares, Debentures and other such cashable financial instruments.

(*ix*) Stores in transit.

6.1.3 Human Resource (as Human Assets Engaged in Productive Activities)

The most important resource comprising of employees of different categories and working at different levels of skills and ranks, in various functional areas. Human Resources when engaged on a regular basis in business enterprise operations, they become Assets so long they perform and make positive contributions.

6.2 Conceptual Assets

These refer to:

- Knowledge and Experience with employees, with management and with the organization as whole, and relevant to the line of business operations.
- Trademarks and Brand Equity/Brands established.
- Copyrights/Intellectual Property Rights.
- Information available and relevant to the line of business.
- Market Image/Reputation.

6.3 Monetary Assets

These refer to:

- Reflected as part of current assets (para 6.1.2 above) in monetary values.
- Generated Reserves/Surpluses.
- Public Deposits re-payable (term deposits as temporary assets).*
- Inter-Corporate Deposits returnable (term deposits as temporary assets).*

- Deposits against depository works (by external or associated agencies) (temporary asset).*
- Incomes from other sources/from non-core sector business dealings.
- In special circumstances, grants from Government and other external sources.
- Depreciation fund.

Note: **These are temporary in nature, but adds to monetary strengths at least for the period of deposits, although re-payable amounts will be higher due to interest burden.*

6.4 Asset Management Strategies

Business enterprises, as compared to Banks and FIs, are not often adequately conscious about their asset base/asset holdings and related (an needed) management strategies, and therefore, tend to ignore NPAs, so long the overall operational performance reflects good results and profits. This rather non-serious attitude may suddenly lead to an unexpected critical level of NPA increase beyond the permissible limits (with respect to TO* and PA), thus putting the enterprise into a credit crunch, specially for working capital availability due to low/poor credit-rating. Therefore, asset management, like the operations management, also deserve adequate attention and regular monitoring for enabling corrective measures as and when situation so demands. Asset Management efforts have to necessarily concentrate on the following strategies to the best extent possible under the prevailing circumstances under which the enterprise operates:

*(TO = Turn Over)

6.4.1 In Case of Fixed Assets

Capital expenditure on fixed assets has a long-term implication since it locks up money for a long period, and cannot normally be converted into ready cash quickly and easily. Hence, enterprise may have to consider the following aspects rather seriously with focused attention:

(*i*) Not to jump into capital investment projects without adequate feasibility studies and investment analysis and appraisal; consider all short-term and long-term implications.

(*ii*) Adopting judicious approach to capital expenditure; avoid luxury in such investment ('if Maruti 800 serves the purpose, why purchase a Maruti Esteem?'). When an enterprise operates with marginal viability, resorting to luxury in day-to-day operations, will amount to unwise and immature style of management, which should best be avoided.

(*iii*) To be sure about the technological process for which plants and machinery are proposed to be purchased and installed; both the selected technology life-cycle and the product life-cycle *vis-a-vis* market/customer demands/preferences be examined adequately for ensuring sustained marketability and market share of the products and services; existing competition and status of competitors.

(*iv*) Evaluating the operating costs of the plant and machinery proposed to be procured and installed (energy consumption level, lub oil and fuel oil consumption level, number of operators required to be engaged for optimal use etc.); examine more economic options if available.

(*v*) Examining alternatives to Capital investments: what happens if you do not go in for this investment?

(*vi*) Ensuring proper upkeep of the fixed assets already installed so that they remain productive and do not become non-performing and a drain on resources and therefore, becomes a liability, rather than assets.

(*vii*) Ensuring that capacity and size of the proposed machine/equipment are compatible with the product technological process; need not opt for bigger size just because it is cheaper, there are implications on cost of operations.

(*viii*) Making efforts to dispose off old/obselete machines and equipment as quickly as possible; continued possession of them may become burdensome and a constant liability.

(*ix*) Taking only those accessories and toolings/fixtures, etc., for machine tools which are essentially required; need not take more than required quantity and size just because price advantage is given by the supplier; you may unnecessarily lock up money for items which may not be required or sparingly required.

(*x*) Deploying trained/skilled personnel to operate the plant and machinery to avoid mis-handling and mishaps.

(*xi*) Exercise strict control on inventory of spare parts and dedicated consumables, tools and fixtures, etc.

6.4.2 In Case of Current Assets

(*i*) Keeping a constant watch on inventory holdings and make best efforts to keep them as low as possible (without of course affecting production and other operational programmes).

(*ii*) Determined efforts should be made to sell off finished goods as quickly as possible and realize sales proceeds.

(*iii*) Determined efforts be made to realize receivables as quickly as possible; constant follow up has to be done; some incentives can be thought of to entice debtors for quick release of payments.

6.4.3 In Case of Conceptual Assets

(*i*) Encouraging knowledge gathering, knowledge build-up, and knowledge sharing within the enterprise.

(*ii*) Giving due respect to the knowledgeable people so that they are motivated to make contributions; also encourage creativity and innovations wherever possible, in line with organizational goals.

(*iii*) Taking effective steps to protect Trademarks, Copyrights and Intellectual Property Rights of the enterprise; preserve knowledge assets.

(*iv*) Encouraging effective communication within the organization to avoid rumours and mis-understandings. However, communication has to be selective and restricted in certain situations; wise management to exercise discretion.

(*v*) Encouraging information exchange and sharing within the organization; discourage selfish approach by any individual or functional agency; however, guard against misuse, pilferage and leakage of company's vital secrets which only the concerned authorities (confidantes of the management) should know and handle.

6.4.4 In Case of Monetary Assets

(*i*) Most judicious and cautious approach be adopted while managing Reserves and Surpluses. If interest liability in commercially borrowed funds are high, consider diverting part of the reserve fund for meeting working capital needs and also for essential capital expenditure.

(*ii*) To be careful and conscious about the liabilities attached to the re-payable financial instruments (Public borrowings, Inter-Corporate deposits, etc.); a sudden emergent situation may get developed resulting in sudden heavy cash outflow causing working capital crises, there should be a contingency plan in place.

(*iii*) For deposits against depository works entrusted by others, take adequate measures right from the beginning to meet commitments made; failure do so may create legal and image problems; in case the enterprise is not geared to undertake such responsibilities, better avoid such dealings.

(*iv*) Having a clean policy about depreciation fund utilization, keeping in mind the statutory requirements and restrictions.

(*v*) Employee PF deposits should be handled with utmost care and observe all statutory provisions; keep in mind that this is a Trust Fund and trust has to be honoured all the time.

(*vi*) Current asset management processes should be as meticulous as possible, particularly inventory control and cash flows, to avoid burdensome and crisis situations, as best as possible.

(*vii*) Delegation of power (DOP) in money matters be practised rather carefully and executives/managers must be educated about its wise applications. Certain amount of vigilance, may be through Internal Audit, be exercised in this respect. Departmental Heads and Senior Management functionaries may have to do some monitoring from time-to-time through appropriate MIRs and budgetary control measures.

6.5 Assets-Resource Relationship

It is to be kept in mind that Assets and Resources are complimentary and supplementary to each other so far as their deployment and usage are concerned. If Assets are healthy and productive, Resources will follow without much difficulty, and both together give positive strengths to the enterprise operations.

6.6 Non-Performing Assets (NPA)

Like the inventory management, management of NPA has to get adequate attention of the enterprise management: efforts have to be made to keep NPA level as low as possible as well as taking measures for converting NPA into PA to the extent feasible under the given circumstances. In larger enterprise with Substantial Asset base, it may be worthwhile to create a dedicated cell to constantly keep a watch on the same and present relevant feedback data to the top management functionaries for enabling strategic decision making for corrective/improvement actions.

6.7 Keeping Stakeholders Informed about Status of Assets

Lastly, stakeholders should be kept informed of the status of Assets, at least once a year, through the annual report/balance sheet.

> ***"Assets shorn of economic value can become a liability in business."***
>
> —*A Financial Consultant*

❍❍❍

CHAPTER-7

ROLE OF EXTERNAL RESOURCES IN ENTERPRISE OPERATIONS

"The companies nowadays serve not only the shareholders, but an increasing number of stakeholders including employees, customers, communities and the activities of the civil and human rights."

—Taken from a book on Business Ethics and Corporate Governance

In the preceding Chapters, we have discussed the roles played by various resources, both from naturally occurring sources as well as from artificially created sources in running the business enterprises, specially the industrial units. It is seen that most of the resources actually come from external sources barring a few from internal sources which gets developed over a period (several years) of operations.

7.1 Internal Resources

The internal resources are mainly limited to:

- Existing organization and the employed manpower.
- Methods and knowledge already developed and available in-house.
- Certain facilities and infrastructure already installed and are in operation.
- Certain materials already in stock (existing inventory).
- Reserve funds a part of which can be utilized for meeting working capital needs, and for certain emergent capital expenditure, in case such exigencies arise.

7.2 External Resources that are Important for Industrial Enterprise Management

7.2.1 Materials from External Sources

7.2.1.1 Procured items

Most of the direct materials, machines and equipment, and the bought out components, finished and semi-finished items, sundry indirect materials, etc., come from suppliers who may be the original manufacturers or trading agents; even certain processed naturally occurring items like gases, timber, cut stones, agricultural produce, minerals/ores, petro-products, etc., are procured from the external sources; this requires effective and dependable supply chain management strategy to ensure regular supply in cost effective regimes.

7.2.1.2 Sub-contracted/off-loaded items

Besides raw materials, components, bought out items for the main products, certain auxiliary items like tools, tackles, special Jigs and fixtures, fasteners, packaging materials, etc., are also procured from external sources. In case of certain components, tools, Jigs and fixtures, although there may exist internal capacity and capability to produce in-house, due to cost considerations, it may be more attractive/cost-effective to procure from outside sources. In fact, off-loading of certain items to sub-contracting sources, is adopted as a good cost-effective procurement strategy to reduce cost of production and making the end products competitive in prices. In fact, this is a widely practised cost-effective procurement strategy adopted by industrial enterprises to maintain competitive edge.

7.2.1.3 'Make or Buy'

'Make or Buy' is a regular feature of procurement strategy specially for a manufacturing unit, this is very relevant to sub-contracted/off-loaded items.

7.2.2 Hiring External Support Services

In order to be competitive in the market, as a cost reduction strategy, even many of the support services like design, repair and maintenance services (routing/special), material handling, packaging, transportation, reprographic services, canteen and medical services, training and skill development activities and the like are being off-loaded to external agencies, thus leaving the core-manufacturing and quality control functions entrusted to the enterprise employees and functionaries posted in various departments.

7.2.3 Technology Acquisition from External Sources

7.2.3.1 Process knowledge and methods

As regards new/advanced technology (methods and knowledge resource) it is often borrowed from external sources, both from the domestic and the foreign collaborators, who supply the required technology and process details at a price and under certain terms and conditions.

7.2.3.2 Techno-commercial collaborations

In case of borrowed technology and other related resources from the collaborators, the following aspects need adequate examination and serious considerations before entering into a tie-up/agreement:

(*i*) It is to be ascertained as to whether the technology offered is compatible with the proposed/existing products and existing facilities?

(*ii*) In what form and mode the technology transfer shall take place (documentation, training of personnel, services of collaborator's experts).

(*iii*) What will be the life-cycle of the technology offered (short life, long life); one time or continuous over the contracted period.

(*iv*) Any financial support being extended (capital investments, working capital support, buy back arrangement, concessional supply of certain critical raw materials, components, etc.); under what terms and conditions.

(*v*) Credibility and reliability of the collaborators.

(*vi*) Third country business dealings, joint-venture in domestic as well as foreign countries.

(*vii*) Territorial restrictions imposed by the collaborators in third party/third country dealings.

(*viii*) Government policy of the collaborators country towards such collaborative arrangements (export-import restriction, restrictions on the technology transfer, restrictions on certain strategic/dual purpose materials/components/items and other related issues).

(*ix*) Terms and conditions on technology updation/upgradation in case such eventuality arise during the contract period.

(*x*) Alternative sources available and a comparative assessment of possibilities, advantages and disadvantages.

(*xi*) Attitude of the proposed collaborator in furnishing required information about their operations and clientele.

7.2.4 Other Relevant External Resources

Besides technology acquisition from collaborators (normally external agency), the following other resources can also be sourced from external agencies:

7.2.4.1 Financial support

- Equity participation by collaborators (funding assistance both for capital investment and working capital).
- Short-term and long-term borrowings from Development Funding Agencies, both National and International.
- Short-term and long-term borrowings from FIs and Banks.
- Public Deposits and Inter Corporate Deposits.
- Through issue of shares and debentures, etc.

7.2.4.2 Management support

In cases where a new high-tech product and related services are being introduced, necessity may arise to borrow the services of management experts either from the collaborators, or from competent Management Consultancy Agencies, to organize operations in the initial stages.

7.2.4.3 Engagement of workers on contract basis

Required numbers of unskilled and semi-skilled workers can be engaged on work-charged basis, through labour contractors/employment agencies. In fact, this is now a widely practised manpower strategy to keep regular manpower strength to the optimum/minimum essential level.

7.2.4.4 Security services

By engaging private security service agencies, this service can be sub-contracted to avoid inflating regular manpower strength with attendant complexities.

7.2.4.5 Cleaning and scavenging services/house keeping

This can also be sub-contracted to external agencies, thus avoiding recruitment of regular manpower.

7.2.4.6 Plant maintenance and services

Certain small and medium industrial units, in order to reduce maintenance manpower and the related infrastructural costs, these services are also being sub-contracted, provided such agencies with skilled manpower are available in the vicinity area, for a dependable service arrangement.

7.2.4.7 Medical service for employees

Many small and medium industrial and other business enterprises are sub-contracting these services to external medical service agencies.

7.2.4.8 Courier service

Through courier agencies operating in the market.

7.2.4.9 Cargo transportation services

Through transportation companies/agencies.

7.2.4.10 Packaging

In some locations, this is also being sub-contracted provided this is cost-effective and reliable agency is available in the area of operation.

7.2.4.11 Project construction works

These are normally being got done through construction contractors.

7.2.4.12 Acquisition of plant and machinery

Plant and machinery, equipment and devices for production and supporting services are to be procured from external sources: both manufacturers as well as dealers/supply agencies.

7.2.4.13 Machine erection and commissioning

(*i*) Manufacturer/supplier of the machines and equipment carry out such works as part of their supply contract.

(*ii*) Certain specialist groups are also rendering such services if need arises and approached; such needs may arise when re-layouting and re-installation of the facilities have to be done, or new facilities being procured and added.

7.2.5 Energy services

Energy supply services like fuels (oil, gas, coal, etc.) and electricity are mostly procured from external sources; however, in certain locations, due to dearth and/or lack of reliable supply, electrical energy is obtained by installing and running in-house generators, mostly by using diesel generating sets; but this method of electrical energy is costlier than those procured from the Electric Supply Agencies through the grid system; therefore, preference will be to get electrical supply from the grid system located in the vicinity area. The connectivity with far away located grid system may be quite costly in the initial stages of installation because of high capital investment cost/high tariff structure imposed by the Electric supply agency for installation of connecting transmission/distribution networks and the dedicated/on-site sub-station.

> ***"The Merchant has no country."***
>
> — *Thomas Jefferson*

❍❍❍

CHAPTER-8

IMPACTS OF RESOURCES ON WORKING CAPITAL MANAGEMENT

> ***"If my mind can conceive it, and my heart can believe it, I know I can achieve it."***
>
> — *Jesse Jackson*

To meet the expenses on execution of various activities and inputs for the day-to-day operation, it is essentially necessary to regularly provide for working funds which is generally called the 'Working Capital'. This fund supply has to be an assured arrangement, in most cases, with Financial Institutions (FIs), Banks and any other funding agencies. In some cases, initially for certain periods (to reduce interest burden/cost of capital), working capital requirements can be met out of any reserves/separable equity funds available with the enterprise owners/promoters, but for regular operations, this may not be a wise option, since business operations are supposed to generate own surpluses, a part of which can be ploughed back to meet the working capital funding requirements, and this cycle must go on, with periodical borrowings from the FIs/Banks, etc., as and when such exigency arises.

Referring to the aspects and issues discussed in preceding chapters, it can be inferred that the major focus of the Working Capital Management will have to be towards optimal cost effective management of deployment and utilization of various resources that are essentially required for viable and successful operation of the enterprise. Therefore, there is a definite relationship between resources inputs and the working capital deployment and management.

In the following paragraphs, we shall discuss the various aspects of Working Capital Management in business-cum-industrial enterprises.

8.1 Definitions and Scope of Working Capital Management

(*i*) For an industrial enterprise, the requirement of finance arise mainly for two purposes as stated under:

(*a*) to fund expenditure for acquiring and installing capital facilities called the 'Fixed Assets', *i.e.*, buildings/sheds, plant and machinery, support services and other infrastructural facilities used for production and related operational activities. Such expenditures are categorized as Capital Expenditure.

(*b*) to meet expenses on various elements of day-to-day operations, *i.e.,* to provide for working fund for various day-to-day expenses as already described in the opening paragraph of this Chapter, for enabling production of saleable products and services, (or for meeting various expenses in trading activities in a non-industrial business enterprise). Such expenditures are covered by Working Capital funding.

(*ii*) While the capital fund for capital expenditure ('*a*' above) on 'Fixed Assets' may be required one time in a span of several years (unless of course expansion, upgradation/modernization of facilities are undertaken subsequently from time-to-time) and the same may also be spent in more than one financial year, the funds for 'Working Capital' are required to be arranged to meet ongoing operational needs and is budgeted on a year-to-year basis (for the Revenue/Operations budget year). Working capital is, therefore, required to meet sundry expenses on raw materials, tools, tackles, components, shop accessories, energy and fuels, consumables, labour charges, wages, payments to the contractors/ suppliers, operational expenses towards various overheads and support services, *i.e.,* for meeting expenses on all such items and activities which are essential for earning revenues/incomes and generation of operating surpluses/profit margins out of the investments made.

(*iii*) Working capital actually keeps the business going since physical assets like machinery, land, buildings, etc., cannot by themselves generate any saleable products and services, unless they are adequately and regularly fed with materials and provided with varied other relevant inputs and support services. Therefore, finances required to buy such materials as well as for meeting expenses towards support services are really the working capital funding requirements.

(*iv*) With a given set of fixed assets, human and other resources for productive use, a matching level of working capital availability is essential. While any thing higher than the optimum level will not generate higher production or sales, like-wise anything lesser than an essential level of working capital may adversely effect the operational efficiency of the enterprise and result in opportunity loss in terms of partial utilization of fixed assets' potential and of other deployed resources. Therefore, proper management of working capital is imperative for successful and efficient business operations.

(*v*) From the physical and financial accounting point of view, working capital is money locked up in inventories (raw materials, components, spares, toolings and fixtures, semi-finished and finished goods awaiting dispatch/sale), sundry debtors and other current assets (like cash, advances made to suppliers/others, etc.), **Minus** money locked up with the business in the form of sundry creditors, bills payable, etc.

(*vi*) Composition of Working Capital will vary according to the nature of the business particularly whether it is a purely trading business or a manufacturing-cum-marketing organization. There are other factors too which cause variation, *viz.*, customary credit terms in the industry, the kind of business it is engaged in, general financial climate and conditions, and so on.

(*vii*) For a purely trading or marketing organization the composition of working capital would be as follows:

(*a*) Inventory: Finished goods only;

(*b*) Receivables: Sundry debtors, Bills receivable;

(*c*) Other current assets, cash, sundry advances for the values to be received, etc.

Total Current Asset $A = (a + b + c)$;

(*d*) Sundry creditors, bills payable, advances from customers etc.;

(*e*) Outstanding liabilities (to employees and outsiders)

Total Current Liabilities $B = (d + e)$;

Working Capital $= (A - B) =$ Current Assets – Current Liabilities.

(*viii*) For a manufacturing-cum-marketing organization, the inventory as at (*a*) above will also include besides finished goods, two other items, namely:

- Raw materials (of all types), components, spares for fixed assets, toollings, fixtures, etc.;
- Work-in-Process (WIP).

The rest of the elements as indicated above will remain by and large unchanged.

8.2 Significance of Working Capital Management

(A) Practising Managers working in any functional area in the enterprise in the course of discharge of their duties and responsibilities they take such actions which lead to financial commitments requiring working capital funding to meet the resultant expenses. Therefore, any careless action and avoidable commitments made may result in blockade of funds causing mismanagement of working capital and thus bring in financial losses to the enterprise. Working capital funding in many occasions is covered by hypothecation of goods and services yet to be generated for sale. Working capital funding is a difficult and risk-prone affair. Therefore, conscious efforts are to be made continuously to ensure optimal use of available working capital fund to maintain viability of operations. In fact, mismanagement of working capital is one of the major reasons for industrial sickness in many enterprises, big or small. When things get going rather smoothly, tendency of complacency sets in to blurr the vision and hence leading to crisis. There are also causes of delibrate and fraudulent diversion of working capital funds for purposes other than core business operations and this may hasten sickness/crisis in operations.

(B) Management of working capital has two aspects: *viz.*, the requirement aspect and finance aspect:

(*i*) The requirement aspect relate to the components of working capital: on the positive side of such components are 'Inventory' and 'Debtors', and on the negative side, is the component of 'Creditors'. Therefore, working capital management in the requirement side boils down to the management of Inventory, Debtors and Creditors.

*(*ii*) On the finance aspect, there are three financial ratios which are important and useful in keeping a constant watch on as well as controlling the above three parameters (Inventory, Debtors and Creditors); these ratios are:

- Invetory-to -Turnover ratio;
- Sundry debtors-to-Turnover ratio;
- Sundry creditors-to-Turnover ratio;

Note: **To understand significance of 'Key indicators' and 'operating ratios'. Interested readers may read the book mentioned at Sl. No. 8 (B) in Annexure 9.*

The financial aspect of working capital management, therefore, essentially means controlling the cost of finance involved. The cost of finance varies according to the source of finance and such costs have to be viewed from various operating angles, *viz.*, real cost and opportunity cost, direct cost and associated cost, implicit cost and explicit cost.

Bank interest rates, overdraft interest rates, credit rating of the organization, changes in the statutory levies, credit periods, outstandings from the customers/others are some of the important factors which effect cost of working capital.

(C) Some of the steps which may help in optimal Working Capital Management may be mentioned as under, particularly for a manufacturing-cum-marketing organization:

(*i*) Adopting carefully selected marketable products and services with market friendly technology, in acceptable quality at a competitive price. **(The Starting Points of Business Ventures.)**

(*ii*) Careful selection, procurement and installation of Fixed Assets and keeping them in proper order to generate saleable products in acceptable quality and with optimal productive quantity and at a competitive cost.

(*iii*) **Optiminal inventory management:**

- Procurement of right material in right quantity at right price at right time; avoiding excess build-up of stocks, avoiding purchase of sub-standard/low grade materials; avoiding/ minimizing rejections of incoming materials.
- A voiding wastages of/excess use of materials, high rate of rejection due to wrong/defective manufacturing, and due to sub-standard/outdated technology/process, and due to negligence.
- Adopting proper material planning and inventory control measures and techniques including computerized material management efforts.
- Avoiding pile-up of finished goods and making all out efforts to sell them off and realize sales proceeds as quickly as possible.
- Conscious efforts to stick to sequential dispatches as per customers requirement; erratic supplies may antagonize and eventually drive away customer.
- Value engineering and design optimization to reduce material consumption and wastage and to optimize product costs.

(*iv*) Optimal deployment and utilization of other resources like man-power, fixed assets, cash, investments, power, fuel, etc.

(*v*) Conscious and concerted efforts for cost reduction, cycle time reduction, avoidance of luxury and extravaganza in operational styles.

(*vi*) Vigorous efforts for quicker realization of sales proceeds/out-standings from customers, and debtors.

(*vii*) Avoiding excess withdrawal of funds from banks/financial institutions, creditors, thus reducing interest burden.

(*viii*) Good amount of efforts for proper cash-management (inflow-outflow balancing), surplus generation, judicious deployment of surplus funds, judicious expenditure.

(*ix*) Optimal sub-contracting strategy and judicious off-loading for components, services, finished items (judicious 'Make or Buy' decisions).

(*x*) Avoiding sudden changes in the process, product-mix, working culture, operating strategies, management styles, personal policies, marketing policies, etc. (a sudden system shock can create confusion and even havoc); imperative changes should be smooth and compatible.

(*xi*) Avoiding capital investments on facilities without rigorous and proper evaluation and analysis, and avoiding infructuous or non-essential capital expenditure, particularly spares and consumables for maintenance and repair services.

(*xii*) Avoiding unnecessary/excess commitments for purchases, wages (overtime payments etc.), non-essential indirect materials, etc.

(D) The significance of Money-flow Cycles involved in the Working Capital Management in an industrial enterprise is represented in the Fig. 8.1.

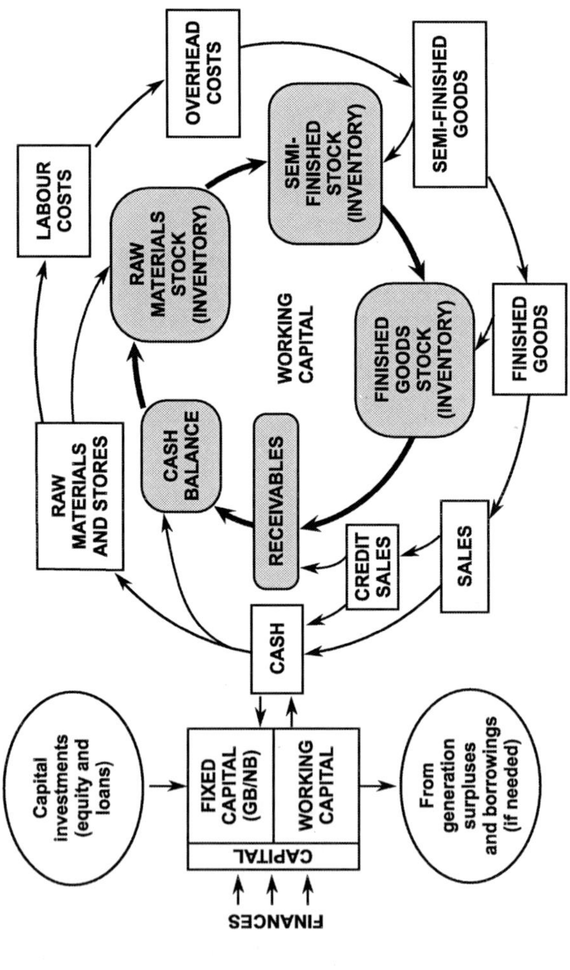

Fig. 8.1 Money flow cycles involved in working capital management.

8.3 Impacts of Resources in Working Capital Management

Here we take up for discussion only the most critical resources without which industrial ventures cannot even sustain, not to speak of growth and development, the objectives which give the impetus for constancy of purpose.

8.3.1 Money

In business, industrial or non-industrial, every aspect of result-orientation ultimately boils down to money and monetary affairs, since it is universally expected that the operations of the business venture shall generate profit-margins in monetary terms on a regular basis. Therefore, availability of adequate cash inflows at the required stages of the. operational activities, assumes a critical dimension, since without cash/fund inflow, everything may come to a standstill.

8.3.2 Materials

As we have already discussed in the preceeding Chapters, materials constitute 35% to 65% of cost of the end-products produced by industrial units depending on the type of products and the technological processes followed. Therefore, optimal level of procurement, storage/inventory holding, deployment and utilization is very important: treating and handling material management aspects rather casually and without proper planning and control, will have serious detrimental effects on working capital funding management (blockage of fund, increased interest burden) and thus in turn, effecting the operational viability.

8.3.3 Machines

Plant and machinery and other infrastructural facilities (fixed assets) together with tools, tackles, fixtures, etc., are essentially required for producing saleable products and services; therefore, their optimal deployment and usage in a cost-effective manner is very important; inefficient management of this resource may lead to a drain on financial resources, particularly on working capital funding, causing burdensome interest liability, besides adversely affecting productivity and profitability.

8.3.4 Management and Organization

Competent management personnel and the organizational set-up provide the leadership as well as directional thrust for any organization to operate successfully with a sense of purpose and constancy. Passive and lackadaisical management may lead to disarray and ineffective work culture, thereby affecting the very existence of the enterprise.

8.3.5 Man

As in the case of management personnel (owner, promoters, top level functionaries) referred to above in para 8.3.4, other categories of human resources deployed contribute towards important functions, the integration of which provide the driving force for running the affairs of the enterprise in a productive and purposeful manner. Therefore, properly trained and skilled manpower with right kind work-attitude and work environment, is the vital resource a business enterprise will cherish to possess; human endeavours directed in a right and purposeful manner, can do wonders to the achievements of the enterprise.

8.3.6 Methods and Knowledge

All human endeavours in business and industry have to depend on certain articulated well thoughtout methods and relevant knowledge inputs. As already discussed in Chapter-2 (paras 2.7, 2.7.1, 2.7.2), methods and knowledge go hand in hand to provide for important inputs to the business operations; lack of these will create hurdles and delays at every step with resultant detrimental effects on the enterprise viability.

8.3.7 Energy

We have discussed about the sourcing and deployment of this resource in the preceding Chapters; here we can reiterate the fact that lack of or absence of energy input can almost kill the business endeavours and lead to darkness everywhere literally speaking. Energy cost is an important element of working capital expenses and needs adequate attention and control for operational cost reduction

> ***"Never put off doing something useful for fear of evil that may never arrive."***
>
> *— James D. Watson, Co-discoverer of the structure of DNA*

❍❍❍

CHAPTER-9

INVENTORY CONTROL: A TOOL FOR MATERIAL RESOURCE OPTIMIZATION

> ***"Not everything that can be counted counts, and not everything that counts can be counted."***
>
> *— Albert Einstein*

Materials of different kinds and specifications are required as an essential input resource for an industrial enterprise producing saleable products. The role of the materials is as important as the product itself because material contents in the final products cost may be of the order of 35 to 65 per cent, depending on the type of product and the technological process involved. Therefore, materials management aspects, inventory control in particular, assume high degree of importance and shall require considerable and regular attention of the enterprise management.

In order to achieve a cost effective operational regime through measures like cost-reduction across the board, competitive pricing, and efforts towards maximizing profit margins, the enterprise management will have to adopt determined and calculated operational strategies that may include, amongst other relevant matters, optimizing the deployment and utilization of material resources at different stages of operations.

Materials Management is a complex function in an industrial enterprise and has a vast scope of activities including those relating to Material Planning and Inventory Control (MPIC as is generally known).

We are confining our discussion in the following paragraphs to the topic on MPIC and related issues with respect to material resource optimization.

9.1 Material Planning and Inventory Control

Note: *The practising managers in industrial enterprises are generally aware of the term 'MPIC' and related material management aspects, and therefore we need not dwell upon the fundamentals here, but focus on relevant practical issues.*

9.1.1 Material Planning

Material planning process has to take into consideration the following to be effective enough for the desired results:

(*i*) **Forecasting and Estimation of Requirements:** This has to be done as per the stipulated/budgeted physical production programmes as well as other related services/supporting activities that have to go along with product realization objectives. Care has to be taken that:

(*a*) In the enthusiasm for main product related priorities, other essential requirements should not be forgotten or ignored; such oversight or lesser priorities may sometimes result in hold-ups in the over all operations; for example, unexpected stock out of an indirect materials like computer stationery can result in work-bottlenecks, or stock out of a critical spare part may stop the functioning of a machine tool critically required for production of certain critical components.

(*b*) In the anxiety for playing safe regarding sudden or unexpected stock outs planning for excess material is often resorted to; this may result in a cascading effect causing undesirable build up inventory holding, thus blocking rather scarce and costly working capital.

(*c*) On the other hand, too miserly planning may create operational hold ups, particularly when, for certain reasons (valid or otherwise), excess material of that category gets consumed fast and results in stock-out, starving the production line or concerned support services.

(*d*) Considering the past trends as indication, procurement/stocking of certain percentage of excess stock of some category of items may have to be planned, but this has to be done judiciously; in such decisions, impulsive wisdom should best be avoided and the decisions are made based on proper quantitative analysis:

Notes: (*i*) *There are a number of quantitative techniques available (viz,ABC, EOQ, XYZ Analysis, etc., which are traditional; presently, IT-enabled software systems like SAP*/SAP-R3*/ my-SAP*/NET suite/Net-ERP/Net suite-CRM/Net-Flex etc. are being offered by Management Consultants. We shall discuss these later at the appropriate stage in this chapter.*

*(*ii*) *These businesses planning softwares have been developed and marketed by SAP-AG of Germany; they are the largest group in this field.*

(*ii*) Identifying supply sources, locating dependable vendors/ suppliers who can meet both, qualitative and quantitative requirements of the enterprise on a sustainable/regular basis.

(*iii*) Vendor evaluation and registration processes.

(*iv*) Planning for not only procurement, but also for proper storage, necessary conservation, and thereafter, distribution to the consumers/users (both internal and external).

(*v*) Drawing up materials budget (physical and financial) and the follow up action plan earmarking the scope and responsibilities of various departmental/sectional managers/other functionaries.

(*vi*) Drawing up programmes for stocking, styling and standardization in association with other concerned functional groups, to enable reduction in variety of categories and size-ranges, thereby reducing the complexities involved in maintaining and controlling of stocks and custody.

(*vii*) Maintaining proper records of all materials related to processes in practice and of the linkages/responsibility sharing with other functional areas.

(*viii*) Maintaining continuous rapport and liaison with both internal customers (user departments) and the suppliers.

(*ix*) To remain abreast with the globalized business environment, orient all material related activities on computerised systems of operations. If the enterprise is aiming at obtaining TQM certification, IT-enabled working in such critical functions becomes imperative for an impressive performance and image. The same is also true for a possible adoption of ERP in business operations.

9.1.2 Inventory Control: A Tool for Material Resources Optimization

Keeping the inventory holdings within the prescribed norms (norms prescribed by statutory provisions, banks/FIs, credit-rating agencies, enterprises' own recommended norms) in terms of financial values *vis-a-vis* the turnover levels, is a rather challenging task for the enterprise management (and for that matter, for the Materials Management functionaries), particularly for the enterprises operating with:

(*i*) high value and high volume products that require a wide variety of raw materials, components, Semis, brought out items, sub-contracted job-sharing, etc.

(*ii*) variable off-take rates of finished products by the markets/ customers.

(*iii*) a wide range of indirect materials requirements.

(*iv*) certain high value but long-lead-time items/scarce items which are difficult to procure at a short notice (within the prescribed procurement time).

(*v*) frequent changes in specifications necessitated by changing market demands/customer preferences.

9.1.2.1 Inventory control techniques

In view of the issues discussed above, inventory control function will be a sort of tight-rope walking all the time for materials management managers. To ease such stresses and reduce uncertainties, certain traditional as well as certain IT-enabled techniques have since been developed and put into practice over the last 6 to 7 decades with good results; some of these can be mentioned as under:

(*i*) *Traditional techniques like ABC, EOQ, XYZ Analysis;

(*ii*) *IT-enabled techniques using computer softwares like SAP/SAP-R3/MySap, Net ERP, Net suite, etc.

9.1.2.2 Parameters of inventory control techniques

Whether it is the traditional techniques, or the IT-enabled techniques as mentioned above, the analytical input data that may be used for inventory control purposes, may be generally as under:

(*i*) Value-based (price/cost wise) segregation and control.

(*ii*) Procurement time based (short-lead or long-lead-items) control.

(*iii*) Direct materials: critical, non-critical.

(*iv*) Indirect materials: critical, non-critical.

(*v*) Short-shelf life, long-life item wise segregation and control.

(*vi*) Strategic and non-strategic usage and supply/procurement constraints.

(*vii*) Import restricted or OGL items and related issues.

(*viii*) Off-loaded/sub-contracted items and related issues.

(*ix*) Consumption rate/pattern based control.

(*x*) Customer-preferred/specified items.

(*xi*) Any other categorization to meet specific needs of the enterprise (*e.g.*, multilocational away-centre inventory control through WAN-based IT systems).

9.1.2.3 Managerial ingenuity and experiences are vital

Inventory control is rather a tricky process like the share market dealings, and lot of working knowledge experience and ingenuity on the part of the concerned managers will be necessary to tackle the subject to a reasonable degree of success. Managers are to be trained in this specialization so as to be able to successfully handle the responsibilities with confidence under ever-changing situations.

Notes: *(*i*) *Those interested in acquiring detailed knowledge on the subject, are advised to read books on the subject and also undergo training programmes as and when the oppo-rtunity comes by.Enterprise management are expected to* *be aware of such training needs and arrange accordingly; in a globalized competitive business environment services of competent managers are essential for successful operation.*

(*ii*) *As for IT-enabled system application in inventory control, systems software as mentioned at paras 9.1.2.1 (iii) above are not readily available for learning and application. The concerned management consultancy groups impart training and help in implementation only against substantial payments against relevant contracted arrangements.*

(*iii*) *IT-enabled systems can be adopted successfully provided the enterprise's work processes and paper work systems and procedures are aligned/revamped and concerned employees are well-trained for implementation of such computerised working systems.*

(*iv*) *Once an organizational decision has been taken to adopt any IT-enabled system, it has to be taken up rather seriously and executed assiduously to the stage of complete implementation; half-hearted lackadaisical approach will only result in disarray, confusion and agony, besides infructuous expenditure and efforts.*

9.1.2.4 Inventory control for non-production areas

Inventory control in non-production areas will pre-dominantly deal with certain categories of indirect materials such as various types of consumables for support services areas, office and computer stationeries, services shop accessories, items required for canteen and medical services, sundry items for administrative, security and safety services, spare parts for machine tools and equipment, consumables and implements for quality control, transportation services, etc. Since there is a general tendency to focus mainly on direct materials for saleable products and related customer services, these indirect materials as mentioned above, get lesser priority and attention; therefore, there are higher chances of non-moving and slow moving indirect material inventory build-up, and at times, the locked up money may be considerable, thus putting a burden on the working capital resources. Depending on the magnitude of such inventory holdings, it may be worthwhile to earmark a separate dedicated managerial group to tackle such indirect materials inventory to avoid excessive stock build-up (or even low stock/stock out situations) beyond the permissible limits.

9.1.2.5 External implications on inventory control processes

So far, in the preceding paragraphs, the discussion was with respect to internal control and management of inventory. Now in the following paragraphs, we are discussing certain aspects of external influences in the process of inventory control:

(*i*) **Customer Related Issues:** Certain enlightened progressive customer organizations, particularly those functioning with ISO-9001-QMS, TQM/Business Excellence work culture, also ERP system, may resort to rather vigorous monitoring for the ordered items; and in pursuant of this, they may, besides, other things, try to monitor the supplier-enterprises' inventory holdings status as well, by resorting to:

(*a*) hooking up their computer network with that of the supplier enterprise to monitor the inventory-status of various critical input materials/components, etc., dedicated or linked to the customer order/contract number.

(*b*) they may bring up inventory related issues during the review meetings with the supplier enterprise to high light deficiencies in material supply/stock position which may effect delivery schedules of the ordered material/equipment/product.

(*ii*) **Supplier Enterprise** may highlight their difficulties in procuring certain specified materials and seek revision/alternative specifications; they may also tune-up their inventory holdings with that of the client enterprise's requirements at least for the items dedicated for the client enterprise. This may require exchange of data for which both organizations will have to interlink their information/data exchange procedures and processes; IT-enabled system networking may be put in practice to facilitate such interactions to maintain good rapports with the suppliers **(Subject to DATA-Security measures.)**

(*iii*) **Funding Agencies:** Such as banks/FIs and other concerned may also like to monitor besides other aspects, the status of inventory holding of the client enterprise with respect to their working capital as well as NPA-Management affairs; they have to ensure as to how the loans extended by them are being utilized within the prescribed parameters.

(*iv*) **Credit Rating Agencies:** Inventory holding status is one of the critical parameters that the Credit Rating Agencies regularly monitor in order to form an opinion about the financial management competency of the subject enterprise, because the status of inventory holdings is considered to be an important element of Working Capital Management. Accumulation of dead/unwanted/slow moving inventory and increasing trend in NPA reflect symptoms of un-healthy financial management trend. Credit-rating at an acceptable level (B, BB, BB+, A, AA, etc., gradings) is crucial in getting funds, particularly working capital funds, from the banks/FIs, etc. This is also an important factor when the enterprise goes in for public issue of shares, bonds, etc., to mop up finance from the capital market.

(*v*) **Impact of External Monitoring:**

(*a*) The external monitoring of inventory status as mentioned above puts the client enterprise constantly on alert mode and thus prompt it to tone up its material management affairs for a reasonably good, if not best, performance, under the given circumstances. Therefore, well meaning and enlightened enterprise management may welcome this to the extent that these do not lead to divulgence of vital confidential data beyond a prescribed limit

(*b*) *Care and precaution have to be taken that more than necessary data/information need not be passed on to the external agencies since if these get into unscrupulous agents, they may exploit these data to damage the interest and even the image of the client organization. It should be clearly sorted out (with written agreement preferably) with these external agencies about strictly maintaining the confidentiality of such vital organizational data and preventing misuse of the same.

Note: **However, with the present-day computer-network- based information/data exchange systems in vogue, it will be difficult to ensure such confidentiality to the desired strict level; inspite of safety-system in place, cyber-pilferage and exploitations are common place these days.*

9.1.2.6 Inventory control as an element of working capital management

We have seen in Chapter-8 that inventory holdings in an industrial unit is a very important element in the working capital funding and commitments, particularly in such enterprise where cost of the material contents in the final product cost is rather substantial, in some cases may be even above 60%. For a manufacturing unit, maintaining a certain level of inventory is unavoidable, but conscious efforts are to be made to keep the inventory level as low as possible to avoid blocking of working capital fund; as the experience gets built-up over a period of time (may be months, even years), aim should be to achieve an optimal level of inventory holding matching with the physical output level, but keeping the cost factor always in view. However, it is easier said than done. No production management functionary will like to do a constant tight rope walking on material front when his machines and human resources are sitting pretty on his head starving of work loads. On the other hand, financial management and materials management functionaries will like to keep inventory level as low as possible; not that production management functionaries are not aware of the implications of high inventory holdings, but they have their own anxieties and functional compulsions. In such circumstances, enterprise management collectively have to play their moderating role. To avoid such contradictory situations developing, appropriate systems, standards and control procedures are to be formulated and put into practice so that every one's cause is taken care of in a rational way; after all, the unified strategies, as discussed above in paras 9.1.1 to 9.1.2.5 are to be preferred and adopted by all the agencies concerned to meet, besides other things, the prime objective of meeting customer commitments, delivery schedules, as well as maximizing productivity and profit margins, the fundamental concepts of positive result-oriented business operations.

9.2 Modern IT-enabled Multi-Feature Inventory Management **

Most of the IT-enabled Inventory Management Packages offer the following multiple working features:

9.2.1 Integrated Inventory

All inventory items can be displayable through assigned web/network specific characteristics such as captions, images, pricing, work-order/customer order linkage, supply sources, levels of inventory holdings in each category, vendor-wise status, delivery schedules, and any other information specific to the enterprise's special requirements for monitoring and control. As and when desired, an integrated status report in total inventory holdings for various categories of items can be generated.

9.2.2 Customer Specific and Volume Pricing

With suitably selected softwares and back up system, it is possible assign different pricing for different types of customers, as well as assigning different prices for whole sale, retail or on line sales.

9.2.3 Multi-Location Inventory Control

With suitably selected softwares and back-up system, it is possible to centrally manage and control inventory held at multiple locations; also, in the process of purchase and sales transactions, it is possible to choose the warehouse location that should receive, or fulfil the customer order; this offers a lot of flexibility in supply chain management with respect to multiple vendors and different customer orders; such an arrangement reduces inter-location paper work communication and delays.

9.2.4 Multi-Currency Pricing of Inventory

With selection of appropriate softwares and back-up system, it is possible to set prices in each of the foreign currencies in which the trading is to be done. When orders and invoices are created for foreign customers, the system can automatically select the correct currency and price, thus saving valuable time and avoid confusion.

9.2.5 Inventory Integration with Customer Relationship Management (CRM)

Integrated inventory management tied up with different customers and different sales representatives allows maintenance of a direct linkage with customers and enhance customer relationship management efforts with respect to inventory holdings, and supply chain management.

9.2.6 Inventory with Multiple Units of Measure

With properly selected software and back-up system, it is possible manage multiple units of measure for selling, buying and costing each item across various sales channels, including enterprise's own website, retail stores, partner or whole sale channel. This also helps in tracking inventory costs and regulate total costing for profit booking.

9.2.7 Inventory Lot Numbers

With properly selected software and back-up system, it is possible to maintain history records of each lot through out the product's life cycle; the system can also assign an expiration date to each lot numbers (specially for short-shelf life items) and enter a special noting about this in the relevant place. Lot of items can track the specific cost for each lot as products are bought and sold and this enables a lot number to be entered when building or receiving a lot into the inventory as well as when executing an order for a lot item. It is also possible to incorporate in the system, an appropriate warning so as to notify as to when a lot item is about to expire. Thus it is possible to track the history of each lot item throughout the operational system as well as the customer transactions, making it easier to recall an item should such exigency arises.

9.2.8 Other Options of IT-enabled Inventory Control Process

Besides the above-mentioned major inventory control processes, there can be many more assorted options which can be built-up in the IT-enabled system. A selected few can be mentioned as under:

- Warehouse management with multi-locational inventory;
- Bar code printing;
- Graphical view of inventory levels;
- Inventory commitment picture;
- Inventory Bulk ordering decision process;
- Stock transfer;
- Inventory serialization;
- Inventory control and tracking for special customer orders/projects;
- Support for Matrix (combination of multiple items in one lot) items and item images;

- Audit trail for inventory adjustments;

.............and so on*

Notes: (*i*) **For a multi-product enterprise with multiple segments of markets/clientele, there can be a need for many such options of inventory control.*

(*ii*) ***These IT-enabled Inventory Control processes are also widely applicable for no-industrial trading and retail business sectors. Retail marketing and distribution organizations such as Wal-Mart (USA), Woolworths (Australia), Tresco (UK), Carrefour (France), to mention a few of the most reputed ones, who deal with hundreds of varieties of commodities and consumer products from multiple locations (allover the country/various regions of the globe), necessarily need to adopt such inventory control system for a set of sustainable and viable operations. Many Indian companies have also now (2007) started Retail Marketing and established outlets in various cities (for consumer products, agri-goods, processed and raw food items, garments, cosmetics, crookeries; utensils and many such items of day-to-day use, even consumer durables and luxury items).*

> ***"Practise as if you are the worst, perform as if you are the best."***
>
> — *Anonymous*

❍❍❍

CHAPTER-10

MANAGEMENT OF ENERGY: A VITAL RESOURCE FOR ENTERPRISE OPERATIONS

> ***"I radiate heat as the sun, and hold back as well as send forth the shower; Arjuna, I am immortality as well as death; even so, I am both being and non-being (at the same time)."***
>
> *— Shri Krishna Bhagawan to Arjuna, (sloka-19, Chapter-IX, Bhagavat Gita, Gita Press Gorakhpur)*

In the preceding Chapters, we have discussed about the sources as well as the usages of Energy as one of the vital resources for business enterprise operations, particularly in the industrial units. In the following paragraphs, we shall discuss the impacts of prudent energy management strategies for business operations—both in the non-industrial as well as in industrial enterprises.

10.1 Energy Scenario: World and India

10.1.1 World Scenario

Energy Security, Energy Availability and Energy Supply sources have, in the recent years, emerged as a set of top-priority issues before the various International and National for a engaging in deliberations and interactions/ negotiations on the status of World Trade, Economic and Technological Development and the Energy needs and joint efforts to meet the requirements of various countries and emerging societies, specially in view of the growing world population and the desire for better standards of living. As a result of growing needs, there is a perpetual shortage of energy supply throughout the world and there is not much hope of large-scale improvements in the foreseable future. Barring a few techno-economically advanced countries like USA, Canada, Sweden, Russia, Japan, Australia, UK, France, Germany and also certain Oil/Gas reach countries like Saudi Arabia, Kuwait, Iran, Libya, Iraq, Venezuela, most of the 200 odd countries of the world are facing energy deficiencies in one form or the other. The data presented in **Annexures 1 and 2** reflect the status of energy reserves of various countries of the world *vis-a-vis* their population, consumption and availability.

10.1.2 The Indian Scenario

The scenario in India at present is rather worry-some, and difficult since there is a perpetual shortage of electrical energy, ranging from around 33% to 40% on peak-load demand. Besides, India has to import a very substantial quantity of petroleum products (Oil, Gas, Crude, etc.) from other countries to meet its essential minimum needs for power generation, transportation and industrial usages. The recent boom in economic and industrial developmental activities in the country has also resulted in increased demands for energy creating a rather difficult situation which may not improve appreciably over the next two decades because of various resources constraints. Beside the fossil fuels-based thermal power generation, increased efforts are also being made at national level for additional power generation from hydro-power sources, as well as harnesing other Renewable Sources of Energy like Wind and Solar power generating plants. Also substantial quantities of bio-mass generated in urban and industrial areas are being used/planned for use for load-centre/captive thermal power generation. However, there is an imperative and urgent need for serious and strategic thinking, on the part of Indian Business Enterprises, both non-industrial and industrial, towards efficient and economic management of available energy supply to the best extent possible and feasible.

While **Annexures 1 and 2** present, certain data/information about world's energy source, potentials, *vis-a-vis* demands/availability, those in **Annexure 3** seek to provide certain data on the energy resources of India.

10.1.3 Related Issues

Keeping the above scenario in view, the following issues need attention and appreciation by energy consuming enterprises:

(*i*) The traditional sources of energy supply, largely derived from fossil fuels (coal, lignite, petroleum, natural gas) are fast depleting because of continuous and ever increasing exploitation and consumptions (predominantly in the form of electrical energy).

(*ii*) Various countries/emerging societies all over the world with increasing population are hankering after improving the quality of life and general standards of living, and hence need for more and more energy supply in every sector of human endeavours and activities.

(*iii*) A technological breakthrough for a cheaper/more economic alternative for large scale energy supply (mostly in the form of electrical energy being the most convenient and efficient form of energy supply) is still a far cry inspite of many ongoing serious International efforts through various R&D projects (*e.g.*, Thermo-Nuclear Fusion Reactor (ITER), Fast Breeder Reactors, utilizing

Coal bed methane as well as Methane Hydrate Crystals from ocean bed, larger Wind turbo-generator sets, more efficient and larger size H_2 Fuel Cells, more efficient and large size Solar photovoltaic panels, etc., to mention a few prominent ones.

- **Hydro-power generation potentials** wherever, harnessable are being explored and hydro stations have been set up/are being set up in various countries including India. In some countries like Canada, Norway, China, India, substantial hydro-power potentials exist; in India as against the total estimated potential of 1,50,000 MWs, so far only around 36,000 MWs could be put into operation (24%) till 31.07.08.

10.2 Strategic Steps Needed to be Considered

10.2.1 Need for Regulation of Consumption Pattern

In view of the scenario mentioned above at paras 10.1.1 to 10.1.3, there is an imperative and urgent need for both non-industrial and industrial consumers to adopt certain conscious policies and practical strategies to:

(*a*) Reduce consumptions to the essential minimum and optimize usage of the available quantum by adopting cost-effective and energy efficient devices and processes.

(*b*) Avoid wastages and pilferages/abuse with rather strict control/ drastic corrective/improvement measures.

10.2.2 Energy Management in Non-industrial Enterprises

10.2.2.1 Energy supply/availability taken for granted

It is generally observed that there is a tendency amongst the non-industrial business establishments to take energy supply and availability, particularly electricity supply, for granted, since there is a general lack of appreciation in such establishments that there is a shortage of electrical energy in the country; in some regions, rather severe shortage due to the gap existing between generation capacity and demand. This attitude on the part of the non-industrial enterprises probably emanates from the following general perceptions:

(*i*) The volume of total electricity consumption is much smaller as compared to those in the industrial units, hence it is not of much consequence.

(*ii*) The over-all expenditure towards energy consumption is a rather small percentage of the total costs of operations/Turn over, and therefore, not discernible enough to catch serious attention of the enterprise management.

10.2.2.2 Frequent disruption in electricity supply forcing attitudinal changes

If we analyse the data (on electricity consumption) in business organizations: like banks, consultancy offices, BPO centers, trading houses, laboratories, call centres, hotels, educational establishments and the like, we may find a general pattern emerging as stated above; so long there is profit margins, who cares about the cost of energy. Although in the recent years, because of recurrent disruptions in the power supply, some attitudinal changes have been forced on such establishments, there is still scope for substantial improvements in energy management aspects there.

10.2.2.3 Steps for reduction of consumption and wastages

Steps which may help Non-Industrial enterprises to reduce consumption and wastage of energy:

(*i*) Adopting energy-efficient building structures so that natural sun lights can be utilized to the maximum extent feasible for lighting in rooms/halls, thus reducing electrical energy consumption for lighting.

(*ii*) In winter, solar water heating system can be installed on the roof of the building. It is also possible to circulate hot air generated from such solar installations for room heating through appropriately designed ducting and radiator system.

(*iii*) Use of summer air-conditioning system, which consumes substantial amount of electrical energy, may be limited to essential minimum. Care should be taken in selecting proper and energy efficient air-conditioning plants; also the plant size should be optimum matching with the cooling loads and over-capacity avoided.

(*iv*) In case of Diesel Generating sets (DG sets) are being used, a constant watch be kept on the cost of power generation including the costs of diesel and other inputs, since in most cases, electrical power generated through DG sets will be much more costlier than that purchased from the Electric Supply Company's grid/ distribution System.

Note: *DG sets when in operation, also generate air pollution in the vicinity area; exhaust gases are also obnoxious for people working in the area, causing health-hazards.*

(*v*) Employees at all levels are to be made adequately conscious about energy-economy and wastage-avoidance measures; also when not in use, lighting, heating and other devices in the offices, laboratories, stores etc. be switched off.

Note: *Respective Area Managers/HODs may have to monitor/check from time to-time-to inculcate a sense of urgency/ responsibility amongst the employees about the need for energy savings.*

(*vi*) Install energy-efficient gadgets and equipment.

(*vii*) It is to be kept in view that each business enterprise has certain social and national obligations which include, amongst other things, avoiding wastage/misuse of scares resources: electrical energy is one of them. Over use and wastages of energy deprive other needy consumers of their essential needs.

(*viii*) It is also to be appreciated that business enterprises, because of national economic development objectives often get priority allocation of scarce electric power supply by depriving public at large; therefore, business establishments have a special responsibility towards energy savings and wastage avoidance objectives.

(*ix*) If DG sets are used for private power generation, even here also scarce diesel oil being used, mostly imported with a substantial out-go on foreign exchange resources, which is always in short supply and thus a perpetual burden on the national economy; over-use/non-essential use of diesel oil also deprive consumers in other sectors of economy and the public at large. Therefore, business enterprises using substantial quantity of diesel oil also have moral and social obligations towards the national economic constraints. The same obligations are applicable in case of Natural gases/LPG and coal.

10.2.3 Energy Management Strategies for Industrial Units

By the very nature of operations, industrial units consume substantial quantum of electrical and other fossil fuel based energy (mainly heat). Energy being an essential input resource, the costs incurred for the same are also considerable; depending on the type of industry and the technological processes followed; expenditures incurred towards fuels and electricity consumptions may be anything between 2% to 5% of the turnover (Value of production output). Even 1% saving in energy input may help in improving profit margins to a higher level. Energy savings, in some cases, can help reduce cost of production, and therefore improve profitability. It may be worthwhile to adopt certain relevant strategies as enumerated below, for effecting energy savings/reduction in consumptions:

(*i*) Adopt measures as listed above under paras 10.2.1 (*a*, *b*) and paras 10.2.1.3 (i to ix) to the extent they are relevant to the working of the industrial enterprise.

(*ii*) Since industrial drives and heating devices consume the major portions of the energy inputs, efforts should made to select, procure and install energy-efficient machines and equipment (particularly machine-tools, furnaces, ovens, etc.); and keep a regular watch on their consumption pattern *vis-a-vis* their productivity/outputs.

(*iii*) As regards the distribution system, care should be taken that/ there is no leakage or wastages because of defective distribution net works which also otherwise is risky since such leakages can result in fire hazards and other mishaps.

(*iv*) In case of fuels (oil, gas, coal, etc.) adequate care should be taken for their proper handling, transportation, storage and distribution to avoid wastages (due to spillages, etc.), pilferages and excessive usage beyond the prescribed norms.

(*v*) Make arrangements for adequate recording of and periodical review of supply and consumption and compare the data with those from other similar enterprises to establish a set of reasonable norms of consumption *vis-a-vis* production outputs and productivity.

(*vi*) It may be useful to carry out periodical (at least once a year) Energy-Audit of all load-centres to determine the level of wastages/excessive usage and take remedial measures for reduction/improvements even in the case of sub-contracting/off-loading of certain operations/ items for operational economy/cost-reduction, the contribution of energy costs should also be considered in case in-house option (if making the items in-house) is adopted. (Make-or-Buy decision).

(*viii*) The costs incurred towards maintenance and administration of energy procurement and distribution should also be considered when calculating the cost figures for energy and fuels consumptions.

(*ix*) Lastly, but not the least, adequate safety measures must be in place for safe handling, storage and distribution of energy and fuels (as applicable).

Bureau of Energy Efficiency (BEE), a Government of India agency, has taken several measures and has made it mandatory for industries, other producers as well as manufacturers of electrical appliances to design and manufacture energy efficient equipment/goods. There is a lot of literature on the subject available from BEE, BIS and other concerned agencies.

10.3 Future Challenges

In the year 2020, nearly eight billion people will inhabit the earth, (as against 6.5 billion in 2007) one and a half billion more as compared to the present strength. Supplying these people with electrical energy in a manner that is reliable, economical and ecologically acceptable and thus meeting the domestic demand as well as the energy demand of entire national economies is one of the great challenges of the future.

As is the case today, power generation in the year 2020 will comprise a mix of various sources of energy with the objective of bringing the demand-supply reliability, economy, environmental and climatic acceptability into harmony. Fossil fuels such as coal or natural gas will continue to be the most important sources of energy in 2020. The contribution of the renewables, in particular wind power, will, however, increase. Also, increased level of usage of solar energy both for domestic as well as for commercial purposes, are expected through development and introduction of appropriate viable technologies.

> ***"We are all faced with great opportunities brilliantly disguised as impossible situations."***
>
> *— Charles R Swindoll*

❍❍❍

CHAPTER-11

TOTAL QUALITY MANAGEMENT (TQM) APPROACH HELPS IN RESOURCE OPTIMIZATION FOR BUSINESS EXCELLENCE

> *"Good ideas are not adopted automatically. They must be driven into practice with courageous patience."*
>
> — *Hyman Rickover*

11.1 Total Quality Management (TQM)

It is a comprehensive concept for attaining and practising all round excellence in business operations. The scope of TQM work-culture extends much beyond the traditional emphasis only on the product-quality and customer requirements, but seek to encompass all the processes and all the human activities that make up the total business operations. TQM focuses on both people and processes, oriented towards higher degree of customer satisfaction leading to customer delight.

European Forum for Quality Management (EFQM) defines TQM as "Effective Management of Business Enterprise through focus on its people and processes by company-wide Customer driven Leadership."

11.2 TQM through Appropriate Resource Deployment and Utilization

From the above definition of TQM, it is evident that the TQM concept of business administration has direct and indirect linkages with the effective management of resources namely people (human resources) and the processes that get associated with other resources such as machines, materials, methods/knowledge, management/organization, monetary matters, motivational aspects (incentives), energy usage, etc.

All such resources get deployed in varying proportions for achieving customer/market driven goals and priorities, oriented towards both, global as well as national perspectives. Broadly speaking, management and administration of business enterprises, both industrial and non-industrial, in the ultimate analysis, boil down to effective and efficient deployment and utilization of various available resources relevant to the kind and scope of operations. In this endeavour, Leadership's role will be crucial for successful implementation of TQM objectives through resource optimization.

We shall further discuss the 'TQM-Resources-Leadership' relationship in the following paragraphs. Fig. 11.1 seeks to represent the above mentioned relationship which is expected to attain perpetuality for successful sustenance and probable growth towards Business Excellence.

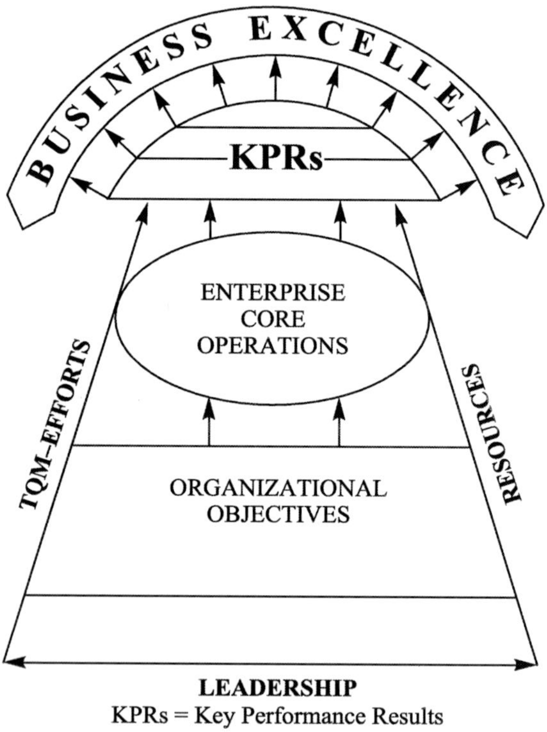

Fig. 11.1 TQM resources leadership.

11.3 The Basic Concepts of TQM

Organizational Quality can be achieved by creating appropriate operating systems, but in enforcing quality, in the way we work and behave, the need for creation of a mind set is imperative. Quality Gurus like Deming, Juran,

- Personal Quality Goals
- Established Personal Quality Accounts.
- Finish what they start.
- Be Ethical
- Avoid mistakes.

} The five ingredients for a personal quality agenda which greatly helps in inculcating TQM work culture in the organization.

Claus Moller and Harry Roberts deliberately identify personal quality as the starting point for Total Quality, insisting that managers set for themselves:

"Search for personal quality begins with self-appraisal"

The above quotation clearly indicates that every manager should make a self-analysis as to how he is going to be a business leader. Here, a leader need not necessarily be a Orator, but has to be a good communicator; he should be a doer to set examples to his subordinates in leading his team towards total quality. Personal integrity coupled with professional competence make a business manager effective since he commands respect amongst subordinates as well as peers and even with the management.

11.4 Total Quality: The Focal Attributes

Total Quality means to get business effectiveness through:

1. People Focus,
2. Process Focus,
3. Customer Focus,

11.5 Total Quality Management: The Objective Focus

Total Quality does not mean mere fulfilment customers' requirements, but it is to provide products and services in a manner so as to evince Customer Delight. It starts from the internal customers and leads to the external customer as indicated in the Fig. 11.2.

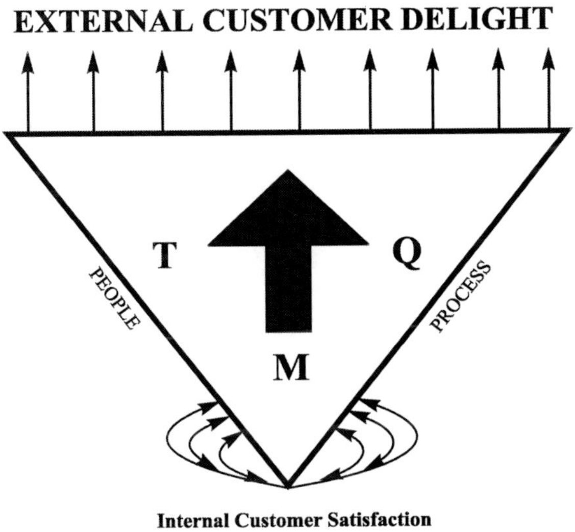

Fig. 11.2 Total quality management starts from the internal customers and leads to the external customers.

Note: **While we all understand as to who are the external customers, the internal customers in a business enterprise refers to those* *internal agencies who are supposed to receive services and supplies from other functional groups within the organization, in order to fulfil their part of the assignments and responsibilities towards meeting commitments made to the external customers. Therefore, for the various functionaries in the organization, for achieving effective management of the total affairs aiming for business excellence, both internal and external customers are important and need to be paid due attention and priorities.*

11.6 TQM: Business Effectiveness Through 'People Focus'

People focus refers to the following operational aspects (with reference to Human Resources):

- In TQM, people in the organization play a major role, since it is the people who run the enterprise.
- People have to be prepared to share common vision, practice values and be ever willing to accept change for betterment and continuous improvements.
- The organizational functionaries to prepare and perform the tasks by undergoing appropriate training programmes/workshops, so as to educate and motivate themselves as well as the employees at all levels.

Some of the exercises/techniques used for enhancing human resource performance and contributions towards Business Excellence, are enumerated below:

(*i*) Effective performance appraisal system.
(*ii*) Effective performance reward system.
(*iii*) HRD programmes and activities.
(*iv*) Well defined job responsibilities.
(*v*) Consensus decision making (democratic participation approach in management).
(*vi*) Behavioural inputs to improve attitudes by setting relevant standards as well as by setting examples.
(*vii*) Trust building exercise.
(*viii*) Team building exercise.
(*ix*) Vision Workshops to enable appreciation of long-term objectives of the organization.
(*x*) Time management; practising and sharing success stories.
(*xi*) Quality Circles.
(*xii*) Suggestion scheme.
(*xiii*) Self-inspection.
(*xiv*) Cross functional teams to support unified approach towards organizational goals.

(*xv*) Welfare schemes.

(*xvi*) Participative relationship with Trade Unions.

(*xvii*) Any other activity: to build stronger chain of human relationship.

11.7 TQM Through 'Process Focus'

Business Processes include:

Activities (Resource Linkages)

- Design and Product development (Methods, Knowledge).
- Planning (Methods, knowledge, management/organization).
- Buying (Material Management; (Material resources).
- Manufacturing (Machines, man, materials, management/ knowledge).
- Technology (Methods/knowledge).
- Quality Assurance (Methods, knowledge).
- Quality Control (Methods, knowledge, man, machine, material).
- Costs and Accounting (Methods, knowledge, money).
- Marketing (Method, knowledge, man/people).
- Services (Methods, knowledge, man, machine).
- Information sharing (Method, knowledge, management).
- Processes for human resources development (Methods, knowledge, man).

11.8 TQM Through 'Customer Focus'

TQM through Customer Focus has to manifest itself through the following:

- "TQM" company is customer driven at all levels of the organization.
- Customer can be internal or external.
- It has to start from the C.E.O./Top management.
- Customer needs are supreme.
- Fulfilling customer-contract obligations and commitments.
- Deliver little more than customer expectations.
- Cultivate customer-relationship on a long-term basis.
- Control cost through continuous improvement so as to be able to offer goods and services at competitive prices.

11.8.1 Tools/Techniques/Approach for Customer Focus

- Quality Policy Declaration-Open documented. Internal Customer Concept: inter-functional role appreciation within the enterprise for an unified and objective approach throughout the organization.
- Purpose-Mission-Value Statements.
- Quality Assurance through ISO 9001 QMS Certification (QMS = Quality Management System).

- Customer Satisfaction Index; Customer feedback, recording and analysis of feedback data, and responses thereon.
- Quality, Cost, Delivery, Service-supported by appropriate systems, methods, procedures and organized efforts.

11.9 Leadership Role in TQM Objectives

Leadership in an organization forms the Hub of TQM efforts which drives activities pertaining to improvement of all types of Processes, empower and enable its people to perform and pursue customer driven strategies and policies.

Figure 11.3 represents the Leadership as the hub of the TQM endeavours for Business Effectiveness.

Fig. 11.3 Leadership as the hub of TQM.

From the Fig. 11.3, TQM–Leadership obviously has to be from the top echelon of the enterprise management who can lead the dedicated efforts for overall successful operations; this will include, besides other relevant aspects, effective mobilization, deployment and utilization of various resources on a sustainable regime with a constancy of purpose.

11.9.1 TQM-Leadership Calls for

- A Leader has to have an intimate knowledge of what he is supposed to lead.
- Participative Style of management (democratic approach to the extent feasible and practicable under the given circumstances).
- Long-term vision for organizational goals and priorities.
- Commitment to organizational values as well as to the stake-holders (customers, employees, suppliers and the society at large).
- CEO himself to lead TQM-activities with the assistance of TQM coordinator. *
- Establishing suitable organizational structure to carry on TQM activities.
- Acceptance and implementation of required changes in the organization.
- Sharing information (within the organization) should be the leader's compassion.
- The leader has to be the symbol of justice and fairplay, the embodiment of organizational values.
- The leader not only has to focus on operational aspects, but also has to have some priorities towards the aspects of management of Resources and Assets since they are also critical for successful sustenance and growth.

Note: *****TQM coordinator, generally a senior official nominated by the CEO, to coordinate both with the internal and the external agencies.External agencies will include TQM–Auditors who evaluate the client enterprise's progress and achievements towards TQM implementation on a qualitative and quantitative (measurable) assessment.*

11.10 TQM: The Global Scenario

11.10.1 Resource Crunch and Competitive Survival

With the increasing pace of globalization of trade and commerce in the last one and half decade or so in the various regions of the world and gradual opening up of economies and markets, both by the developed as well as by the developing countries, although still restricted in some aspects (particularly agricultural produce and energy-resources related technologies, certain high end dual purpose technologies, and the like), the market places everywhere are becoming highly competition oriented, specially for the industrial products and services. A substantial number of countries are trying to enter the emerging markets to get a share of the global trade (estimated to be around

US $ 15,000 billion/2007). Increasing world population (estimated at around 6.5 billion in 2007) and ever increasing aspirations of better standards of living in various countries, the demands for products and services are also going up substantially every year. All these developments are also making the customers/consumers every where more enlightened, quality conscious as well as environment- conscious, and therefore becoming more and more choosy and demanding about their requirements. In such a scenario, more and more business enterprises in many countries across the globe are going in for adoption of TQM as a global business strategy to capture new markets, retain and enhance market shares, and successfully face competition. And this is happening in both the public/government as well as private sector business enterprises. For certain large and medium size corporations, adoption of TQM-work-culture as a business strategy has become rather imperative for viable sustenance and possible growth. European Union is a pioneering agency in adopting the TQM-movement for the European business/industrial corporations. The European Forum for Quality Management (EFQM) has evolved and propagated a Business Excellence Model presented in Fig. 11.4. This model has been/is being adopted by a substantial number of business/industrial corporations in many other countries including those in India.

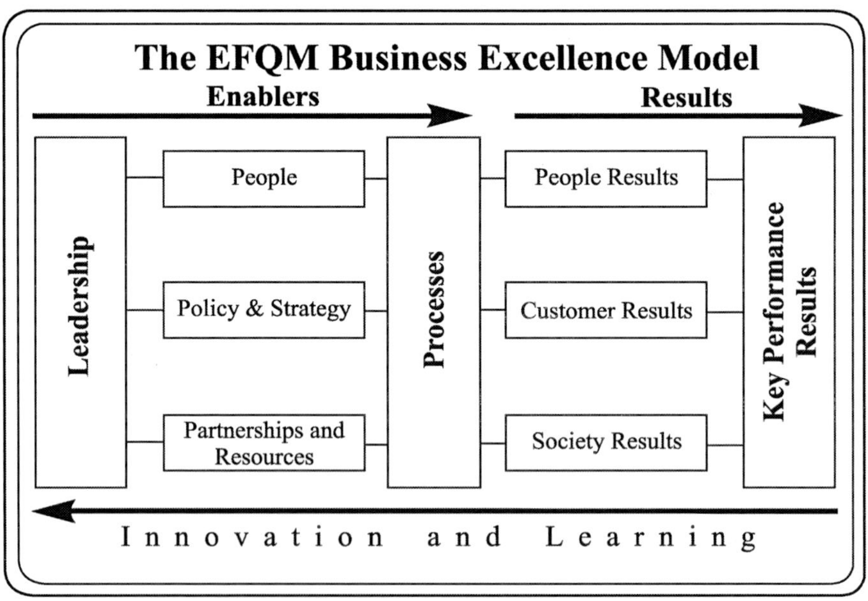

Fig. 11.4 Business Excellence model.

In addition to the EFQM Model as stated above, there are a number of other Business Excellence Model developed in different countries, more about this is stated at para 11.11.

11.10.2 TQM: The Indian Scenario

Confederation of Indian Industries (CII) in association with Export-Import Bank India (EXIM Bank) has undertaken the pioneering role in introducing the TQM-movement in India and propagated amongst the Indian Industrial enterprises the EFQM. Model of Business Excellence Fig. 11.4. So far (2007), over 100 Indian enterprises are actively pursuing the TQM-work-culture and many more are planning to follow suit. Many others are also pursuing adoption of Deming Cycle Model of Business Excellence. On the other hand, some large business houses like Tatas, Kirloskars, Hindustan Lever, to name a few are developing their own model of TQM/Business Excellence work culture in their group companies.

The TQM movement is fast catching up in India and more and more business enterprises are adopting TQM-work culture for not only enhancing their business prospects, but also to keep abreast with the globalized trade and commerce practices, thus attaining for themselves a place of pride in the international business arena. There are already many a success stories in India and many more are aspiring to join the victory march. Many successful Indian business corporations like the Tatas, Birlas, Reliance, Ranbaxy, Videocon to name a few, have substantially expanded their business operations in many other countries through Mergers and Acquisitions (M&A) as well as by setting up their own subsidiaries/off-shore units. ERP and TQM-oriented working systems are definitely playing important roles in such endeavours, besides other relevant business strategies. As experience gets built-up with the passage of years, more and more refinement in the business processes will evolve for enhancing business effectiveness for successfully facing emerging global competition and capturing newer markets/enhancing market shares.

11.11 TQM Assessment and Award Models

11.11.1 Different TQM Assessing Models

For assessing the effective implementation of TQM activities in an organization models have been developed in different countries that are interested in introducing the TQM Culture.

Some of the TQM Models that are being propagated

- The Mckinsey TQM Model.
- The European Quality Award Model.
- The Andersen Consulting Model.
- The Malcom Baldrige Award Model.
- The Juran Model.
- The Deming Cycle.

11.11.2 EFQM–Award Model: The Indian Preference

Most Indian industrial corporations/companies have chosen to adopt the European Quality Award Model for TQM-activities which are basically developed on 9 criteria such as:

- Leadership
- Policy and Strategy
- People Management
- Resources
- Processes
- People Satisfaction
- Customer Satisfaction
- Impact on Society
- Business Results

In India, 'CII-EXIM Bank Award for Business Excellence' also assess the performance of a client enterprise against these nine criteria.

11.11.3 Diagramatic Representation of EFQM Award Model

The TQM Assessment Model as per EFQM looks as Fig. 11.5:

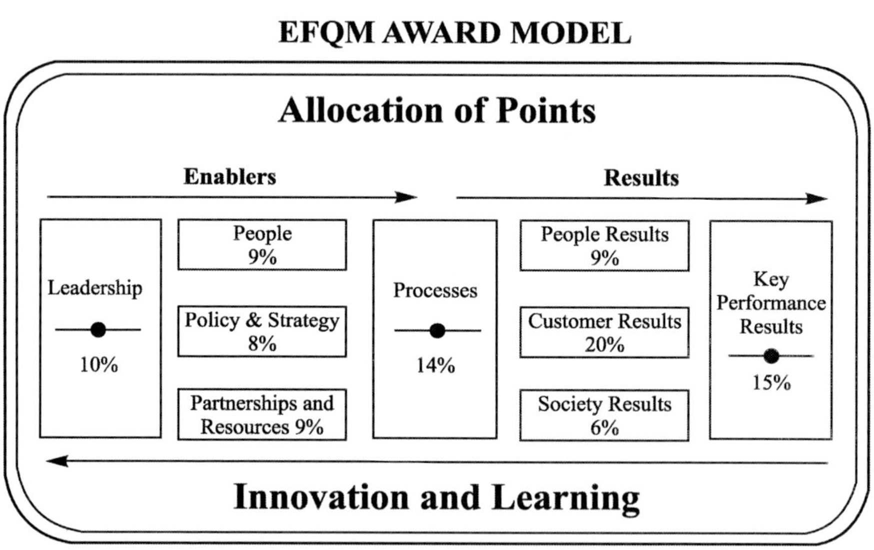

Fig. 11.5 TQM assesment model as per EFQM.

11.11.4 Resource-Support for the 9-Criteria

Referring to the nine assessment criteria mentioned at para 11.11.2 and the score allocation chart in Fig. 11.5 it is obvious that the assessee enterprise has to assiduously gear up its all round activities with back-up systems, procedures and matching work-culture to achieve performance level at a sufficiently satisfactory level so as to meet the assessment criteria in both quantitative and qualitative terms.

This will be possible only when the assessee enterprise is capable of efficiently and effectively manage its over all operations including optimization of the resource deployment and utilization.

11.12 Enterprise Resource Management (ERM) has an Important Role in TQM Work Culture

Enterprise Management and the key functionaries working towards adoption of TQM work-culture for attaining business excellence must appreciate that efficient and effective management of various resources will be an important factor in achieving such objectives. In order to successfully implement the TQM work-culture the key functionaries in the enterprise must know and assiduously work for certain basic working principles as listed under:

Taking Positive Steps to	Linkage to Relevant Resources
Communicate with staff at all levels regularly both formally and informally.	Management, Human Resource.
Make oneself accessible to staff.	Management, Human Resource.
Promote two way communications at all levels.	–do–
Listen to people with genuine concern and warmth.	–do–
Classify peoples' skills and match with the organization's needs.	Management/Organization, Human Resource, Method.
Identify training needs of the employees in the organization and relate these with individual capabilities/requirements.	Management/Organization, Human Resource; Method and Knowledge, Money.
Assess the effectiveness of all training activities Encourage commitment to as well as achievement in total quality.	Human Resource, Method, Management, Human Resource, Knowledge.
Use in-house Programmes/meetings to encourage involvement of people.	Management/Human Resource, Method, Money
Empower people to act and evaluate their action.	–do–

Contd...

Taking Positive Steps to	Linkage to Relevant Resources
Help identify priorities, improvement activities in each individual's functional area.	–do, Method/knowledge.
Provide necessary resources, training and other support to such improvement activities.	Management/Organization, Methods, Knowledge, Human Resource, Machines, Materials, Money.
Promote and develop people through team work.	Management/Organization, Human Resource, Methods.
Discuss with individuals and match organization's target with their own objectives.	Management/Organization, Human Resource, Methods/Knowledge.
Review and update these targets/ objectives.	–do–
Recognize and appreciate the efforts/ success of individuals as well as that of the team at the appropriate time.	–do–
Understand and respond to needs of customers, contractors and other agencies effectively and in time.	Management, Methods, Knowledge, Organization.
Spread the principles and practices of TQM in every forum through lectures, presentations, articles, etc.	Management/Methods, Knowledge.
Deploy the resources (financial and non-financial) effectively in the best interests of the organization.	Management/Methods, Knowledge, Money, Machines (facilities), Material Human Resource.
Exploit existing technology to secure competitive edge.	Methods, Knowledge, Human Resource, Machines, Money.
Explore new processes, system and technologies.	–do–
Relook at every process for its needs and effectiveness	–do–
Focus on "Critical" processes that cut across various functions and thus effect the business.	Methods, Knowledge, Human Resource, Management, Organization, Machines.
Establish clear ownership for every process.	Organization, Methods, Knowledge, Human Resource.

Contd...

Taking Positive Steps to	Linkage to Relevant Resources
Set standards for all processes and monitor performance against such standards.	–do–
Review and update these standards systematically.	Human Resource, Machines, Material, Methods.
Stimulate creative talents of people for achieving improvement and break through in technologies.	Management, Methods, Knowledge. Methods, Knowledge, Human Management, Machines, Money.
Encourage active involvement in community activities, preserving global resources, reducing and preventing nuisance and hazard to neighbours.	Management, Methods, Knowledge Human Resource.

> ***"If you want to know the end, look at the beginning."***
>
> — *African Proverb*

❍❍❍

CHAPTER-12

ENTERPRISE RESOURCE BALANCING: INTER-ACTIVE RELATIONSHIP MATRIX TO ENABLE PRIORITY TARGETING

"You can never solve a problem at the level on which it was created."

— Albert Einstein

12.1 Inter-Resource Relationship Matrix

In the business enterprises, operating with a multitude of work and cost centres, the trickiest part of the resource management is the process of constantly balancing the deployment and utilization of various available resources in such a manner and proportion that their contributions, singularly or collectively, get channellized in an unified approach towards accomplishment of the organizational goals as well as achieving the desired results. Such balancing acts are easier aimed at than done, because of complexities arising out of the multiplicity of operating variables that are at inter-play in the various inter-related functional areas.

The complex relationship-matrix makes it rather difficult to clearly identify and quantify the impacts as well as contributions made by various resources, singularly or collectively. However, with appropriate organizational systems backup and work-procedures put in place, supported by matching data-discipline and data processing facility, it is possible to work-out a set of effective methods of balancing the deployment and utilization of various resources, particularly the physically discernible resources, so that these play complementary as well as supplementary roles for each other.

Such a relationship-matrix when actively pursued may result in a force-multiplier effect on their impacts and enhance the overall performance of the enterprise.

While such resource-balancing exercise has to be a regular operational strategy, it may be worthwhile to attempt, in the following paragraphs, to establish a inter-resource relationship-matrix for the six physically discernible resources:

(1) Man
(2) Machine
(3) Material
(4) Money
(5) Energy and
(6) Management

So as to enable focused attention to and planning effective actions for enhancing business prospects as well as organizational effectiveness:**

Notes: **(*i*) *The relationship-matrices being presented in the Table 12.1, by and large, are generally known to the practising managers working with business/industrial enterprises, but since most of them are primarily focused towards their specific assigned functional responsibilities, they may not pay much attention to the inter-related aspects of resource management; the predominant tendency will be to leave the matters related to resource-balancing to be the task of the top-management functionaries; but such a perception may not be conducive for overall organizational effectiveness and efficiency.*

While the leadership and directional thrusts have to come from the top-management functionaries, the line managers' roles are critical in successfully implementing the programmes drawn up and making the enterprise resource-conscious across the board; otherwise there are bound to be pockets of passive and in-effective work-culture and weak links in the chain of organizational endeavours.

(*ii*) *Even if it is conceded that most of the modern-day business managers are reasonably conscious about organizational objectives and inter-functional relationship, there are always advantages of re-capitulating and re-emphasizing the nuances of the critical operational aspects of the business enterprise in order to inculcate a sense of constancy of result oriented purpose amongst the line managers.*

Table 12.1 Relationship-matrices

Resource	Inter-resource relationship matrix for inter-active work culture	Key result focal priorities and targets
1. Man (Human Resources) ➤	Manpower requirements to optimize resource deployment and utilization with respect to: **(A) Machines:** • Number of machines to be procured and the procurement/ purchase organization; • Number of machines to be installed and the erection commissioning organization; • Number of shifts to work for; • Number of operators required for each machine, each shift including contingency resources; • Number of personnel required for maintenance and up keep, trouble-shooting, etc. • Number of supporting services personnel required (administrative, planning, record keeping, quality control, welfare, safety, security, material handling, etc.).	• Manpower studies; • Manpower budget; • HRM (recruitment, deployment programmes). • HRD (Trg. & Dev.) programmes (including retraining); • Industrial Relation.
➤	**(B) Material:** Personnel required for: • Material Planning and Inventory Control (MPIC) and related organization. • Procurement/purchase functions. • Storage, conservation and custody. • Distribution and disposal. • Related administrative and support services including material handling, safety and security, record keeping, etc.	• MPIC related systems and procedures, processes. • Procurement Policy and procedures; • Vendor Development policy; • Sub-contract/BPO policies; • Storage and Distribution; Systems & Procedures.

Contd...

Resource	Inter-resource relationship matrix for inter-active work culture	Key result focal priorities and targets
Man *(Contd.)* ➤	**C. Money:** Personnel required for managing Monetary Resources with respect to: • Financial Management and Budgetary affairs including Working Capital and Capital Investment matters; • Accounting and Book-keeping; • Internal Audit; • Cash and Treasury functions; • Costing and Sales proceeds realization, customer contract/service related matters; • Related administrative services and record keeping matters.	• Supply Chain Management and Logistics. • Budgetary and Budetary Control Systems • Funding strategies including Working Capital Management. • Cash flow Mgmt. • Costing and control/auditing. • Performance appraisals and MIRs; • Delegation of Power.
➤	**D. Energy:** Personnel required for: • Energy/Power procurement/power generation, distribution; • Maintenance and upkeep of energy supply/power supply systems; • Related administrative and support services, record keeping, etc.	• Energy/Power supply arrangement and distribution set-up. • Energy/Power procurement and utilization policy.
➤	**E. Management** (Organization) Personnel required to man: • Top-management functions, • Middle management functions, • Junior management and supervising functions, • Operating and supporting staff as mentioned under A, B, C and D above, • Management services functions like centralized Planning, Productivity Services/Industrial Engineering, Security, Safety, and other supporting services areas.	• Organizational set-up for Apex functions. • Organizational set-up for main functional areas including operations. • Organizational set-up for each support service areas. • Business Development Organization. • Quality Management Organization. • HRM and HRD Organization. • Engineering/Design, R&D and Product Dev. Organization. • Organization for ISO 9001-QMS, TQM/EMS (in case these activities are being done or planned to be done).

Contd...

Resource	Inter-resource relationship matrix for inter-active work culture	Key result focal priorities and targets
2. Machine ➤	**(A) Man (Human Resources)** • As spelt out at 1 (A) above for mutual role sharing;	• Manpower planning for machines. • Training and skills development for operators and maintenance personnel.
➤	**(B) Material:** Material requirements to be identified and arranged with respect to: • Machines to be deployed and utilized for execution of annual production/operation plans drawn up; • Technological process implementation; • Machine utilization plans drawn up; • Machine maintenance and upkeep programmes drawn up.	• MPIC related systems and procedures. • Materials Budget and budgetary control system. • Value Engineering approach. • Vendor development policy and systems. • Standardization efforts. • Stocking and Styling. • 5-S work-culture in Shops.
➤	**(C) Money:** Monetary resources (funding) to be arranged for: • Capital expenditure towards procurement and installation of Fixed Assets (machines and other infra-structural facilities); • Expenses to be incurred for maintenence and up-keep of machines and other production and operational facilities (spare parts, consumables, labour charges, incidentals, etc.). • Expenses for toolings, jigs, fixtures shop accessories, etc., for machine tools and other equipments (for production as well as for supporting services activities).	• Facility planning; PPR/DPR; • Capital budgeting. • Budget provisioning for operating expenses, spares, consumables, maintenance and upkeep.

Contd...

Resource	Inter-resource relationship matrix for inter-active work culture	Key result focal priorities and targets
Machine *(Contd.)* ➤	**D. Energy:** Machines and equipment/devices required for: • Power generation/power receiving stations. • Power/Energy supply and distribution systems. • Devices for measurement of consumption and for control (safe operation, system protection, avoidance of excess consumption/wastages and pilferages)	• Facility-oriented energy policy. • Selection of energy efficient machines and related processes • Systems for machine related energy audits and avoidance of wastage/excess consumption.
➤	**E. Management:** Organizational set ups for: • Machine procurement/purchase. • Machine erection and commissioning. • Machine maintenance and upkeep.	• Capital Investment Strategy. • Project Management. • Strategies for maintenance and upkeep of plant and machinery (in-house, hired services). • 'Jishu-Hozen' (autonomous maintenance) work-culture.
3. Material ➤	**A. Man** (Human Resources) • Issues mentioned at 1(B) above also apply here.	• Issues stated against 1(B) above also apply here.
➤	**B. Machine:** Arranging and installing facilities, Machines and equipment for: • Material handling and transportation. • Storage and conservation of materials. • Material issue and distribution.	• Capital Expenditure on machines and equipment. • Maintenance infrastructure and organization. • Focus on issues stated against 2(B) above.

Contd...

Resource	Inter-resource relationship matrix for inter-active work culture	Key result focal priorities and targets
Material (*Contd.*) ➤	**C. Money:** Monetary resource allocation (funding) to be made for: • Procurement of various raw materials, components, bought-out items and other direct materials. • Procurement of sundry indirect materials both for production as well as for other support service functions. • Meeting expenses towards storage, conservation, distribution and disposal.	• As stated against 1(C), 1(B) and 2(B) *above (NOTE: Appropriate combination of priorities and targets to be selected for focused action).* • Delegation of Power.
➤	**D. Energy:** Power/energy required for: • Material handling equipment. • Lighting, cooling, airconditioning, dehumidication services, etc., in stores and offices related to material management functional areas. • Material transportation and shipping activities.	• Ensuring availability of Power/energy as required. • Energy auditing from time-to-time and taking measures for avoidance of wastage/ excess consumption.
➤	**E. Management:** • Appropriate organization for procurement/purchase activities. • Appropriate organization for MPIC, Stores, distribution and disposal. • Arranging and managing appropriate infrastructural facilities. • Providing support services (administrative security, record keeping, etc.)	• Procurement Policy. • Materials Management related systems and procedures. • Budgeting and budgetary Control. • Costing (PSL, SRV/SIV, etc.). • Delegation of Power. • Supply Chain Mgmt. and logistics.
4. Money (Monetary Resources) ➤	**A. Man:** Monetary resources required for: • Recruitment processes. • Paying salaries and wages. • Meeting expenses towards training and skill development. • Meeting expenses towards employee welfare and amenities. • Meeting other human-resource oriented expenses.	• Manpower budget. • HRM and HRD plans and programmes. • Funding arrangements and related budgetary allocation and control.

Contd...

Resource	Inter-resource relationship for inter-active work culture	Key result focal priorities and targets
Money *(Contd.)* ➤	**B. Machine:** Monetary resources (funding) required for: • Purposes stated at 2(C) above, • Meeting expenses towards operation of machines and equipment installed-both for production as well as support service areas.	• Capital Investment project appraisals and cost-benefit analysis. • Costing for machine operation and utilization levels. • Depreciation policy and status of depreciation fund. • Interest burdens on fresh capital expenditure towards replacements, modernization, capacity expansion, etc.
➤	**C. Material:** Funding for materials with respect to: • Purposes stated at 3(C) above also apply here.	• Materials budget *vis-a-vis* production/operation programmes drawn up. • Inventory Control. • Budgetary control for material related expenses.
➤	**D. Energy:** Providing monetary resources for: • Procurement and installation of power/energy supply machines, equipment and devices; • Equipment and devices for power /energy distribution, control, protection and measurement systems. • Expenses towards fuels and other consumables, maintenance/repair spares. • Expenses towards related administrative and support services.	• Energy/Power Management Policy (buying or own generation or a mix of both). • Organizational measures for reducing/avoiding wastages pilferages, etc. • Enery Audits. • Technology/process upgradation/improvement to reduce power consumption.

Contd...

Resource	Inter-resource relationship matrix for inter-active work culture	Key result focal priorities and targets
Money *(Contd.)* ➤	E. **Management:** The management of monetary resources is a crucial function in business enterprises and has to take care of: • Putting in place appropriate organization and functionaries for management of Finance and Accounting functions. • Funding sources and funding policies and procedures. • Cost of Capital (both for capital investments and working capital needs) issues. • Budget preparation and exercising budgetary controls and disciplines. • Deciding on investment needs. • Deciding on accounting and book keeping policies, procedures and practices. • Cash flow management and commitment management and control. • Financial performance appraisals. • Keeping a watch on status of Assets in and Non-Performing Assets (NPA) in particular. • Internal Auditing for keeping a watch on wasteful/unjustified expenditures. • Preparing and presenting Balance Sheets. • Take care of statutory and legal requirements with respect to financial transactions. • Carryout Accounting and record keeping. • Exercise due control on financial implications of business contracts and other financial instruments (Letters of Credit, Bonds and Fixed Deposits, Bank Guarantees, etc.).	• Appropriate Financing and Accounting policies and related systems and procedures; • A sound budgeting and budgetary Control System; • Financial performance monitoring system and MIRs; • Deployment of qualified and experienced Finance & Accounts managers; • Appropriate liaison with Banks and other FIs; • Delegation of power; • Computerized working and record keeping.

Contd...

Resource	Inter-resource relationship matrix for inter-active work culture	Key result focal priorities and targets
5. Energy ➤	**A. Man:** • Human resources working for/in business /industrial enterprises have to deal with /utilize energy/power in appropriate forms to execute the tasks assigned to them for achieving desired results. • The issues mentioned a 1(D) above also apply here.	• Issues mentioned against 1(D) and 4(D) above also apply here. • Particularly for industrial enterprises, adoption of effective and efficient energy management strategies will be important for maintaining cost-effective operation (reducing cost of production/operation)
➤	**B. Machine:** • Issues mentioned at 2(D) above also apply here; • Arranging energy/power supply for machines and equipment being used for production and support services; this is a critical resource input for sustained operation.	• Issues mentioned against 2(D) above also apply here. • Issues mentioned against 4(D) also apply here.
➤	**C. Material** • Issues mentioned at 3(D) above also apply here. • Energy/power supply will be a critical input for enterprises supplying and or manufacturing various raw materials, components, bought-out items, semi finished items, etc.	• Issues mentioned against 4(D) above also apply here.
➤	**D. Money:** • Issues mentioned at 4(D) above also apply here.	• Issues mentioned against 4(D) above also apply here.
➤	**E. Management:** Putting in place • Appropriate energy/power management strategy and matching organization. • Deployment of trained persons to deal with power supply systems and installations • Appropriate measures for wastage avoidance.	• Issues mentioned against 4(D) above, also apply here.

Contd...

Resource	Inter-relationship matrix for inter-active work culture	Key result focal priorities and targets
6. Management ➤ (Organization, Policies, Strategies, etc.).	**A. Man:** It is the people of appropriate back-ground, skills and experience who conceive, establish and manage/lead the business enterprises. Therefore, the issues mentioned at 1(E) above also apply here.	• Deciding on organizational vision, mission and objectives (short and long term) and providing leadership. • Framing of organizational and operational policies, system and procedures. • Deciding organizational set-ups for various functions. • Business development strategies. • HRM and HRD Policies. • Industrial Relation Policies. • Technology and Quality Management policies. • Customer and market driven strategies. • Delegation of Power. • Environmental Management Policies. • Public Relation and image building Policies • Policies on Business Ethics and Corporate Governance.
➤	**B. All other resource.** (Machine, Materials, Methods/Knowledge, Money, Energy): Management has a role to play for acquisition, deployment and utilization of all resources that are necessary to succesfully run a business/ industrial enterprise.	• Procuremnt policies; • Deployment stretegies; • Utilization and operational control; • Dealing with all issues mentioned above against 6>A.

Contd...

12.2 Concluding Remarks

(*i*) Other abstract resources namely–'Motive' and 'Methods (Knowledge)', have their respective roles in the management of all the resources mentioned above: without appropriate 'Motive' no human endeavour takes off and without matching 'Methods (knowledge inputs)', it is almost impossible to achieve tangible results in business ventures

(*ii*) Practising managers have to constantly think in terms of optimization of deployment and utilization of various resources through inter-active role appreciation; measurement and quantification of contributions made by various resources will be a challenging task, but the same are important for business operational analysis for enabling corrective and improvement actions.

> ***"Success will not lower its standard to us, We must raise our standard to success."***
>
> — *Randall McBride*

❍❍❍

CHAPTER-13

ERM VERSUS ERP: ROLE APPRECIATION WITH RESPECT TO ENTERPRISE OPERATIONS

"Successful management of a business enterprise heavily depends on the optimization of its resources and assets under the given circumstances."

— Taken from the brochure of a reputed Financial Institution

13.1 Resource Management: Scope and Purpose

Whenever the subject of Resource Management in business enterprises comes up for discussion, most corporate managers rather instinctively tend to veer such discussions around ERP (Enterprise Resource Planning), the topic which has assumed widespread recognition as a modern business operations management tool, particularly for industrial and multi-commodity and multi-locational trading enterprises, operating in a globalized competitive business environment.

Referring to the opening paragraphs (Remarks) in Chapter-2, while ERP's scope is specifically focused on application of certain IT-oriented softwares for day-to-day operations in certain critical/selected functional areas, **ERM (Enterprise Resource Management)** on the other hand, is a generic concept of business management and administration through the composite processes involved in acquisition, deployment and utilization of various available/required resources in optimal proportions. Efficient and effective utilization of deployed resources pose challenging tasks before the enterprise management and the key functionaries, since fulfilment of these tasks at a reasonable/acceptable level are also critical in successfully running the enterprise in a viable and sustainable regime.

While the primary objective of a business enterprise is to earn a reasonable return on capital employed, to be realized through generation of saleable products and services, adequate attention is also needed to manage effectively and utilize optimally the available resources as well as the assets generated out of it, since these resources and assets form the very foundation of the enterprises operating structure; degraded/deteriorated resources and assets will surely lead to the weakening of this structure, and may cause sickness and eventual collapse.

There are a large number of cases of such failures due to mismanagement/in-efficient management of available resources, inspite of good market prospects and standing. The mismanagement referred to above also arise out of unethical business practices and fradulent diversion of resources from the core-business area to other peripheral personalized priorities/channels, thus starving the main business lines, causing sickness and eventual collapse.

It is also to be understood by business managers that adequate availability of only the monetary resources alone does not guarantee viable sustenance unless conscious efforts are made continuously to manage all other critical resources productively with due care and in sustainable proportions: it will be a Balancing Act all the time for the enterprise management.

In the preceding Chapters, we have already discussed about the roles of various resources as critical inputs for successfully running business ventures. The management functionaries, particularly at the middle and senior/top levels will have to assume direct responsibilities for proper deployment and utilization of various resources at different stages of operations, even up to the stage of after-sales services to be rendered to the customers. In fact the execution of ERM tasks in a way becomes one of the important focal attributes of the TQM/Business Excellence processes towards attaining Business Effectiveness across the entire organization.

Since both ERM and ERP are being propagated as elements of modern businesses management process and practices, it will be imperative for corporate managers to first appreciate the total scope of ERM before attempting to take a grasp on ERP practices, so that a comprehensive approach is taken for business management and administration. Such an approach will be quite helpful in successfully introducing and adopting ERP processes, should the enterprise choose to do so, provided of course, adequate attention is also paid towards training and skills development of the deployed employees, as well as putting in place, matching IT-enabled systems back-up.

13.2 'TQM VERSUS ISO 9001-QMS: ANALOGOUS TO 'ERM VERSUS ERP'**

Like TQM versus ISO 9001-QMS, where TQM preaches for a comprehensive Business Excellence effort, whereas ISO 9001-QMS focuses on quality of products and services with respect to customers' requirements and satisfaction; similar analogous relationship between ERM and ERP can be drawn up for their respective scope of applications in business enterprise management and administration. In the following paragraphs we are attempting to define the scopes of coverage for both ERM and EPR for the purpose of clarity so that business managers can appreciate the differences and fine tune their approach towards the assigned tasks according to the needs of the enterprise:

Notes: ***Before we embark on drawing up a comparative analysis of the roles of ERM and ERP, it may be pertinent to state the following about the inception and evolution of ERP as a business management tool:*

(*i*) *ERP was introduced in the USA in early 1980s as a business management tool initially in the manufacturing sector enterprises, dove-tailing the process intimately with Electronic Data Processing (EDP) as applied to certain functional areas like preparing salary and wage bills, bills of materials, purchase orders, listing of payables and receivables, ledgers' entries and financial accounting. With the development of micro-processors in 1970s followed by the advent of PC in late 1970s/early 1980s, the application of ERP as a business operations management tool got a big boost and became increasingly adoptable for different sectors of business operations management.*

(*ii*) *BaaN of Holland and SAP of Germany undertook pioneering efforts in 1990s to introduce ERP in Indian enterprises.*

ERM vs. EPP

ERM Scope	ERP Scope
• ERM is a generic concept for a comprehensive management of various resources in the optimal regimes with respect to their acquisition, deployment and utilization.	ERP is a business management tool for function specific operations with IT enabled application softwares developed for the purposes.
• ERM processes, like the company's long-term objectives, require strategic thinking to be followed by strategies for effective implementation of the set targets.	ERP processes rather intensively focus on application of function-specific softwares with continuous emphasis on achieving market-driven targets in quantitative terms: physical, financial and impressional but tangible.
• ERM processes generate a set of new resources mainly in the form of Assets - both physical and monetary, together with conceptual (knowledge/methods) which can be recycled into the business endeavour; this cycle can go on with a sense of perpetuality.	ERP process regularly generate feed back data/information that can help in timely intervention by operating managers for taking corrective/course correction actions/measures.

(Contd.)

ERM Scope	ERP Scope
• ERM emphasizes on the roles and contributions of various resources as critical inputs for sustainable operations.	ERP processes enables networking of inter-functional activities through data/ information exchange and collation, thus furnishing output data/information to help in operational decision making appropriate to the circumstances prevailing. ERP process also regularly throw up inter-functional and inter-sector performance issues to enable management action for balancing mis-matches and achieving optimization.
• ERM work-culture like TQM, also require regular involvement of top management functionaries to provide leader-ship and directional thrust in conformity with corporate objectives.	ERP processes heavily depend upon the performances of line managers and operating staff for successful application of prescribed/selected softwares in the concerned functional areas with due inter and intra functional net working to facilitate a composite and positive result-oriented outcomes that support customer/ market centric efforts in right time.
• ERM require, besides other organizational priorities, adequate attention towards proper upkeep and maintenance of Assets since Performing Assets (PAs) are critical for sustainable operations; lack of such attention may result in creation of excess Non-Performing Assets (NPAs) which tend to become a burden and adversely effect operational viability.	ERP on the other hand, considers availability of requisite resources and assets as a routine affair assuming that these necessarily have to be provided for in case the enterprise has to operate successfully. ERP focuses on day-to-day performance in meeting market/customer driven targets. ERP however, cannot alone support efforts for long-term objectives; ERP is at best, an effective tool of operations management subject to availability of required resources in adequate/right quantities in right time.

13.3 Concluding Remarks

The very conception of the idea of undertaking a business venture, industrial or non-industrial, has to be based on the possible availability of adequate resources of the relevant kind, in a sustainable regime. When the enterprise gainfully deploys and utilizes its resources effectively and efficiently, assets will get generated out of operations which in turn help in creating further resources and newer assets to support sustenance and possible growth. To bring in a process of perpetuality in such an endeavour, this cycle has to go on and on.

Therefore, managing resources optimally will always remain, besides other critical factors, a central focus for enterprise management. In business enterprises, resources and assets will have inter-active complementary and supplementary roles to play for effective contributions for the best/acceptable results.

The Fig. 13.1 attempts to represent the operating relationship amongst Corporate Objectives, Organizational Efforts, ERM, ERP, Resources, Assets, Operating results and the Business Effectiveness for a business enterprise operating with a perpetual sense of purpose.

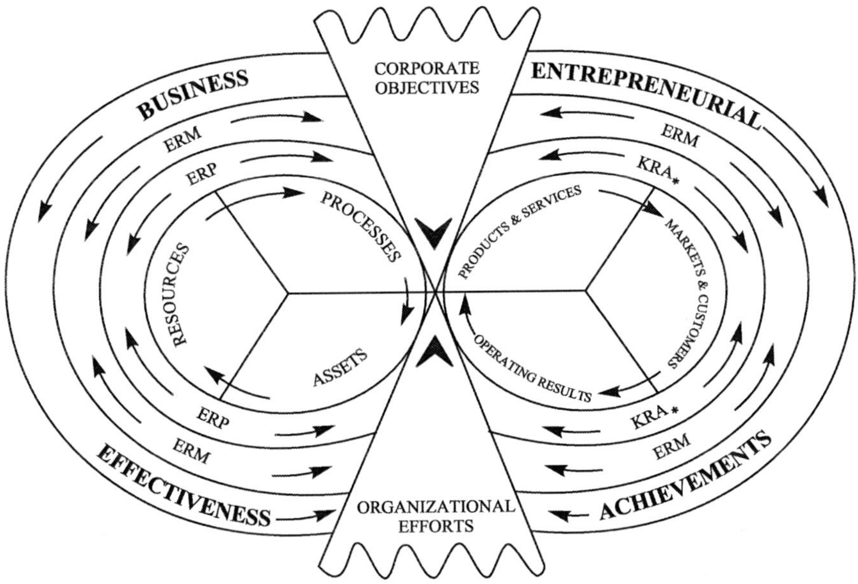

Fig. 13.1 Interactive relationship amongst ERM, ERP, KRA for business effectiveness and entrepreneurial objectives and organizational efforts.

*KRA = KEY RESULT AREAS

> ***"You can never plan the future by the past."***
>
> *— Edmund Burke*

❍❍❍

CHAPTER-14

SYSTEM-SUPPORT TO ENTERPRISE RESOURCE MANAGEMENT

- Systems and Methods Instructions and Procedures;
- Practising Delegation of Power;
- Application of Standards in Business and Industry;
- Quality Management System: Resource Specific Aspects;
- Environmental Management System: Resource Related Issues;
- Total Quality Management (TQM) (Covered in Chapter-11);
- Legal Frame-work Systems to Support Resource Deployment and Utilization in Business Operations.

> ***"The man who doesn't read good books has no advantage over the man who can't read them."***
>
> — *Mark Twain*

In the preceding Chapters, we have discussed various aspects relating to the acquisition, deployment/mobilization, and utilization of resources of different kinds in business enterprises. Since resources get intimately related to the core activities (related to products, services, customers/markets, management of operations, etc.) of the enterprises, these need adequate attention by the enterprise management. However, when the enterprise is a large one with multifunctional set-up, there are bound to be certain amount of difference in perception, approach and interpretation, with respect to the working processes, by the different functional agencies; even the individual functionaries may differ due their own background and assigned priorities. This may lead to intra-organization work-culture mis-match and conflicts, affecting, sometimes rather adversely, the performance of the Key Result Areas (KRA); in such a divergent situation, the unity of organizational purpose may get diluted, even get lost, in the inter-functional disputes and bickerings.

In order to avoid such an inward-looking and sometimes self-centric work-culture ruling the roost, management in the business enterprises, particularly in the industrial enterprises, have to seriously think of/conceive, formulate and put into practice a set of relevant and well designed documented systems and procedures, with a back-up organizational responsibility matrix and declared Delegation of Power (DOP), both for administrative and financial operations. These systems and procedures and DOP have to be both in the function specific formats as well as in the composite corporate formats, with appropriate logical linkages. We shall discuss, in the following paragraphs, various aspects of relevant systems support to enterprise resource management:*

Notes: *(*i*) *Systems and procedures can be rather widespread with both direct and indirect relevancy. However, we are dealing here with only a limited number of directly relatable ones, which are common place.*

(*ii*) *Systems and procedures are as important to Resource Management as they are to the overall operations since both are intimately related.*

14.1 Systems and Methods Instructions and Procedures

In the Business Administration and Management parlance, a system may be defined as a set of instructions, combined in some fashion, directed to some purpose. A system explains how to perform specific activities or tasks: who is to do what, when, and how.

Procedures are further elaboration of systems from the point of view of actual implementation process to be followed, clearly indicating the specific roles and responsibilities for various agencies/individuals to achieve the end results desired.

14.1.1 Role of Organizational Systems

Systems are formulated and brought into practice in an organisation to:

- Provide role-clarity.
- Serve as a common language for working.
- Avoid confusions and conflicts; provide role-clarity.
- Improve work-culture.
- Support efforts for achieving overall excellence.
- Avoid adhocism and personal whims.
- Helps increasing awareness for adoption of better and healthy working systems in the organization.

14.1.2 Nomenclatures in Vogue for Systems and Methods

Systems and Methods can be named under different titles and terminologies in various organizations depending on the organizational culture and preferences, but the purpose is the same:

- SMI (Systems and Methods Instructions):
- WMI (Works and Methods Instructions);

- OMI (Organization and Methods Instructions);
- SP (Standard Procedures);

..........and the like of these.

Notes: *(i) *Systems and Methods instructions and procedures can be a combination of formal and informal ones; however, to avoid confusion and 'buck-passing', these should be in the written and documented form with provision for revision/updation in conformity with the operating circumstances. However, while revising for updating it should be kept in view that basic purpose and disciplines are not diluted.*

(ii) *When a set of in-vogue systems and methods instructions/ procedure become redundant due to change in operating circumstances and processes, they should be cancelled and withdrawn, and new relevant' ones introduced.*

(iii) *When a system/procedure is revised or cancelled/ withdrawn, wide publicity amongst the concerned functional agencies and functionaries must be done to avoid confusion and out dated/wrong working approach getting into practice, creating operational distortions.*

(iv) *Since it is the people in the organization who are supposed to implement/practice these Systems/Methods and procedures, concerned employees at different levels, must be got acquainted and trained through educational training and skill development programmes.*

14.1.3 Functional Linkages of Systems and Methods

Systems and Methods, relevant to Industrial and Business Organizations, can be broadly classified as under; depending on functional applications.

Note: *The list below is representative and not exhaustive as there can be large number of functions in a complex organization.*

Functional Area	Coverage
• General Organizational Systems	Relating to General Administration, Organizational matters, Establishment matters, Personnel Policies (HRM, HRD) and Industrial Relations, TQM and EMS related activities Security, Public Relation/Society Orientation, External Agency relations, etc.
• Planning System	Organizational Objectives Planning

Contd.....

Functional Area	Coverage
	(long-term, short-term); Management Services and coordination-related processes and procedures; Corporate plans related procedures; futuristic action plans and programmes and related systems and procedures.
• Engineering System	Related to Design and Engineering functions and associated aspects; procedural and work instructions, etc., for specific product orientation to cater to customer/market needs.
• R&D Systems	R&D objectives, R&D strategies, procedures for selection, initiation, authorization, investment and budgeting; procedure for closing/abandoning, record generation and data storage; those relating to product development and commercialization, etc.
• Production Systems	Relating to production/manufacturing/assembly/testing/packing/dispatch activities, shop organization, etc., relating to production planning and control.
• Plant Maintenance and services related system	Relating to all activities and processes for maintenance/repairs, upkeep, replacements, re-trofitting of plant and machinery, buildings, other facilities; also for installation of such facilities including acceptance tests.
• Quality Systems	Relating to Quality Assurance, Quality Control Checks, ISO 9001-QMS related activities.
• Financial Systems	Relating to financial management and accounting, costing, PSL, Pay Roll, sales costing, sales billings, cash management, audits, dealing with Banks/FIs; budgeting and budgetary controls, balance sheets and MIRs, financial appraisals, working capital management.
• Commercial Systems	Relating to commercial/sales/pricing-processes, customer services, invoicing, billing, dispatch related matters, customer

Contd...

Functional Area	Coverage
	project monitoring and follow up, tendering, order booking, after sales services, etc.
• Marketing Systems	Marketing objectives and strategy, procedures for various segments of market, procedure for dealership accreditation, marketing outlets and distribution, procedures for tie-up with other agencies, leasing procedures; advertising and publicity; processes relating to Supply Chain Management (SCM).
• Trading Systems	Trading objectives and strategies, procedure for commodities procurement and distribution, dealing with dealers, procedure for customer dealing, sales proceeds realisation, invoicing; Supply Chain Management (SCM), etc.
• Exports Related System	Export objectives and strategies, procedures and paper work system in conformity with National and International trading procedures, shipment procedures, etc.
• Materials Systems	Relating to Materials management aspects like procurement/purchase, receipt, storage, conservation, distribution, disposal, vendor evaluation and registration, vendor development, sub contracting/off-loading, inventory control, logistics and SCM.
• Computerization Systems	This relates to all areas of operation as listed above and systems formulated for enabling computerised systems of working (inputs, output, corrective, record keeping, etc.); adoption and application of relevant softwares and hardwares; softwares for ERP systems in case ERP has been adopted.
• Collaboration/Joint Venture	Objectives and strategies, procedures, related systems for technical and techno-financial transactions, role definition and

Contd...

Functional Area	Coverage
	division of responsibilities, profit/ loss/ liabilities sharing (as the case may be), market sharing, buyback terms, royalty payment procedures, contractual frameworks and inter-organizational interactive relations management, etc.
• Facilities, Infrastructure and Asset Management	Systems and procedures relating to Assets Management planning, Capital investments, acquisition, procurement, installation, upkeep, replacement, disposal, reconditioning, record keeping/asset ledgers, etc. for all types of Capital Facilities/ Fixed Assets, other assets (monetary, knowledge, IPR/Copyright, etc.).

14.2 Delegation of Power (DOP)

In any organization, particularly medium and large ones, concentration of power, both—administrative and financial, with a few top level officials/ managers, often possess practical operational problems, resulting in delays and organizational stress and strain; this situation can best be avoided in the interest of smooth running of day-to-day affairs. Therefore, to the extent possible, feasible and desirable, down-the-line officials, line managers, supervisors, employees may have to be consciously empowered (in some aspects, directly, in others, indirectly) to enable them to take quick operative decisions and follow-up actions. Such empowerment is called **'Delegation of Power'.** For industrial and business organizations, particularly medium and large ones, this becomes imperative for smooth operation.

Besides smoothening out operational complexities, DOP also enthuse the employees, particularly executives/managers and inculcate in them a sense of involvement, responsibility and belongings (but remember the well known Management Dictum: "Authority can be Delegated but not the Responsibility").

Delegation of Power is practised in two distinctive but co-related managerial/administrative jurisdictions: 'Administrative Authority' and 'Financial Authority'. The Delegation of Power for both the above will be based mostly on ranks/levels and hierarchy in the organization (and rightly so to avoid confusion and short-circuiting of roles).

14.2.1 Delegation of Power for Administrative Authority***

This may relate to:

(*i*) Recruitment, posting, training, transfer, deployment/re-deployment, promotion\demotion, disciplinary matters, vigilance, security, welfare, etc.

(*ii*) Establishment related matters.

(*iii*) Day-to-day functional and operational assignments/matters.

(*iv*) Procurement, tendering, storage, distribution, transportation, works.

(*v*) Public Relation, dealing with external and internal agencies.

(*vi*) Disposal of surplus assets/re-deployment of assets, re-deployment of manpower.

(*vii*) Statutory matters relating to the Factory, labour force, establishment etc.

..........And such other things related to operations.

14.2.2 Delegation of Power for Financial Authority***

This will be based on specific ranges of financial values and may relate to all the above 14.2.1 (i to vii), additionally the following are also to be covered:

(*i*) Budgetary sanction, budgetary control.

(*ii*) Expenditure and commitment control.

(*iii*) Tendering and tender finalisation.

(*iv*) Contracts of all kinds having financial implications (including those relating to collaborations/joint ventures).

(*v*) Financial transactions of all kinds including those relating to Banking/Financial Institutions, Creditors, Debtors, suppliers, employees (wages, other payments), contractors, subsidiaries, collaborators shareholders, etc.).

(*vi*) Capital Investment and Trade Investments.

(*vii*) Cash Management/Fund Management (including deployment of surplus funds, assets, etc.).

(*viii*) Working Capital Management, Public Deposits, Inter-Corporate financial Dealings.

(*ix*) Internal Audit, Statutory Audit, Government Audit, other statutory matters having financial implications.

(*x*) Commercial/Sales activity related financial and accounting management billing invoicing, etc., matters relating to payables and receivables.

(*xi*) Costing including sales costing.

(*xii*) Matters relating to administrative and miscellaneous expenses and miscellaneous incomes.

.........And such other finance and accounting related activities.

Note: ****Since in Industry and Business all activities revolve around monetary affairs and transactions, in practice, the Delegation of Power under both the above categories (14.2.1 and 14.2.2) becomes inseparable in most cases.*

14.2.3 Practising Delegation of Power (DOP)

Engineers and other business administration professionals working in industrial and business organizations are expected to try to find out, study and educate themselves about the organization specific DOP. Many progressive and reasonably well-managed organizations have documented Delegation of Power like Organizational Systems and Methods. Copies, of such documents are supposed to be available in the departments and preferably with practising executives/managers. Executives/managers must understand the underlying meanings and implications of various clauses and gather courage and confidence in putting them to practice. If the intentions are clear and prescribed procedures are being followed then there is no need for unwarranted fear or reservations in practicing the authorised delegation of power. In fact, willful avoidance may be taken as a sign of incompetence by the Management. On the other hand, overzealous approach by way of manipulations/short circuiting for exceeding one's delegated powers may lead to a controversial situation. Therefore, an executive/manager is supposed to develop the capabilities of taking rational, well balanced and timely decisions within the framework of the organizational approved procedures and delegation of power.

14.3 Application of Standards in Business and Industry

Application of standards are very important, not only for engineering and design procedures, but also for various other activities and processes that are to take place in construction projects as well as on the shop-floors during manufacturing: assembly and testing, quality control checks, packing and dispatches to customer, besides ensuring acceptable quality of input materials, material testing, documentation etc. The application of standards may also assume significant role in engineering-trading houses, consultancy firms, construction companies, inspection and contracting/sub-contracting agencies. For Universal acceptability in the market, it is essential to follow certain common standards which may be National like BIS/IS in India and International ones like DIN, BS, ASME, ASTM, IEC, API, ISO, etc. Even in the individual organization there can be corporate standards and plant standards for streamlined working within the organisation. For practising engineering and business administration professionals, adequate knowledge of standards/codes and their application/relevance are essential, as without such knowledge, practice of engineering and techno-commercial matters will definitely be incomplete and troublesome for business dealings.

14.3.1 Representative Listing of National and International Standards Organizations

For the benefit of the practising business management professionals, the following is a representative listing of standard-series and standardisation/ regulating bodies widely used/known the world over:

ISO	=	International Standards Organization, (Geneva)
BS	=	British Standards (UK)
DIN	=	Deutsche Industrien Normein (Germany)
ANSI	=	American National Standards Institute (USA)
BIS	=	Bureau of Indian Standards (India)
ASME (USA)	=	American Society of Mechanical Engineers (USA)
ASTM (USA)	=	American Society of Testing and Measurements (USA)
API	=	American Petroleum Institute (USA)
VDE	=	Association of German Electrical Engineers
IEC	=	International Electro-technical Commission
ISO-9000-QMS ISO-9001-2000 ISO-9004-2000	=	Quality Management Systems Propagated by ISO, Geneva
ISO-14001	=	Environmental Management System
IEEE (US&CANADA)	=	Institute of Electrical and Electronics Engineers
CEN	=	European Committee for Standards
NEMA (of USA)	=	National Electrical Manufacturers Associations (USA)
FAO	=	Food and Agricultural Organization (of the UN)
WHO	=	World Health Organization (of UN)
FPO	=	Standards Specified by the Ministry of Agriculture (India)
IND/P&T	=	Standards Specified by the Ministry of Communication
IND/PHARMA	=	Standard Specified by the Ministry of Health (India)
IRS	=	Standards Specified by Research, Design and Standards Organization (ROSO) of the Indian Railways
IRC	=	Standards Specified by Indian Road Congress
JSS	=	Standards Specified by the Ministry of Defence (India) for defence production and defence/ military supplies/procurement.
GOST	=	Russian National Standards.
JIS	=	Japanese National Standards.

Notes: (1) *Besides the above, there are National Standards Organizations in various countries which are members of ISO (Geneva).*

- **Address of ISO =**
  International Standards Organization,
  Central Secretariat,

Post Box-56, CH-1211,
Geneva-20, Switzerland.

- **Address of BIS =**
Bureau of Indian Standards,
Manak Bhavan,
9, Bahadurshah Zafar Marg,
New Delhi-110002.

(2) *Refer 'Handbook of BIS' (Published every year) for:*

(*i*) *Listing of all Indian Standards;*

(*ii*) *Listing of National Standards;*

(*iii*) *Other relevant information.*

14.3.2 Technical Services Function: A Nodal Agency for Standardization Efforts

A discussion on application of standards, systems and procedures will be rather incomplete without appreciating the role of Technical Services function which in most enterprise, act as the nodal agency for standardization and other technical services as mentioned below.

Technical Service function in an engineering/industrial/manufacturing/ trading organization may generally deal with the following activities:

(*i*) Provide reprographic facilities for documentation, drawings (including Micro-filming), etc.

(*ii*) Provide archival services for documentation/standards/reference materials.

(*iii*) Provide library services for technical and non-technical books, magazines, periodicals, etc.

(*iv*) Keep custody of various National and International Standards and make copies/extracts available to users as and when needed.

(*v*) Arrange to procure updated/latest issued standards for the benefit of users.

(*vi*) Coordination for the formulation and circulation of various corporate and plant standards amongst the units/departments/ branches.

(*vii*) Keep liaison with the National Standards Organization for obtaining information to keep the standards directory updated. Also coordinate for giving comments/suggestions to the National Standards body as and new draft standards are formulated and circulated.

(*viii*) Adopt computerised working to the extent practicable for quick dissemination and retrieval of information on standards and related matters, and also for archival inventory records/ status, etc.

Note: *In some organizations, Technical Services function may also deal with activities like Corporate Affairs, contracts coordination, legal cell, liaising with external agencies/ collaborators/joint venture partners, engineering-commercial coordination with major customers/consultant for major projects, departmental training coordination, etc.*

14.4 Quality Management System (QMS): Resource Specific Aspects

Quality Management System (QMS) primarily refers to the organized efforts supported by appropriate organizational facilities and procedures for ensuring quality of products and services. Quality Management by way of adoption of quality-culture and practices have become imperative in the globalized competitive business environments; it is now a question of survival with dignity. A large number of business enterprises are now going in for ISO-9001-QMS certification and hundreds have already obtained the same, and many more are aspiring to get the same.

Note: *As per the latest concept of assuring product quality, the workers and supervisors are being encouraged towards 'Self-inspection' of their own outputs at various stages to reduce deviations and rejections, thus eliminating/reducing the dependence on 'Inspection and Quality Control' by others which tend to be a regulatory pressure which most workers detest.*

14.4.1 ISO-9000 Series of Quality Management Systems (QMS) and Relevant Standards (an Awareness Brief)

14.4.1.1 ISO-9000 series of standards

ISO-9000 Series of Standards, formulated by the International Standard Organization (ISO), seek to formally define a system necessary to assure that the technical, administrative and human factors affecting the quality of an organization's products and services are under control and, further that the formal system must be implemented in a manner that its effectiveness can be demonstrated to the Organization-management, to the customers and to an independent third agency for the purpose of verification.

14.4.1.2 Main standards (ISO-9000, ISO-9001, ISO-9004)

ISO-9000 Series of Quality standards as per the latest valid prescribed systematic formats comprise of the following three main standards as applicable to business and industry producing/delivering products and services to customers to their satisfaction in a consistent manner:

(*i*) **ISO-9000: Quality Management System - Fundamentals and Vocubulary.** ISO-9000 is in fact a referral standard which describes fundamentals of quality management systems and specifies the terminology for quality management systems.

(*ii*) **ISO-9001: Quality Management System - Requirements: ISO-9001** specifies requirements for quality management systems for use where an organization's capability to provide products that meet customer's requirements and applicable regulatory requirements which are needed to be demonstrated.

(*iii*) **ISO-9004: Quality Management System - Guidelines for performance evaluation:** ISO-9004 provides guidance on quality management systems including the processes for continual improvement that contribute to the satisfaction of an organizations's customers and other interested parties.

14.4.1.3 Other supplementary standards

The above main standards are further supported by the following supplementary standards:

(*i*) **ISO-10005** : Quality Management-Guidelines for Quality Plans;

(*ii*) **ISO-10012** : Quality Assurance requirements for measuring equipment.

(*iii*) **ISO-10013** : Guidelines for developing Quality Manual.

(*iv*) **ISO-19011** : Guidelines on the conduct of environment and quality audits.

An Organization can only be Assessed and Registered/Certified to ISO-9001-2000 QMS (the latest valid version); the previous standards in the form of ISO-9002, and ISO-9003 have been discontinued after December 2002.

14.4.2 Resource-Specific Reference in ISO-9001-2000-QMS Standard

Clause-6 of ISO-9001-2000 QMS state the requirements of Resource Management in a business/industrial enterprise through focus on:

6.1 Provision of Resources : Recognizing the need for resources in running a business enterprise; it requires the enterprise to provide for the required resources (for sustained operation; this obviously include funding/monetary resources and material resources, besides others).

6.2 Human Resources : Make appropriate arrangements for recruitment/posting and deployment/utilization of manpower, provide for their training and skill development.

6.3 Infrastructure : This requires making provisions for various facilities like builtup premises, machines and equipment and supporting services infrastructures like water supply, power supply, lighting, roads, transport and communication, etc., to facilitate production activities.

6.4 Work environment : To provide for proper and conducive working environment for employees motivation, safety, welfare, reasonable compensation and incentives, etc.

Note: *Interested managers may please go through the full text of the three main ISO-9000 standards (Para 14.4.1.2 (i, ii, iii) above) to get conversant with the provisions of the ISO-9000 QMS.*

14.4.3 The PDCA Cycle

The Management approach towards QMS: Fig. 14.1 represents sustained efforts by the enterprise management to implement the provisions of ISO-9001-QMS Standards towards building up a quality culture across the organization.

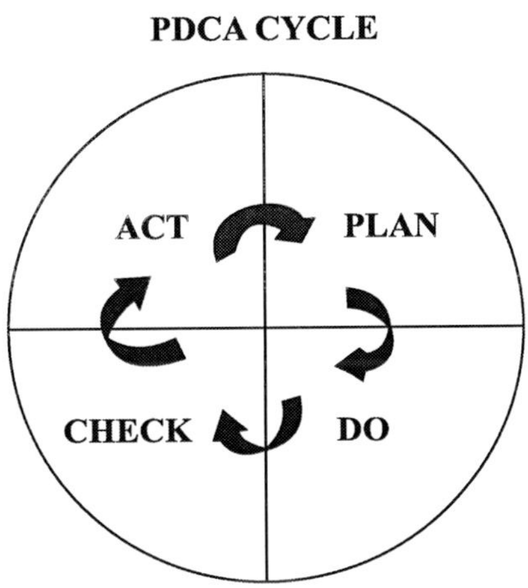

Fig. 14.1 PDCA cycle.

14.5 Environmental Management System (EMS): An International Effort to Fight against Ecological Degradation, Overexploitation of Natural Resources and to Regulate Industrial Pollution

With the growing population on the earth over the centuries, there have been ever-increasing exploitation of natural resources to meet the growing demands for consumption as well as for enhancing the standard of living. The rapid rate of industrialization and accelerated agricultural activities in the last two centuries resulted in over-exploitation of the natural resources so much so that not only the natural resources are getting rapidly depleted but such overexploitation is also adversely affecting the environment to the detriment of the ecosystem and the mankind. Realising this, individuals and the societies in various parts of the world have started thinking to adopt measures to conserve and preserve the environment and stop/minimize ecological degradation.

The issues like global warming, emission of green house gases, depletion of ozone layer in the upper atmosphere, depletion of green cover, rising of sea level, shrinking of glaciers, acid rain, increased concentration of harmful gases in the atmosphere, pollution of surface and underground water sources and also land pollution are some of the burning issues faced by the modern world. Most of the inputs of modern industries are non- renewable natural resources which are fast depleting. The major energy sources like coal, natural gas and oil are being consumed at an alarming rate and may not be available in sufficient quantities for use by our future generations. Therefore "Sustainable Development" is the buzzword now. The importance and urgency to conserve the natural resources and to reduce environmental degradation are now being realized the world over and efforts are on to minimize adverse impacts.

In view of the above, it is the utmost duty of all nations, all organizations and all the citizens of all nations to conduct their activities in environment friendly ways, conserve natural resources, control and if possible eliminate/ minimize pollution so that development could be made ecologically sustainable. Therefore, enlightened organizations world over are adopting environmental management systems to control impacts of their activities and products on the environment and to conserve valuable natural resources. The whole business philosophy is now changing. Now an organization is judged not only by its financial performance but also by its environmental performance and positive contributions to the society at large.

14.5.1 Evolution of ISO-14000 Series of Standards

The genesis of ISO-14000 series can be traced to the United Nation Conference on Human environment in Stockholm in 1972. In this conference more than 113 countries were represented by participation of more than 1000 delegates from 350 organizations.

This conference resulted in a global action plan for the environment in which United Nations Environment Programme (UNEP) headed by Mr. Harlem Brundtland was formed.

In 1987, the Brundtland Commission published a report titled "Our Common Future" calling for industry to develop effective Environmental Management Systems.

By the end of 1988, more than 50 world leaders had publicly supported the report. In 1989, the UN decided to convene the United Nations Conference on Environment and Development (UNCED), generally known as the 'Earth Summit'. This Conference was held in Rio-de-Janeiro, Brazil, in June 1992.

In August 1991, ISO and IEC (refer para 14.3.1) established the Strategic Advisory Group on the Environment (SAGE) to make recommendations regarding international standards for the environment. SAGE studied the British Standards Institution (BSI) standard BS7750 and other starting points for an ISO version.

In January 1993, ISO created the Technical Committee 207 with the responsibility to develop uniform international standards on Environment Management Systems (EMS).

Realising the need for a uniform and systematic approach towards environmental quality attributes, the International Organization for Standardization (ISO) has produced since 1996 a series of International Standards on EMS which include following standards (already issued):

ISO-14000 Family of Standards (a selective listing)

ISO 14001 : 1996 - Environmental Management Systems Specifications with guidance for use.

ISO 14004 : 1996 - Environmental Management Systems: General Guidelines on principles of systems and supporting techniques.

*ISO 14010 : 1996 - Guidelines for Environmental Auditing -General Principles.

*ISO 14011 : 1996 - Guidelines for environmental Auditing -Auditing procedures.

*ISO 14012 : 1996 - Guidelines for environmental auditing-Qualification criteria for environmental auditors.

ISO 14015 : 2001 - Environmental Assessment of Sites and Organizations (EASO).

ISO 14020 : 2000 - Environmental labels and declarations - General principles.

ISO 14021 : 1999 - Environmental labels and declarations - self declared environmental claims (Type II environmental labelling).

ISO 14024 : 1999 - Environmental labels and declarations - Type I environmental labelling Principles and procedures.

ISO 14031 : 1999 - Environmental management - environmental performance evaluation Guidelines.

ISO 14040 : 1997	-	Environmental management - Life cycle assessment - Principles and framework.
ISO 14041 : 1998	-	Environmental management - Life cycle assessment - Goal and scope definition and inventory analysis.
ISO 14042 : 2000	-	Environmental management - Life cycle assessment - Life cycle impact assessment.
ISO 14043 : 2000	-	Environmental management - Life cycle assessment - Life cycle interpretation.
ISO 14050: 2002	-	Environmental management - Life cycle assessment - Examples of application of ISO standards.
ISO 19011 : 2002	-	Guidelines for quality and/or environmental management systems auditing (*This standard replaces ISO 14010, ISO 14011 & ISO 14012)

14.5.2 Environment Management System and ISO-14001 Standard

ISO 14001 is world's most recognized and accepted standard which provides a framework for environmental management system. It was prepared by International Standards Organization (ISO) and was released in 1996; it specifies requirements for establishing elements of EMS, *viz.*, Environment policy, determining environmental aspects and impacts of processes, activities, products and services, planning environmental objectives and targets, checking and corrective actions, and management review.

ISO 14001 provides an internationally recognised standard against which an organization's EMS can be assessed and certified. It is flexible enough to be applicable to any organization irrespective of its activities or size.

14.5.3 Elements of Environmental Management System (EMS) ISO-14001

Environment Management Systems (EMS) standard provide a framework for the organization to manage their **Resources** better, and improve their environmental performance. The management system approach of ISO 14001 is also based on the well known PDCA cycle approach (Fig. 14.1). The six elements of ISO 14001 are:

	Element	Phase	
1	Environment policy	---PLAN	This activity cycle has to go on and on for a sustained efforts towards maintaining the recommended standard.
2	Planning		
3	Implementation and operation	---DO	
4	Checking and corrective action	---CHECK	
5	Management review	---ACT	
6	Continual improvement		

14.5.4 Integration of ISO-9000 QMS and ISO-14000 EMS

International Organization for Standardization (ISO) has set-up a technical advisory group (ISO/TAG 12) for addressing the integration of ISO-9000-QMS and ISO-14000 EMS series standards. The objectives of TAG 12 are as per the following:

Assess the need of Business and Consumers in the field of ISO-9000 and ISO-14000 standards taking account of integrated QMS (Quality Management System) and EMS (Environmental Management System) standards and recommend a strategic plan for the achievements of compatible QMS and EMS Standards by integration either directly or via. alignment of the ISO-14000 series of standards.

As per the latest interlinkages of these standards, the structure and clause requirements of ISO-14001 are fully compatible with that of ISO-9001 and OHSAS-18001. (OHSAS = Occupational Health and Safety Management System).

14.5.5 International Scenario

EMS is gradually becoming a condition of doing business in many markets and regions. Some governments may require ISO 14001 Certification from suppliers of specific goods and services.

14.5.6 Indian Scenario (2007)

ISO 14001 Certification has started taking roots in Indian Industries; Presently over 100 companies which include Chemical, Engineering, Petroleum, Processed Food and Hotels are working towards establishing and implementing ISO-14001 Standards, Presently (2007 status), over 50 industries have already implemented ISO-14001.

14.5.7 Benefits Adopting ISO-14001 EMS Certification

Environmental issues are becoming an important part of business planning. We must analyse and find what on earth can sustain and renew itself for life to go on. The future of mankind lies in a cleaner environment. It is duty of all organizations to work towards environmental conservation and resource conservation. Environmental Management is increasingly being accepted as a part of good business management strategy. If an organization has a sound environmental management system, it is certified against ISO 14001; apart from contributing to environmental conservation and resource conservation and control of pollution, the organization directly and indirectly gains through the following:

1. Provides a structured frame work for environmental management system.
2. Recognition for organization.
3. Increased business opportunities.

4. Better regulatory compliance.
5. Healthy working conditions.
6. Benefits arising due to lesser accidents.
7. Gets confidence of Insurers and financiers.
8. Good will in the society.
9. Good will among employees.
10. Economic benefits arising out of efficient use of Natural Resources.

14.6 Total Quality Management (TQM) the Enterprise Work-Culture Towards Business Excellence

This has already been covered in detail in Chapter-11.

14.7 Legal Framework Systems for Business and Industry: Legal Reference/Relevant Laws/Acts: Commonly Applicable and known to Trade, Commerce, Busines and Industry*

Practising managers and other business management professionals working in business and industrial enterprises should also know about the existence of the following, so that in case of exigency, can take some remedial/ preventive preliminary action before approaching Legal consultants/ Experts on the subject for further follow-up action:

Notes: *(*i*) *The Laws/Acts go on being amended from time to time; consult legal advisors to find out the latest.*

(*ii*) *The idea of presenting this topic is not to make the professional as legal experts, but to make them aware of such legal requirements, and get reasonably conversant.*

14.7.1 Specific Labour Laws: Selected Listing

- The Apprentices Act, 1961
- The Contract Labour (Regulation and Abolition) Act, 1970
- Misconduct/Dismissal/Discharge and Domestic Enquiry Procedures
- Minimum Wages Act, 1948
- Workmen's Compensation Act, 1923
- The Employees' Provident Funds and Misc. Provisions Act, 1952
- The Employs' State Insurance Act, 1948
- Equal Remuneration Act, 1976
- The Industrial Employment (Standing Orders) Act, 1946
- The Maternity Benefit Act, 1961
- The Payment of Gratuity Act, 1972
- The Child Labour (Prohibition and Regulation) Act, 1986
- Employers' Liability Act, 1938

- The Payment of Wages Act, 1936
- The Payment of Bonus Act, 1965
- Factories Act, 1948
- Industrial Disputes Act, 1947
- Shops and Establishments Act (Each State may have separate Acts)
- Trade Union Act, 1926.

14.7.2 Trade Unions

There are a large number of Trade Unions operating in various Industrial Establishments, Agricultural Industries, Coal and Mining Sectors, Railways, Insurance and Banking Sectors, etc., most of them directly or indirectly get affiliated to the following well-known major National Trade Union Organizations:

- INTUC : Indian National Trade Union Congress.
- AITUC : All India Trade Union congress.
- CITU : Centre for Indian Trade Unions.
- BMS : Bhartiya Majdoor Sangh.
- HMS : Hind Majdoor Sabha.

14.7.3 Some Other Related Laws Covering Business, Trade and Industry (Selected Listing Only)

- Companies Act 1956/Companies (Amendment) Act, 1974
- Indian Explosives Act, 1884 and Subsequent Amendments
- Indian Boiler Act, 1923 and Subsequent Amendments
- Environment Protection Act, 1986
- Air (Prevention and Control of Pollution) Act, 1981
- Water (Prevention and Control of Pollution) Act, 1974
- Law of Contracts: "The Indian Contract Act, 1972" covering aspects like agreements, contracts, proposals, discharge of contract, breach of contracts, guarantees, indemnity, pledge, etc., and related legalities
- Commercial Laws, Laws of Partnership, Law of Arbitration, Laws of Negotiable Instruments
- Sale of Goods and Hire Purchases
- Law of Insolvency
- Indian Electricity Act, 1910 and as Amended by Act 50 of 1991
- Indian Electricity Rules, 1956 (updated till 1992)
- Right to Information Act, 2005
- Indian Copy Right Act of 1914, of 1957 and Amendments on the same introduced in 1983, 1984 and 1999
- IT Act, 2000 (Cyber Law)

- Negotiable Instruments Act, 1881
- Income Tax Act, 1961
- Essential Commodities Act, 1955
- The Insolvency Act, 1920
- The Societies Registration Act, 1860
- The Customs Act, 1961
- The Insurance Act, 1963 and 1972
- The Partnership Act, 1932

"If an idea is worth having once, it is worth having twice."

— Tom Stoppard

❍❍❍

CHAPTER-15

SOME MISCELLANEOUS TOPICS RELEVANT TO RESOURCE MANAGEMENT IN INDUSTRIAL ENTERPRISES

- Contract Management: A Critical Process in Customer and Supplier Relationship.
- Innovative and Creative Approach to Business Enterprise Management.
- Cultivating Industrial Realtion: A Positive Step Towards Human Resource Optimization.
- Human Aspects of Resource Management.
- Role of Information Technology in Enterprise Resource Management.
- Excellence in Factory Management: Adopting.
- 'Jishu-Hozen' (Autonomous Maintenance): A Revolutionary Concept in Plant Maintenance.
- Business Ethics and Corporate Governance.

"Everyone has inside him or her a piece of good news. The good news is that you do not know how great you can be."

— Dr. APJ Abdul Kalam,
Former President of India

15.1 Contract Management: A Critical Process in Customer and Supplier Relationship

In business enterprises, contractual situations prevail in many of the critical operational areas, be it internal or external. Taking the case of an industrial enterprise, the contractual processes are predominantly relatable to certain critical resources such as **Man** (Human Resources), **Machines**, **Materials**, **Methods** (Knowledge) and **Money**. For the acquisition, deployment, and utilization of these critical resources, the contractual processes may be both internally directed and externally directed. We shall take each of these for further elaboration in the following paragraphs:

• The Contractual Relationships with Respect to Resources

15.1.1 Man

Called Human Resources (HR) in business management parlance, the term generally refers to employees at all levels, management functionaries, promoters, labour-service providers/contractors and other stakeholders who contribute human efforts of different kinds in running the enterprise.

15.1.1.1 Employees and management functionaries

Their services are hired either as regular employees or on fixed tenure basis. In both cases, terms and conditions of engagement are spelt out in writing; these necessarily have to include ranking, assignments, compensation packages, perks, service conditions, etc. When the employee accepts in writing and join the service, a contractual arrangement has been entered into with all legal implications covered by the relevant laws of the land.

15.1.1.2 Promoters

As soon as the enterprise is formed through the 'Article of Association' and is registered as a Company, certain contractual processes, obligations and legalities come into force and play, and the members get bound by those.

15.1.1.3 Labour service supply contractors/agencies

For certain labour intensive services, the enterprise may, instead of having regularly employed workforce, hire the services of a labour force on contract for temporary engagement, through the external agencies, generally called 'Labour Contractors'. Once engaged after due paper-work formalities, a contractual arrangement has been entered into with all legal implications as per the relevant Labour Laws.

Sometimes, individuals are also hired temporarily on work-charged basis. In such cases, there can be both written terms and conditions, or on an un-written mutually acceptable understanding on terms and conditions of engagement. In such cases, the legal rights are almost absent.*

Note: **In such cases, engaging enterprise management must ensure compliance of applicable labour laws to avoid legal complica tions and violation of Statutory provisions.*

15.1.2 Machines

This generally refers to all kinds of facilities like Plant and Machinery, equipment, and other infrastructural services like buildings/sheds/offices, services installation like water supply, power supply, communication, transportation, roads, railway siding, storage facilities, etc., which are essentially required to facilitate production of saleable products and services to meet customer/market requirements and also help in successful/viable sustenance of operations.

15.1.2.1 Machines for own use

For acquiring and deploying these resources, which are mostly of Fixed Assets nature (capital facilities), procurement processes followed with placement of orders with negotiated and agreed terms and conditions, thus leading to a contractual arrangement. In case of construction projects for buildings, sheds, roads, services lines etc. through due process of tendering, contracts are entered into either only for works portion as Works Contract, or there may be a composite contractual arrangement for material/ equipment Supply-cum-Works (works comprising of labour and supervision).

15.1.2.2 Machines for selling to customers

In case the enterprise is the manufacturer and/or supplier of such machines and equipment (and related services) to customers, then here also, after due process of tendering/tender offers and negotiations, order thus received generally falls in the category of 'Supply Contact' with associated obligations/commitments and legalities as reflected in the agreed terms and conditions stipulated in the contract.

15.1.2.3 EPC Contracts

In case of certain large engineering/technologically complex projects like setting up of a Thermal Power Station or Petro-Chemical Complex, a composite contractual arrangement generally known as EPC-contract may be adopted with scopes involving Engineering/Design, Procurement and Construction (EPC); in such a case the original manufacturer or the authorised supplier/agent undertake execution of the project on a turnkey basis for the whole project, or a separately identifiable subproject within the framework of the client organization's specified terms and conditions and scope of work.

15.1.3 Materials

15.1.3.1 Materials for own use

Taking the case of an industrial enterprise, as already discussed in the preceding Chapters material is a critical resource and mostly have to be procured from external sources. Procurement/Purchase Policies and procedures which include tendering activities, once the purchase/supply order is placed, the same becomes a contractual arrangement with all associated obligations, legalities and commitments reflected through the incorporated terms and conditions.

15.1.3.2 Materials to be supplied to customers

In case where the enterprise is the seller of materials (raw materials, components, semi-finished and finished items, purchase resold items, etc.), then once the formal order is finalized and placed/received, the same conforms to a contractual arrangement with associated obligations and legalities.

15.1.4 Methods (Knowledge)

In business operations, often services of experts/consultants are hired to acquire required process knowledge and to get guidance for certain specific purposes. There can also be technological collaboration arrangements with expert-groups/agencies for developing capabilities for manufacturing of products as well as developing in-house expertise for rendering saleable services to customers. For such services as above, contractual arrangement will have to be entered into for clarity of purpose and ease of executional follow-up for fulfilment of contractual obligations with attendant commitments and legalities.

15.1.5 Money

Although money is a link resource, its availability is always associated with lots of conditions and restrictions particularly for the organized business operations. Once the industrial enterprise, after necessary capital investments, goes into production/operation mode, a continuous flow of fund in the form of working capital becomes critical for successful sustenance. Money borrowed from banks, other financial institutions, from other companies, and also from other sources including public borrowings (by issue of bonds, shares, etc.), always come forth through certain contractual arrangements with attendant obligations, legalities and guarantees. **The same is true for loans taken for capital investments as well.**

15.1.6 Managing Commercial Contracts

All the contractual situations discussed above ultimately revolve round monetary transactions in one form or the other and these have to be necessarily covered by certain mutually agreed terms and conditions duly put down in writing, to avoid uncertainties, misunderstanding, intentional or un-intentional violations and digression at a later stage leading to a dispute situation. Therefore, formulating and finalising a mutually agreed contract-document is imperative in business and commercial transactions. Such contracts are generally called Commercial Contracts.

15.1.6.1 Kinds and types of commercial contracts

(A) **Kinds of commercial contracts:**

Commercial contracts may be of different kinds depending on the:

- Subject of the contract; Kind of the contracting parties and their area of business/operations.

- Legal/Statutory implications/requirements and regulations concerning the subject of the contract: both domestic and international.
- Time frame of the contractual arrangement; it may also be advisable to define contract closure conditions to avoid differently at the completion and closing stage.

(B) **Types of commercial contracts:** Commercial contracts broadly relate to the following business transactions/operational processes:

(*i*) Purchase/Procurement, supply of goods and services.*
(*ii*) Construction/Project construction, erection and commissioning.*
(*iii*) Marketing and Trading.
(*iv*) Selling of products and services to customers.
(*v*) Design and engineering of products and projects.*
(*vi*) Technology transfer and acquisition.
(*vii*) Funding/financial services, Banking services.
(*viii*) Training & skills development (HRD) programmes.
(*ix*) Consultancy services (of any kind).*
(*x*) Manpower supply contracts.*
(*xi*) Transportation, shipping, other logistic support services.*
(*xii*) Maintenance & Repair Services, after sales services/AMCs.
(*xiii*) Security services.
(*xiv*) Recruitment and selection.
(*xv*) Printing and Reprographic services.
(*xvi*) Rental of premises, land, buildings, accommodation, machinery, etc.
(*xvii*) Leasing arrangements for accommodation, equipment, machinery, vehicles, etc.
(*xviii*) House keeping services.
(*xix*) Canteen and welfare services.
(*xx*) Medical and Health care services, insurance schemes.
(*xxi*) Insurance services for business and industrial operations.
(*xxii*) Educational services.
(*xxiii*) Scavenging and community cleaning services.
(*xxiv*) Telecom services.
(*xxv*) Power supply services.
(*xxvi*) Computer/IT services.
(*xxvii*) Others not listed above but may be required for smooth operation of business/industrial enterprises.

Notes: *(*i*) *In case of EPC contracts, these activities may get covered by a composite contractual arrangement for large engineering/instruction projects on a turnkey basis.*

(*ii*) *In case of certain construction and infrastructure projects like setting of a power plant, construction of roads, bridges, flyovers, shipping terminals, etc., considering the project funding methods, the contracts can be in any of the following categories;*

(*a*) *BOLT* = *Build Operate Lease Transfer,*
(*b*) *BOO* = *Build Own Operate,*
(*c*) *BOT* = *Build Operate Transfer,*
(*d*) *BOOT* = *Build Own Operate Transfer.*

15.1.6.2 Basic approaches that are necessary for conceiving and taking up processing of commercial contractual arrangements

(*i*) Conceiving and formulating the purpose and objects of the contract.

(*ii*) Contractual risk perceptions, *force-majeure* conditions applicable, competence of contracting parties to successfully shoulder the responsibilities and obligations, arbitration/dispute redressal mechanism, etc.

(*iii*) Deciding on an organizational policy framework for dealing with commercial contracts, keeping in view the legal/statutory requirements and regulations.

(*iv*) Putting in place necessary procedures (with Delegation of Power) for tendering/calling for offers, evaluation of offers, negotiation and finalization and execution.

(*v*) Identifying agency/persons responsible for operation of the contractual arrangements and follow-up thereon.

15.1.6.3 Drafting of commercial contracts*

This is a tricky job and this can be done properly by an experienced person(s) conversant with various aspects related to the proposed contractual arrangement. Not only the techno-commercial/technical aspects are to be dealt with, the legal implications and requirements are also to be well thought of and incorporated. Company's legal officers and Chartered Accountants have to play their role here in association with concerned (and conversant) technical persons (particularly if the contract is for a techno-commercial arrangement).

Best way to do such a job is to adopt the following approach:

(*i*) Study earlier similar contracts already in operation or executed.

(*ii*) Study similar contracts available with associated enterprises.

(*iii*) Obtain a copy of draft contract from the other party (which is normally done) and build/modify on the same as per current requirements specific to the contracting parties and objects.

(*iv*) Tie-up points which are absent in the earlier/present draft, but are necessary for inclusion now, to make it as comprehensive as possible, to take care of present and foreseeable future circumstances.

Notes: *(i) *If this activity is a regular feature in the organization, there has to be a contract management group, may be under the Legal department or Company Secretariat or even under the Commercial department, depending on the organizational working arrangements and work culture.*

(ii) *There are training courses available in certain institutes on this subject, and it may be worthwhile to train some executives/managers who are supposed to deal with such matters.*

15.1.6.4 Certain important aspects which must be understood and considered while drafting and incorporating in the proposed commercial contracts

(i) Incoterm (Incoterms ICC-560/2000) particularly for international contracts.

(ii) Warranty, Guarantee clauses and the difference between the two (the operative part).

(iii) Arbitration clauses (arbitration process/mechanisms to be adopted in case of dispute).

(iv) *Force Majeure* conditions (define).

(v) Price Escalation clauses (if any), (better to define a formula).

(vi) Legal Heirs/Obligation Transfer clauses.

(vii) Liquidated Damages (LD) and Penalty Clause for delayed delivery/execution**.

(viii) Payment Terms, Negotiable instruments, payment collection mechanism (Letter of Credit, Bill discounting, Documents through Banks, early/quick delivery incentive, etc.).

Note: ***Practically very difficult to enforce and execute unless proper information and data are maintained right from the beginning; also the language has to be very specific and clear.*

(ix) Interface of contract with guidelines of International Trade Regulatory Bodies like WTO, WCO, Regional International Trade Blocks, Export/Import Regulatory Agencies, Funding Agencies (World Bank, ADB, EURO-fund, etc.).

(x) E-Commerce related clauses (if applicable).

(xi) Incorporation of Tax Liabilities/issues: language of this clause should be as clear as possible, leaving no ambiguity to create difficulties/disputes later.

(xii) Foreign Exchange related clause, particularly exchange rates, applicability of rates, period/date, forward coverage, backward coverage currency, etc.

(*xiii*) Other aspects not mentioned above but are relevant to the proposed contract (such as Lease Financing, Buyback arrangements, Working Capital support, contract-closure conditions, etc.).

15.1.6.5 Operating commercial contracts

(*i*) This is an important activity and should be dealt with, on behalf of the enterprise, by experienced and matured officials duly authorised. They are supposed to be conversant and as thorough as possible about the purpose, terms and conditions incorporated and the obligation and legalities involved in the contractual arrangements entered into.

(*ii*) Execution of the contract needs to be regularly monitored by the concerned officials, till the contract is closed. IT-enabled contract monitoring system should preferably be adopted and trained persons engaged to do the job; appropriate IT-softwares to be selected and installed.

(*iii*) Record keeping (preferably through computerised system) should be as best as possible and adequate attention given, appropriate back up system should also be in place for emergent situations.

(*iv*) Reviews should be done periodically at senior levels and corrective follow-up actions taken.

(*v*) In case deviations noticed or needed this should be sorted out as quickly as possible; delays may complicate matters.

(*vi*) In case of any dispute arising, efforts be made to sort out mutually through discussions and through written communications. In case dispute cannot be sorted out mutually, Arbitration process can be resorted to. Best efforts be made to avoid court cases.

15.2 Innovative and Creative Approach to Business Enterprise Management

> ***"Science alone is not Technology,***
> ***and***
> ***Technology alone is not Innovation."***
>
> — *Akio Morita,*
> *Former Chairman, Sony Corporation*

15.2.1 Innovations in Enterprise Management

As per the EFQM (European Forum for Quality Management) Business Excellence Model Glossary of Terms (TQM-related), innovation is defined as **'the practical translation of ideas into new products, services, processes, systems and social interactions'.**

In an industrial enterprise, there is always ample opportunities and scope for innovative working, almost in all areas of functioning, but all said and done, in an industrial situation, the focus and priorities always revolve round product development efforts and manufacturing activities for saleable product realisation which in turn help in financial returns on capital employed. However, broadly speaking, in an industrial enterprise, innovation can be practised in some core functional areas with certain degree of tangible results:

Note: *Below is the Listing of some major functional areas only; the list is not exhaustive.*

(1) Engineering and Design for Product Development

Innovations can be for:

(*i*) Software development for engineering calculations.

(*ii*) Optimization of design for structural detail: adoption of CAD system.

(*iii*) Adoption of value engineering concepts.

(*iv*) Optimization of material specifications and quantities, material substitution for economic/cost effective construction and manufacturing.

(*v*) Orientation to customised designs if market demands so.

(*vi*) Reverse Engineering approach in diversification and in upgradation of current products.

(2) Production Technology

Innovative approach can be for:

(*i*) Optimization of application of machine tools and other production equipment for cost-effective operations, introduction of CNC system, robotics/artificial intelligence.

(*ii*) Optimization of cutting tool selection and application regimes.

(*iii*) Optimization of shop floor technological flow to improve mobility and reduce process fatigues/sluggishness/congestions.

(*iv*) Ways and means to avoid/minimize wastages and rejection level (size rationalization, tailoring charts, in-process QC).

(*v*) Optimization in manufacturing cycle time.

(*vi*) Efforts to improve shop-floor work-organization (5S system, etc.), material handling and shop accessory facilities, etc.

(*vii*) Optimization of labour utilization and machine utilization.

(*viii*) Minimization of accidents.

(3) Plant Maintenance and Services

Innovative thinking and action can be for:

(*i*) Ways and means for reduction of machine down time.

(*ii*) Optimization of inventory management for spares and maintenance/repair consumables.

(*iii*) Adoption of preventive maintenance action plans, introduction of online fault diagnostic system.

(*iv*) Adoption of contingency plans for meeting emergent situation.

(*v*) Organizing proper record-keeping and retrieval systems for history of all machines and equipments.

(*vi*) Organizing available manpower for optimal utilization/deployment.

(*vii*) Improvising and improving training methods.

(*viii*) Improving environment and ecological management.

(*ix*) Adopting 'Jishu-Hozen' Autonomous Maintenance concept.

(4) Procurement and Storage Management

Innovations can be introduced for:

(*i*) Streamlining tendering process and procedures.

(*ii*) Improving documentation and formats to avoid confusion and processing delays.

(*iii*) Streamlining vendor development and registration process.

(*iv*) Improving storage and distribution processes.

(*v*) Adopting Internet/e-procurement process.

(*vi*) Optimising inventory control process.

(*vii*) Improving processes for receipt and custody of incoming materials, conservation, and distribution network.

(*viii*) Improving processes for quick sorting out/settlement of rejection cases.

(5) Sales and Marketing

Innovative ideas and systems can be adopted in the following areas:

(*i*) Adoption of Multimedia advertising and communication.

(*ii*) Improving system for quick redressal of customer complaints.

(*iii*) Introducing attractive sale and after-sale-service packages for customers (credit-sale, lease financing, quantity discount, quick-payment discount, free training facility, etc.).

(*iv*) Involving customer in quality control processes.

(*v*) Adopting E-commerce, High Seas-Sale methods where relevant; and the like of it for successful marketing efforts and facilitating quicker sales-proceeds realization.

(6) Human Resource Management (HRM)

Innovations can be for:

(*i*) Streamlining/adopting scientific method of selection and recruitment process: devising process instruments and procedures for quicker and efficient evaluation of prospective recruits.

('Hire for attitude, Train for skill')

(*ii*) Improving/improvising training and skill development methods: introduction of job-oriented programmes for workers and supervisors.

(*iii*) Adopting contemporary and futuristic strategies for improving industrial relations and motivations, including employee participation in selective areas.

(*iv*) Adopting entrepreneurship training programmes for executives and managers.

(*v*) Introducing appropriate incentive and reward schemes for improving motivation and organizational loyalty towards effective contributions.

(*vi*) Reducing bureaucratic system of working, introducing employee-friendly-administrative processes, reducing paper-work, practising DOP.

(*vii*) Introducing/improving employee welfare measures and other motivation steps.

(*viii*) Encouraging and monitoring measures for improvement of work-area environment, environmental and ecological aspects reduce/minimize adverse impacts.

(*ix*) Adoption of tactful strategies to deal with government agencies and local bodies to maintain cordial and mutually beneficial relationship.

(*x*) Adopting strategies for maintaining good public image and public relation.

Innovation can be introduced/adopted in any area of function provided the top management encourage and the employees are motivated.

Experience in some reputed large business and industrial organizations has shown that given the environment, resources and encouragement, many employees rise to the occasion and their innovative contributions have resulted in savings/additional incomes to the tune of crores of rupees in a financial year; many of them are winning National Awards, besides helping the organization attain lofty heights in the business world as well as in the society at large.

15.2.2 Practising Creativity in Enterprise Management (Creativity Adds Value to Business Operations)

Creativity comes from imagination and imagination often leads to innovative ideas. Therefore, in a way, creativity comes into play when innovative ideas are put to practical translation for an objective result. While creativity can manifest itself in many forms and in every conceivable human endeavours, the results can be both beneficial and detrimental depending on the intent with which the creativity is perused.

Creativity in business endeavours generally get associated with innovations that help in providing the enterprise with an impetus for continually striving for meaningful and satisfactory sustenance, growth and for attaining excellence. In fact, many talented people working for the enterprise, given due encouragement, incentives and resources, will try to practise an innovative work culture which may lead to creativity in many aspects of operations. In a competitive market scenario, innovation and creativity have to go hand in hand to support successful sustenance and growth, besides helping in attaining excellence wherever, possible and practicable. In the following paragraphs, we are listing out briefly the areas of operations in business and industry where creativity can be practised:

Note: *The list is representative and not exhaustive.*

(*i*) **Product Design:** This is an area of activity where there are constant efforts being made to make the product quality, reliability and aesthetics attractive and competitive. Even for the existing established products, creative ideas can give a new look to the configuration and aesthetics thereby help enhancing the marketability and boosting sales/market share. This is very much relevant to consumer products for emerging markets as well as to meet the needs of the changing customer preferences. In a globalized competitive business scenario, creativity in products-design and aesthetics assume high degree of importance.

(*ii*) **Marketing:** Creative ideas can give a big boost to advertising, communication and presentation techniques thereby enhancing product and process acceptability and saleability in the market. In fact, multi-media presentations with creative ideas, are making even the sundry products and processes appealing to the consumers/customers at large and boosting sales.

(*iii*) **Process development and improvement:** While innovative ideas can make the processes (and the resultant products and services) cost-effective and competitive, creative ideas when translated to reality, can vastly improve the processes and enhance their credibility/acceptability in various areas of operations where such creative ideas get generated and applied judiciously.

(*iv*) **Service Providing:** With the growth of population occurring all over the world, emerging newer societies and growing aspirations for higher standards of living, the markets for service providers are increasing at a rapid pace. Even medium and large service providing enterprises like hotels, hospitals, electricity utilities. telecom services, transportation companies, etc., are increasingly off loading part of their peripheral services to a second generation low cost services agencies to make their operations cost effective and viable. Lot of creative ideas are being generated for bringing in innovative methods in providing services to make the same attractive to consumers and thereby expanding their market; even new markets are also being developed to provide services which were not available earlier to the sundry consumers/customers.

(*v*) **Training and Development:** With expanding population, business opportunities, and enterprising endeavours, need for skilled and trained manpower is also increasing. In a global context, for successful sustenance and possible growth, roles of people working in the organization are becoming critical given the resources and environment. Therefore, traditional methods of training and skill development may not serve the purpose effectively. Innovative ideas have to come into play to align the requirements in conformity with the changing scenarios/ requirements; and thus creative training tools may have to be devised and employed to made the programme application oriented so that trained persons can fit into the scheme of operations of the employing organization with ease and confidence, and to the satisfaction of the employers.

15.3 Cultivating Industrial Relation: A Positive Step Towards Human Resource Optimization

The conduct of affairs pertaining to the day-to-day working relationship between the owners, management and the employees (and their representative for a like Trade Unions, Executive Association, Supervisors Association, etc.) is generally perceived as the activities and processes that relate to the term 'Industrial Relation'. However, in a broader view, the scope of 'Industrial Relation' may go beyond the traditional concept of employer-employee interactive relationship, and may also encompass the working relationships even with other externally associated agencies like customers, shareholders, suppliers, contractors, service providers, banks/FIs, Auditors, regulatory state/local bodies, etc., who have considerable direct and indirect influences and impacts in the running of operations of the industrial enterprise. Therefore, while framing the industrial relations policies and procedures these external factors may have to be kept in view, more so when the industrial units are operating in an era of globalised competition and market, thus needing a reasonably good reputation besides the operational performance; the perception that such external agencies can be dealt with only through the process or 'Public relation' exercise, is not very logical, since public relation process predominantly deal with image-building exercises which may or may not address the various issues with respect to the working/business relationship with these external agencies as mentioned above. There is, however, a difference in strategies in case of dealing with employee specific affairs and those pertaining to the associated external agencies. We are, however, limiting our discussions here to the 'Industrial Relations' issues pertaining to the employees and their representative for a in the following paragraphs for general appreciation or the subject.

15.3.1 Personnel Policies: The Starting Point

The starting point of 'Industrial Relation' in any industrial enterprise, is already incorporated in the 'Personnel Policies' adopted by the enterprise management, particularly the policy frame-work formulated and adopted towards:

(*i*) recruitment process and compensation packages;
(*ii*) posting and deployment;
(*iii*) promotion policy/career growth prospects;
(*iv*) amenities and perks, welfare measures, social securities;
(*v*) incentive schemes/reward schemes;
(*vi*) training and skills development, re-training, re-deployment;
(*vii*) retirement policy and terminal benefits, post retirement benefits;
(*viii*) retrenchment policy, and terminal conditions;
(*ix*) disciplinary matters;
(*x*) workplace security and safety.

Employees, by and large, judge an employing organization and the management with respect to the above issues and adopt an attitude which have great influence and impacts on their behavioural pattern towards the industrial relation matters.

15.3.2 Participative Style of Management

Experiences over the last three decades in some successful corporations in India have shown that employee participation in day-to-day affairs, which affect their working life and performance, have substantially improved industrial relations, productivity and a sense of belonging/loyalty. Depending on as to whether the enterprise is a Public/Govt. undertaking or a Private Sector organization, the degree of employee participation in running the affairs of the enterprise may vary, but the positive impacts are visible and discernible, wherever this policy has been adopted with certain degree of commitment.

15.3.2.1 The employee participation process, by and large, may get into practice through the following approaches

(*i*) Recognising Employee Representative fora like Trade Unions, Executive Associations, Supervisor-Association, etc., within the framework of relevant statutory laws and regulations and the Company's declared policies.

(*ii*) Providing necessary facilities and infrastructure to the above employee fora, to the extent feasible, with respect to the statutory provisions.

(*iii*) Formation of **Joint-Committee at the Apex Level** (particularly if the corporation is a multi-unit and/or multi-location conglomerate, employing a large workforce).

(*iv*) Formation of a plant level **Plant Council** encompassing various major-functional areas; again with declared objectives and terms of reference and supporting procedures.

(*v*) Formation of Shop Councils at various shop levels with declared objectives, terms of reference, and supporting procedures. These shop councils are expected to function within the terms of reference of the Plant Council to avoid conflicting and divergent approach.

15.3.2.2 Beside the above-mentioned fora (other approaches)

Certain other approaches, as mentioned** below, circumstances demanding, can also be put into practice:

(*i*) Special Task groups may be formed to go into certain specific issues that may crop up from time-to-time and suggest remedial/corrective steps.

(*ii*) Task-Groups/Bi-partite Committees can be formed for Recreationary/Cultural and Sports activities to improve/enrich quality of life, besides making positive impacts on attitudes towards work culture and team spirit.

(*iii*) Task-groups/Bi-partite Committees may be formed to monitor and sort out issues/suggest improvement measures for quality, safety, productivity as well as for employee welfare matters like medical, residential, schooling (of employees' children), canteen services, etc.

Note: ***Plant Council and Joint Committees as mentioned above in para 15.3.2.1 may also deliberate on these issues and suggest remedial/improvement measures, besides other operational matters like target fulfilment, productivity, quality, disciplinary matters, customer commitments, national and social commitments, etc.*

15.3.2.3 Benefits of participative approach

The participative approaches mentioned above may help in achieving effective results by way of:

(*i*) Decision-making process quicker and implementable without much hitch.

(*ii*) Sanctity of Decisions: wide acceptability and respect amongst all section of employees.

(*iii*) Participation based on equal opportunity reduces grievances/dissent.

(*iv*) Broad based Representation: brings in added weightage and authority for implementation.

15.3.3 Extraordinary Performance Recognition and Reward Schemes

Suitable performance recognition and reward schemes, formulated and put into practice, backed by appropriate systems and procedures, to make the same as transparent as possible. Opportunities to the talented employees should be provided to enable extraordinary performance in line with the set objectives of the enterprise.

Innovation and Creativity must be recognized and contributions rewarded; the results achieved out of these may immensely benefit the organization, both short-term and long-term. Adopting and successfully practising a suitable Industrial Relations policy require certain degree of commitments on the part of owners/management.

15.4 Human Aspects of Resource Management

15.4.1 Behavioural and Attitudinal

Referring to paras: 2.4, 2.4.1, 2.4.2 in Chapter-2, we have discussed, besides other things, the role played by Human Resources in business endeavours. As regards human behaviour and attitude on various activities, it may be useful to further elaborate on the human aspects of management relating to certain critical resources to enable managers to appreciate the impacts of human behaviour influencing the operations with respect to the specific resources as mentioned below:

(*i*) **Behavioural aspects of Human Resources:** Factors that influence the behaviour pattern of employees in the organized business enterprises:

- Recruitment/selection policies and processes followed.
- Level/status in the organization.
- Compensation package and perks; other service conditions.
- Education and Training background.
- Area of work and the work-culture/environment prevailing there (boss, subordinates, peers, ecological, etc.).
- Promotional avenue/growth prospect.
- Challenges of assignments/responsibilities attached.
- Degree of supervision by seniors/management; degree of mentoring.
- Overall organizational work-culture and environment.
- Others not specified above, but may also influence behaviour pattern.

(*ii*) **Human aspects of Machine Management:**

- Technological knowledge and competency levels of engineers and others engaged in the selection process.

- Technological knowledge and competency in installation, upkeep and maintenance activities.
- Experience and managerial competency in machine resource deployment and utilization.
- Attitude towards productivity, quality and safety.
- Leadership qualities and capabilities for facility management.
- Intra and Inter-functional rapports and role appreciation with respect to facilities provided.
- Capability for crisis management (accidents, machine break-downs/unplanned shutdowns, un-notified absenteeism, excess work loads, etc.).

(iii) **Human aspects of Material Resource Management:**

- Techno-economic knowledge level regarding material specifications and sources.
- Competency in handling processes for procurement, storage, conservation, distribution, inventory control and wastage control/ avoidance.
- Ethical aspects of procurement activities and disposal of surpluses, scraps and obsoletes.

(iv) **Managing Monetary Resources: Human aspects:**

- Adequacy of knowledge and competency of the concerned employees relevant to the tasks of Financial Resource Management.
- Ethical attitudes and sense of responsibility in handling finances/ monetary resources.

(v) **Human aspects of Organizational Knowledge Resource Management:**

- Appreciation of importance of organizational knowledge resources by the senior/top level management personnel.
- Generation/Regeneration of knowledge base and enrichment of knowledge bank are the concerned, employees (all levels) adequately conscious about these aspects and making their contributions to the set objectives?
- **Dissemination/sharing of knowledge within the organization:**
  - is a policy framework and procedure in place to encourage concerned employees?
  - are the concerned employees ethically following the prescribed guidelines?
  - are the concerned employees adequately conversant about the issues related to Intellectual Property Rights (IPR), Copy Right matters and protecting Company Trade Secrets? Who in the organization are supposed to take care of these responsibilities?

(*vi*) **Human aspects relating to Management as a Resource:**

- Competency of management personnel in managing day-to-day affairs, organizational policy matters, short-term and long-term company objectives, and in providing required leadership.
- Adequacy of knowledge and attitudinal disposition of Management personnel towards 'Business Ethics and Corporate Governance', and organizational loyalty.

(*vii*) **Energy Management: Human Aspects:**

- Are the employees made conscious enough about the need of energy conservation, avoidance of wastages and abuse of energy (electricity, fuels, water, gas, etc.)
- Are the employees made conscious about safety aspects in usage and handling of energy resources?

15.5 Role of Information Technology (IT) in Enterprise Resource Management

In the present era of computerized work-practices in every sphere of business operations with attendant benefits, adoption and application of IT-enabled systems and methods have now become essential to maintain a reasonable level of working efficiency which gets reflected through:

(*i*) Quicker and more accurate processing of data.

(*ii*) Time saving and cost saving in data recording, processing, storage and retrieval.

(*iii*) Easier and quicker process of information exchange and analysis of data through computer networking.

(*iv*) Reducing/minimising voluminous manual paper work.

(*v*) Creation of data base which helps in permutation and combination and graphical representation of data.

(*vi*) Quick retrieval of data/information as well as revision/correction on line.

(*vii*) Multi-media networking through LAN (Local Area Networking), WAN (Wide Area Networks), and G-Nets (Global-Networking).

(*viii*) E-mail and Internet Services.

(*ix*) Video-Conferencing.

(*x*) E-Commerce.

(*xi*) E-Procurement.

15.5.1 Computer Software Systems

For effective operation of any computer system, certain instructional programmes made out properly in computer-recognised languages, codes and logics, are to be fed into the computer to enable it to perform the desired tasks such as computation, data processing, imaging, communication, etc., followed by delivery of desired outputs as well. These instructional programmes are generally known as the Softwares.

These Softwares are of two kinds:

(*i*) **Operating System Softwares:** Which tell the computers how to use its various components; when the computer is put on, the embedded operating softwares come into play and start the sequential process of activating and operating various components and associated devices, thus preparing and readying the computer for data processing task.

(*ii*) **Application Softwares:** These are the most important tools developed for the users to get the desired data processing and computation done through the computer. While the operating system software only help the computer itself, the application softwares helps the users to accomplish the specific tasks. A large variety of these are already available and newer ones are being developed everyday by some one somewhere in the increasingly IT-savy world today; there are softwares for every conceivable type of applications not only in business and industry, but also in all other spheres of human endeavours everywhere, and it is very difficult to categorise these multitudes of application softwares today. However, there are some major categories well known in the world of IT/ Computerization, as listed below:

- Word Processing software.
- Desk-top publishing software.
- Spread sheet software.
- Database management software.
- Graphics, Multimedia and presentation application softwares.
- Entertainment/Infotainment and Education Serviecs softwares.
- Utilities oriented software.
- Communication software.
- Weather Forecasting and Climate prediction softwares.
- Book-making (text and styles, page-maker, etc.) softwares.
- Project Management softwares (Prima-Vera, Microsoft-Project 2000, etc.).
- Inventory Control/Supply Chain Management/Materials Management softwares (SAP, BaaN, Net-Sute, my-SAP etc.).
- Engineering calculations and Design/drawing softwares (CAD/ AUTOCAD), Production Management softwares (machine loading and utilization, PPC charts, labour deployment, material input and tool control charts, QC charts, etc.).
- Plant Maintenance Scheduling softwares.
- Health Services and Demographic application softwares.
- Material Science and application research oriented softwares.
- Scientific Research and R & D oriented application softwares.
- Satellite, rocket and missile launching, trekking and control softwares.

- Banking, Financial services and Stock Exchange services softwares.
- International and Domestic Trade monitoring and commodity exchange softwares.
- Air-Traffic control Softwares.
- Environment Analysis and Management softwares.
- Agricultural Development and monitoring softwares.
- Demand Forecasting softwares.
- Economic Research and Analysis softwares.
- National and Organizational Planning softwares.

  ....and many more like these, the list can be endless.

15.5.2 Role of IT in Business and Industrial Management

15.5.2.1 Some major application regimes

As can be seen from the listing of application softwares listed under para 15.4.1 (*ii*) above, the possibilities are widespread and multifaceted. In today's globalized trade and commerce, competition is rather severe and challenging, and therefore, more and more efficient and cost effective working methods and procedures are imperative for successful sustenance and possible growth. In this emerging scenario, one of the most important and essential steps in day-to-day operations will be to introduce and attain higher levels of computerization for IT-enable working to reduce operating costs and optimization of deployment and utilization of available resources.

While there is wide scope of IT applications in business and industrial operations, we are mentioning below a few areas of major activities where IT enabled working may lead to force-multiplier effect on the ongoing operations as well as provide effective support to the planned new ventures/diversified line of operation for long-term sustenance and growth:

(*i*) Corporate/Company/Enterprise planning process both short-term and long-term, strategic planning exercises;

(*ii*) Enterprise Resource Planning (ERP), Enterprise Resource Management (ERM);

(*iii*) Procurement/Purchasing/Materials Management/Supply Chain Management/Inventory Control;

(*iv*) Engineering and Design, R&D functions; consultancy services;

(*v*) Manufacturing/Production management;

(*vi*) Marketing, Sales/Commercial management, Customer services;

(*vii*) Project Management, both capital investment as well as customer projects/contract management;

(*viii*) HRM and HRD functions and establishment matters;

(*ix*) Financial Management and Accounting functions;

(*x*) Quality Control and Stage wise inspection, SQC, QTM, etc.;

(*xi*) Plant Maintenance and Services;

(*xii*) Systems and procedures, standardization (including documentation control).

(*xiii*) Communication and Publicity (multimedia, presentation methods included); advertising.

15.5.2.2 Specific advantages of IT-enabled working

Some specific advantages of IT-enabled computerized working in industrial manufacturing units:

(A) If we consider the business processes of a typical manufacturing organization then with proper IT infrastructure and integrated application regimes in place, data get keyed in only once and preferably at source. Once data is in, it can be made available on demand in real time to every organizational element. In the best case of total computerization and integration, we can achieve the following:

- All data get keyed in at the source thus ensuring data consistency and availability. Data made available to all aspirants/applications as soon as it is keyed in. Trigger in the form of message reaches all associated entities (Computers can't make the recipient read the message and act on it).
- Ideally zero wait time between activities (provided the person at receiving end is not sleeping/missing/waiting for computer).
- Nobody waits/searches for other person to get/provide data (Computers can guarantee data consistency and availability in real time).
- Rule based inter-process communication and interlocking.
- Automation of process where human intervention is not required.
- Information on demand (for decision makers and also help in decision making with 'what if analysis' (alternative options).

(B) Computers have excellent long-term memory. A computer can provide data of past failures, with trend analysis and whatsoever is desired to be extracted from historical data. The data related to suppliers, transporters, customers, lost orders, past enquiries, financial records, etc., can be kept for years together and used. In case of perennial problems related to repeated failures, poor quality, etc., the historical data can be used intelligently by any body desirous of knowing the root cause can of the problem. The computers, on the other hand if used casually, can drown the root cause in a pool of data thus leading to a situation when the root cause can never be known or identified. To take advantage of this capability of computers, it is necessary to use clean and authentic data, define the problem correctly and use intelligent programming to derive the necessary information. Remember computers are not called GIGO (Garbage in and Garbage out) just for nothing.

(C) **Unreliable data:** If the data used for decision-making is wrong or unreliable you are bound to reach wrong conclusion with confidence. This data includes the material specifications, bill of materials, norm hours, material inventory, supplier's data, manufacturing lead time, test and measurement data, material procurement lead times, etc., this is specifically true for all planning and automation applications. If proper data discipline is practised and enforced, the authenticated data inputs can result in computer performing another type of 'GI-GO', *i.e.,* 'Gospel in and Gospel out'.

Conclusion

Computes are much better than human beings in data storage, event handling, doing repetitive monotonous (boring) jobs. The real value of data lies in our ability to use it across the organization. IT-enabled working can help us integrate groups that normally do not work closely together. Sales, purchasing, production, service operations, customers, and suppliers, all forming a coherent team, working together to design, develop, deliver and service the best possible products to the mutual benefit of all parties. With proper IT infrastructure and application, required data/information can be made available on demand in real time to every organizational element thus resulting in accelerating the pace of business with defined and focused efforts.

Information Technology is not the solution to correct fundament flaws in underlying business processes. Some of the business that we do today were formulated at a time when computerization and communication were in their infancy. If the habitual ineffective methods are what the organization knows and relies on to run the business, then no amount of technology is going to help. The organizational elements set their bench marks of time and expenditure, for various activities based on existing practices and these become a part of mind set and ultimately the organization culture. It is these old practices that often become a bottleneck in cutting time by reducing redundant activities because people do not think otherwise ever while computerizing the process. It must be appreciated and clearly understood that if we run business processes the same old way with the same old benchmarks, we are guaranteed to get the same old results. Enlightened approach for an IT-enabled work culture is imperative for viable survival with confidence and pride in facing the ever increasing challenges of global competition.

15.6 Excellence in Factory Management: Adopting the 5S Work-Culture*

The 5S working concepts were developed in Japan to achieve excellent orderliness on the shop-floor in the factories to make them world-class establishments. The 5S factory management techniques aims at instilling in the workers at the shop-floors, a sense of disciplined work-culture which rests on the logic that cleanliness, orderliness and discipline at work-sites are basic requirements for manufacturing high quality products, with little or no waste and with high level of productivity.

***The 5S stands for five Japanese Words: Seri (clearing up), Seiton (organizing), Seiso (cleaning), Seiketsu (standardizing), and Shitsuke (training and discipline).**

15.6.1 Active 5S

The propagators of the technique recommend that before putting the 5S to work, it is advisable to take photographs (colour) of the worksites as they are existing and keep them in record, so that these can be used later for comparison purposes with those photographs taken after the 5S working system has been put to full practice. This will help adopting colour coding for critical analysis and for further stabilization of this work-culture by creating a positive impression on the concerned workforce.

Let us now, understand the significance of the five principles of 5S working concepts.

15.6.1.1 Seri: Clearing up the area

This process aims at identifying at the work-site, items which are needed there and the item which are unwanted/superfluous. This is to be done after clearly defining and deciding the standards for what is really needed, and 'what is not needed' to avoid difference of opinion and excuses. The unwanted/not needed items to be marked with red tags, so that anybody can see what is to be eliminated from the work-site. For a bias free approach, the employees to be posted in the concerned work-site be adequately conversant with the working requirements of the specific work-site be assigned the task.

15.6.1.2 Seiton: Organizing

Organizing is the most far reaching one amongst the 5S steps. After clearing up the area of unwanted/superfluous items, the next step is to organize the area for each and every machine/work-sites by putting the materials, tools, tackles, drawings/documents, etc., in dedicated storage cabinets/bins, etc., and earmarking and levelling by large visible letters, numbers, sign-boards for the specific machines and work-sites. Such identification levels should be in the language and colour codes which can be easily understood by all concerned. The system further recommends that the storage bins, cabinets, etc., be open type without doors so that all can see what is lying there: this reduces the chances of messing up the storage and the surroundings again with the passage of time. The best approach for the shop management/ supervisors is to switch from the 'remedial organizing' to 'preventive organizing' by raising questions like why this mess-up happens and how something can be done about it.

15.6.1.3 Seiso: Cleaning

A regular cleaning system has to be put in practice keeping the three broad categories of cleaning targets : storage areas, machines and equipment, and the surroundings. The cleaning efforts have to be organized in the following recommended manner to consolidate the procedures:

(*i*) divide the work-sites into small areas and identify and list out all the cleaning work that are needed to be done there.

(*ii*) draw up a cleaning responsibility chart and prepare a cleaning schedule and display the same prominently at the respective work-place so that every one can see.

(*iii*) adopt a shift-system for the areas of common interest/joint responsibility of various working groups.

(*iv*) propagate the habit of daily five-minute cleaning schedule at all places, although the time is too short, but over a period of time, things will improve, and efficiently done cleaning work will show more than expected results.

15.6.1.4 Seiketsu: Standardization

Standardize a spotless work place and impress upon all concerned to put in a little effort to keep the work-place clean and tidy all the time. The standardization effort must keep three **'No-principles'** in view for successful implementation: **No unnecessary items, No mess, No dirt;** Re-checking and appraisal are vital to give the system an impetus for perpetuality.

15.6.1.5 Shitsuke: Training and discipline

Training of the work-force which should also inculcate a sense of descipline in them, is an essential part of the practice of 5S work-culture. This training will be an inter-active process which will not only involve preachings but will also recognize the workers' participation in constructive criticism and decision making so that the system gets wide acceptability. The idea is to create a work place where problematic issues can be easily recognized and remedial action taken.

15.6.2 Comparison of Old and New Situations

After the 5S working concepts have been successfully implemented, it is now time to take a set colour photographs of the present situations and display both the sets of colour photographs 'Before 5S' and 'After 5S' positions side-by-side, to demonstrate to all concerned the amazing difference that has come about which has resulted in transforming the factory towards a world class establishment.

15.6.3 Effective 5S

In order to sustain 5S work-culture, the following aspects are to be taken care of:

(*i*) Implement visual control: by way of photographic display as stated in para 15.6.2 above and also circulate the results through handouts for wide publicity.

(*ii*) Introduce a reward-scheme for best performing work-place.

(*iii*) Avoid, by all means, becoming complacent and slackening up.

(*iv*) Constantly strive to make 5S work-culture habitual.

(*v*) Control stock levels : by gradually working to decrease shop-floor inventories without disrupting production and establishing an optimum level.

(*vi*) Make it easy to return things which are surplus or not needed at the work-place: simplify paper work-procedures.

(*vii*) Put names and numbers on all jigs and tools and outline their shapes at their precise storage positions. Ideally, tools should be stored besides the machines with which they are to be used and according to the sequence of work operations.

(*viii*) Organize every thing by a suitable colour code for easy recognition at a glance.

(*ix*) Always clean and check.

(*x*) Maintain standards through out the company; discipline has to begin with following strict standards.

(*xi*) On the spot correction should be done whenever, there is some sign of disorder and this should be got done through the area group-leader for effective results, since his commitments will be crucial for effective 5S work-culture.

15.6.4 Preventive 5S

Once the 5S work-culture has taken root and becomes habitual, the factory management has to assiduously work for maintaining the standard achieved. This will require certain preventive steps to be taken with determination and with a sense of sustained emphasis. The preventive 5S will lay stress on the following:

(*i*) Avoid unnecessary items and prevent their coming back by rationalizing systems regulating supply and consumption.

(*ii*) Shift from lot production to leveled production and from lot deliveries to multiple small lot deliveries; this will reduce chances of excess material piling up at the work-place.

(*iii*) Avoid disorganization in storage; three basic points to be remembered about storage: **Where, What and How Many.**

(*iv*) Create a system which allows only the necessary items to be stored at the work-places.

(*v*) Ensure cleaning regularly and do not tolerate accumulation of dirt and scraps, wastes, residues, etc., at the work-places.

(*vi*) Create facilities like double shields, vinyl curtains, etc., to prevent entry of dust/dirt wherever feasible. Switch to work-methods that prevent dirt from being produced in the vicinity areas.

(*vii*) Prevent degradation of environment: tidiness and cleanliness reflects efficiency.

(*viii*) Emphasis on systematic training, awareness and discipline so that these become a habitual work-culture.

(*ix*) Once a month the factory manager and the top officials should take a round of all the work-places and evaluate the implementation status of 5S steps.

The secret of preventive standardization lies in full application of the three preventive 5S: 'preventive clearing up', 'preventive organization' and 'preventive cleaning.'

Note: **Adapted from an article on the subject appearing in World Executive Digest-May 1994.*

15.7 'Jishu-Hozen' (Autonomous Maintenance): A Revolutionary Concept of Plant Maintenance

> ***"A concept is as good as its successful implementation and practice."***
>
> — *Taken from a Management Institute Brochure*

During the years after the World War II came to an end (in 1945), Japanese government and industrial enterprise, like those in the European continent, embarked on a massive urban and industrial reconstruction effort. In the decades that followed, Japanese industries and business enterprise not only achieved rapid progress and growths in respective areas, but also, in the process, evolved and developed many new revolutionary management concepts and philosophies which provided added impetus to their success and enabled the country to attain the status as an industrialised high growth enterprising nation. As the success stories spread over the world, Japanese concepts of industrial and business management got propagated and to a large extent got accepted/introduced in the enterprises in other industrialized countries in the Europe, Asia and even in the Americas (USA, Canada, Brazil, etc.). The process is still on and a cross-fertilisation of Japanese management concepts and styles and those in other industrialized nations is taking place on a larger scale for mutual benefits of experience sharing and collaborative relationships/arrangements for enhanced economic, trade and technological developments.

15.7.1 Jishu-Hozen-Objectives

'Jishu-Hozen' activities focuses on the equipment to make it perfect *i.e.,* Zero Break-down and Zero defective products processed by the machine tools/equipment on the shop floors. It builds a relationship between the man and the machine through a sequence of 7 steps (refer para 15.7.3. below) where by the machine operator owns the machine to the extent of taking care of its routine maintenance activities as well, besides his assigned manufacturing job.

15.7.2 Jishu-Hozen: A New Work-culture Concept

Jishu-Hozen, a Japanese word for Autonomous Maintenance, implies that the operators themselves maintain their machines in highest standards. These operators are trained to do so through the structured approach of 7 steps of Jishu Hozen as enumerated below. Each step has a focus, an activity to be carried out and certain results to be achieved.

15.7.3 Autonomous Maintenance Methodology: The 7-Step Sequence

(*i*) Perform initial cleaning and inspection;

(*ii*) Eliminate contamination sources and address inaccessible places;

(*iii*) Develop tentative standard for cleaning, inspection and lubrication;

(*iv*) Conduct general equipment inspection training and develop inspection procedures;

(*v*) Conduct general process inspection autonomously (*i.e.,* self-inspired);

(*vi*) Set standards and manage the workplace;

(*vii*) Pay attention to the ongoing autonomous maintenance and advanced improvement activities.

Mainly the operators and cross-functional teams with support and training provided by maintenance personnel, production managers and production engineering staff, carry out these activities.

15.7.4 Goal of Autonomous Maintenance

To develop operators to maintain the equipment and work places and follow uniformity in implementing shop-floor activities to eliminate forced deterioration on equipment. Since operators have to ensure productivity and quality, they are bound to take better care of their machines to maintain their credibility and ensure earning of incentives often given in monetary terms.

15.7.5 Why Jishu-Hozen is Significant?

'Jishu-Hozen' means activities of the machine operator are also focused on the upkeep of the machine he works on, by personally conducting maintenance activities, including cleaning, oiling, retightening and inspection. This in turn raises production efficiency to its limit. Such activities will prevent forced deterioration of the machine tools and other production equipment. Activities of Jishu-Hozen aim to eliminate:

(*i*) Machine failures,

(*ii*) Minor Stoppages,

(*iii*) Defects in the machine and its output,

(*iv*) Other losses (*e.g.,* energy losses, lube oil wastages, rejection, man hour loses, etc.).

Jishu-Hozen activities restore the equipment to their desirable forms, maintain them, and improve them and at the same time develop personnel who are skillful at operations of the equipment as well as its improvement and upkeep.

"Jishu-Hozen" is the operator's own work itself. It is carried out under the shared approach through small group activities closely unified with the factory management structure. Jishu-Hozen itself signifies the constitutional improvement in the relationship between the personnel and the facilities. This entails the changing of worker's ways of thinking and behaviour. By replacing the traditional concept of division of labour between operation and maintenance. Represented by the traditional view that "I am a machine operator, and you are a maintenance man, fix it", Jishu-hozen concept aims at replacing the thinking towards the work culture of "owning and protecting one's equipment by oneself".

15.7.6 Operating Staff get Familiarized with Machine Characteristics

To translate this philosophy into action, the development of personnel who are skillful at machine tools and equipment operations are persuaded further to get conversant with the structure and function of the facilities, as well as to acquire maintenance skills to effect improvements in upkeep and functioning, thus bringing in the attitudinal reform in the concerned personnel. It is also very important to bring about structural and operational improvements of the machine tool/equipment currently being used. In "Jishu-Hozen", as the first step to "protect one's equipment by oneself", work should be started with improvement of basic conditions of the equipment being used (cleaning, oiling, and retightening; *i.e.,* (COT). Then, based on the step method, structural improvement of machine tool/equipment should be effected so that the equipment will be in the form as it should be.

As a result, Overall Equipment Efficiency (OEE) will improve greatly, and the machine operator personally experiences the effect of "Jishu-Hozen" so that his attitude will change towards protecting so as to protect his own machine tool/equipment by himself; thus the constitutional improvement of personnel and the equipment proceed simultaneously.

Also, "Jishu-Hozen" is a self-management activity by small work-site groups and can lead to a multiplier effect on the facility maintenance and upkeep efforts.

Through the development of "Jishu-Hozen" work-culture, the machines operator's willingness and skills increase and encourage him to "protect his own equipment by himself." Literally, he will be able to manage his work autonomously. In 'Jishu-Hozen', small group by itself sets its goal for the attainment of corporate objective; it uses machine tools/equipment as its own tool; and tackles production and improvement activities. Therefore, unprecedented, remarkable result can be achieved through action based job satisfaction for the desired growth and self realization. 'Jishu- Hozen' is the practice of participation in factory management and respect for human endeavours.

"Let us learn from the past to profit by the present, and from the present to live better in the future".

— William Wordsworth

CHAPTER-16

ENTERPRISE RESOURCE OPTIMIZATION

> *"Historically, the rich states of today set off on a path of economic growth when they began investing in infrastructures and education for all."*
>
> — *John Ralston Saul,*
> *Canadian Author*

16.1 The Objectives

In order to successfully manage a business enterprise, certain operational strategies have to be necessarily thought of and put into practice. One of the critical operational strategies will relate to the tasks of optimization of deployment and utilization of various resources made available to the enterprise. However, accomplishing such optimization objectives is easier said than done in view of the multitude of variable parameters and related constraints that have to be rather competently tackled to derive the desired benefits out of resource optimization exercises undertaken. In the case of industrial enterprises, the operating circumstances are much more complex, and therefore, enterprise management as well as the line managers will have to assiduously work towards such optimization efforts, but at the same time, not losing sight of other critical areas of operation which are also important for a comprehensive approach towards successful operations.

16.2 Selective Exercise for Certain Critical Resources

Because of the inherent complexities, limitations and related constraints in the case of industrial units, it may not be practically feasible to undertake optimization efforts across the board at one go, but it may be possible, with a good amount of success, to attempt such exercises selectively for certain functional areas utilizing critical resources such as Human Resources, Machines, Materials, Energy and Working Capital funds (monetary resource), to specify a few priority target areas. Obviously, such optimization exercise has to follow certain scientifically defined quantitative techniques to arrive at acceptable outcomes in quantitative terms. It is also to be appreciated that a resource optimization exercise not only helps in improving operating results, but also helps in establishing organizational processes that may lead to long-term successful sustenance as well as to other tangible and intangible benefits.

The scope of work efforts and costs involved in carrying out optimization exercises can be quite substantial and therefore, a prudent selection of critical target areas has to be done with a rather clear set of objectives, in qualitative and quantitative terms, to justify such efforts, the end-results of which are not always guaranteed to the extent desired. As already stated in para 16.2 above, such exercises undertaken from time to time, will also result in certain positive impacts in toning up the enterprise across the board, towards improving work-culture and efficiency and infuse a sense of constancy of purpose amongst various functional managers.

16.3 Selected Industrial Enterprise for Optimization Exercise (a Case Study Approach)

Having broadly outlining the scope and impacts of optimization exercises in the preceding paragraphs, to be specific in our objectives, we propose to attempt resource optimization exercise for a medium size industrial enterprise manufacturing certain sizes and categories of sheet metal press dies to be used for production of ETS (= Electro-Technical Steel) and MS (= Mild Steel) stampings required by Electrical Machine Manufacturing Industries (EMIs) (Motors and Alternators: both AC and DC). In fact, this Die manufacturing unit is operating as an Ancillary Unit for these Electrical Machines Manufacturing Industrial Enterprises (EMIs). The Dies are manufactured according to the designs and specifications prescribed by these EMIs in conformity with sizes, configurations and materials of the stampings being used by them.

16.4 Broad Technological Details of the Selected Die Manufacturing Unit

16.4.1 Product–Mix

(*i*) Simple dies for notching, slotting and bending: 5 kg to 25 kg-piece weight.

(*ii*) Simple dies for trimming, blanking: Square, rectangular, size up to: 300 mm × 300 mm; piece wt. from 20 kg to 350 kg.

(*iii*) Circular Compound dies for blanking, slotting, notching and trimming: dia up to - 610 mm; piece wt. upto 1000 kg.

(*iv*) Compound dies for multiple piece segmental stampings: (blanking, slotting, notching, trimming) piece wt. up to 3000 kg; size up to 1200mm × 900mm.

(*v*) Assorted jobbing items for milling, jigs and fixtures, etc., piece wt. ranging from 5 kg to 350 kg.

16.4.2 Materials of Construction of the Dies

- Base/body..........made from rolled heavy steel plates, forged stocks.
- Knife edges..........made from tool steel grades, rolled/forged blanks/cutting bars; forged bars;
- Springs..........procured (as bought out items) from external sources as per required specifications.
- Fasteners, ... –do–
- Dowel/Positioning Pins, spacers, Studs, etc. .... made from rolled bars/forged stocks.
- Jigs and Fixtures..........as per specifications prescribed by customers.

16.4.3 Technological Processes Followed

(*i*) Blank cutting, bar cutting;

(*ii*) Machining, (metal cutting mainly), grinding, pressing, tapping, heat-treatment as required; fine machining using EDM-Wirecut machines;

(*iii*) In-process Quality Control;

(*iv*) Assembly and final inspection (visual and dimensional checks)*

(*v*) Material handling and transfers;

(*vi*) Packing and despatch.

Notes: *(*i*) *Trial runs for finished dies, jigs and fixtures manufactured, are being carried out at customer's factory (EMIs) for final acceptance.*

(*ii*) *Third-party inspection/quality checks are done by Accredited Inspection Agency; sometimes, depending on the complexity of the jobs, engineers of the client organization are also involved in final inspection at the die manufacturing unit before despatch.*

16.4.4 Facilities Available/Installed

(*i*) Factory layout (Land, Bldg. Sheds, etc.).	–	Please *see* Annexure-6 (A);
(*ii*) Facilities installed through Capital Investment.	–	Please *see* details in Annexure-6 (B);
(*iii*) List of Machine Tools and other production equipment required for manufacturing activities.	–	Please *see* Annexure-6 (C)

16.4.5 Organizational Set-up and Human Resources Deployed

(*i*) Organizational set-up: A Private Limited Company; Organization Chart at Annexure-6 (D).

(*ii*) Human Resources Deployed (Nos):*

		Regular	Irregular/ Temporary Engagement
Managerial/Executives	=	10	–
Supervisors	=	10	5
Skilled workers (Artisans)	=	100	100
Other unskilled/semi-skilled workers	=	5	15
Other supporting non-executive staff (Administrative, Accounting, establishment, computer and clerical, etc.)	=	7	3
	Total =	132 +	123 = 255

Note: **For 2-shift working (8 hrs-shift: 7-15 a.m. to 4 p.m.; 4 p.m. to 12.30 a.m.; 15 minutes Tea Break and 30 minutes Lunch/ Dinner break in each shift.*

16.5 Capital Investment

- Gross Block (GB) (from Annx-6 (B&C) = Rs. 1545 lakh;
- Net Block (NB) (in the 3rd yr of oprn) = Rs. 1126 lakh;
  * Annual average depreciation @ 10%; (*)

16.6 Operating Regimes (in the 3rd Year of Operation)

(*i*) Days worked in a financial year (from April to March)	=	300;
(*ii*) Working shifts	=	2 shifts of 8 hrs. each ($2 \times 8 = 16$ hrs)
(*iii*) Total hours worked in a year	=	4800 hrs.
(*a*) For production (2 shifts)		
(*b*) Emergency Power supply, water supply, etc. (24×365)	=	8760 hrs for 6 persons in 3-shifts;
(*c*) Security services (including fire fighting)	=	Through External Agency engaged on contract.
(*iv*) Annual Sales Turn-over (TO) ($a \times d$) (*see* below)	=	Rs. 5720. lakh,
(*v*) Annual Physical Turnover		(Metric Tonnes = MT)

(*a*) Shop Production (finished)	= 200	MT;	
(*b*) Sub-contracted/B.O. (Bought out)	= 20	MT;	
Total	= 220	MT	...(a);

(*vi*) Gross Direct material input = 250 MT ...(b);

(*vii*) Average cost of production Ex-Factory cost, per kg. = Rs. 2000 per kg. ...(c);

(*viii*) Average sale value realized (including taxes and duties), = Rs. 2600 per kg. ...(d);

(*ix*) Total value of Production (VP) (a × c) = Rs. 4400 lakh.

(*x*) Average cost of materials in VP = 45% of VP = Rs. 1980 lakh;

(*xi*) Salaries, wages and personnel payments (average) = 12% of TO;

(*xii*) Energy costs (fuel, electricity) = 3% of VP;

(*xiii*) Administrative Overheads (including welfare, medical, canteen services) = 1% of VP;

(*xiv*) Selling & Commercial Expenses = 1% of VP;

(*xv*) Average Inventory Holding = Rs. 1467 lakh (100 days of VP);

(*xvi*) Average Working Capital (WC) needs (Annual) (at 66% of VP) = Rs. 2900 lakh;

(*xvii*) Depreciation and interest burden on Capital Investment = 20% of GB;

(*xviii*) Average interest burden on Working Capital funds = 10% of WC;

(*xix*) Average quantity of scraps generated (Annually) = 5% of 250 MT = 13 MT;

(*xx*) Average annual income from scrap disposal (LS) = Rs. 2.0 lakh; (lump sum)

(*xxi*) Gross Margin/ = 20% of TO;

(*xxii*) Profit Before Tax (PBT) = 18.5% of TO;

(*xxiii*) Profit After Tax (PAT) = 13% of TO;

(*xxiv*) Average Labour Efficiency = 75%;

(*xv*) Average Energy Consumption (Electricity Equivalent in KWhrs) per year (300 KWs for 16 hrs a day);

(*a*) Production Linked = 300 KWs × 300 days

		× 16 hrs;
	=	14,40,000 KWhrs = P;
(*b*) For other services plus idle hrs	=	5% of P = 72,000 KWhrs
	=	K;
Total Energy Consumption P + K	=	1,512,000 KWhrs; Say 1.5 million KWhrs per year

16.7 Resource Optimization Exercise

16.7.1 Operating Resources Under Consideration

As stated in para 16.2 above, the optimization exercises for the case in hand (para 16.3) are being attempted for the following five **operating resources**:

(1) Human Resources,
(2) Materials consumption,
(3) Machine utilization,
(4) Working Capital funding,
(5) Energy consumption.

16.7.2 The Approach to Optimization Exercise

In the following paragraphs and pages, we are attempting to carryout the optimization exercise using the quantitative technique known as '**Variables Search Methodology (VSM) and Design of Experiments (DOE)** developed by **Dorian Shainin a** research engineer-scientist-cum-statistical mathematician of USA well-known for his **"Shainin Techniques"** which prescribed certain practical tools to help industrial manufacturers solve problems relating to operational processes, other critical management processes and optimization of deployed resources.*

Taking into consideration certain intelligent assumptions and estimates based on industrial operating experience and brain storming, the required database for this specific exercise have been stipulated and used. The approach and the results are presented in the tables and charts placed below with relevant data and explanatory notes.

Note : **For relevant books by Dorian Shainin please refer to misc. group of Annexure 9.*

1. Optimization of Resources

Problem: To optimize resources to achieve a Response of 100

Resource Parameters	Codes Adopted
• Human	A
• Material Consumption	B
• Machine Utilization	C
• Working Capital Availability	D
• Energy Consumption	E

2. Optimization of Resources

Design Tolerance for Parameters:

S.No.	Parameters	Design Value	Design Tolerance
1	Human	75% Efficiency	70%- 80% Efficiency
2	Material Consumption	1.10 ton per ton output	1-1.2 ton per ton output 80-90%
3	Machine Utilization	85% availability	availability
4	Working Capital Utilization	66% of Product Cost	60-70% of Product Cost
5	Energy Consumption (KWhrs)	6800 units per ton	6500-7000 units per ton

3. Optimization of Resources

Assumptions:

- Design tolerances are set based on the experience.
- Only Five factors (as above) are considered for the effect of the response.
- Sub-factors related to each parameter are kept at constant and their effect is taken as insignificant. For example, human resource level may be
  - No. of persons
  - Efficiency of person
  - Skill of person
  - Experience of person
  - Working hours of persons
- Rejection and rework level is not taken into account.*
- Response is set at 100 and unit is left open. It may be ton, kg, numbers, percentage, etc.
- Product range is not taken into account.*

Note: **"These are not taken into account to avoid increased numbers of parameters and interaction lavels which result in complex DOE. It was also considered to make the present case as simple as possible for easy understanding of the reader.*

4. Optimization of Resources

Variable Search DOE: Stage-Wise Approach

When parameters are more than 3, as is the present case, a Variable Search DOE tool is used to optimize the resources to reduce the cost for response to be achieved.

In Variable Search DOE tool, following six stages are used:

Stage 0: To identify the design parameters and identifying '–' and '+' setting for each parameters.

Stage 1: To find out whether the parameters and the levels identified in stage 0 are correct or not.

Stage 2: To find out which parameters are important and which of the parameters are not important.

Stage 3: To validate the significant parameters found in stage 2.

Stage 4: Do factorial analysis and find out the contribution of each of the significant parameters.

Stage 5: Make a mathematical equation based on the contribution of significant parameters and optimize the process.

5. Optimization of Resources

Stage 0: Identification of Parameters & '–' and '+' setting

Code	Parameters	+ Setting	– Setting
A	Human	80	50
B	Material Consumption	1.2	0.9
C	Machine Utilization	90	60
D	Working Capital Utilization	70	40
E	Energy Consumption	7000	5000

Remarks:

- *"+" Setting are those values which are the best condition and will produce the response of 100.*
- *"–" Setting are those values which are the worst condition and will not at all produce the response of 100.*
- *All + and – setting are decided based on the experience and brain storming.*

6A. Optimization of Resources

Stage 1: Parameters and Levels are correct or not (Validation of stage "0")

Following three steps are followed:

1. Data Collection

Experiment is done for getting the response (results) at the + and – setting of each parameters as decided in stage 0. The experiment is done three times for each setting. However, experiment is done alternatively, *i.e.,* 1st experiment is done to get response when all parameters are having the values mentioned for + setting, then second experiment is done when all parameters are having the values mentioned for – setting. This is repeated three times. Responses got from these six experiments are shown in the table given below:

Resources	+ Setting	– Setting
1st Run	95	50
2nd Run	96	55
3rd Run	94	60

Remarks : *Only three runs are defined in this DOE concept.*

6B. Optimization of Resources

Stage 1: Parameters and Levels are correct or not (Validation of stage "0")

2: Validation - establishing relationship matrices

Resources	+ Setting	– Setting
1st Run	95	50
2nd Run	96	55
3rd Run	94	60
Median	95	55
Range	2	10
D	40	
d	6	
D/d	6.67	

Remarks:

D is the difference of two medians. In this example it is 95 – 55 = 40 d is the average of two ranges and is equal to 6 in this case, i.e., (10 + 2)/2

6C. Optimization of Resources

Stage 1: Parameters and Levels are correct or not (Validation of stage "0")

3. Conclusion

As D/d ratio is greater than three, the level of parameters decided for "+" and "–" settings are correct and the values decided are validated.

Remarks:

If D/d is less than three, the values decided for each setting are not correct. Do not proceed further for stage 2. Decide different values for each setting and repeat the experiment and calculate D/d ratio.

7A. Optimization of Resources

Stage 2: Parameters are important or not

Follow the steps to calculate and plot the values on graph (refer Graph 1) to judge whether parameters are important/significant or not

- Calculate the median of "+" and "–" settings responses achieved during three runs (trials). The median for "+" and "–" settings are 95 and 55 in this case.
- Calculate the average of these two medians. Average of median is 75.
- Calculate UDL and LDL for both "+" and "–" settings with the help of the formula as given below:
  - UDL= Median + 1.5d and LDL = Median - 1.5d where d = average of two ranges as calculated in stage 1.
  - For "+" setting
    UDL = 95 +1.5 × 6 = 104 and LDL = 95 – 1.5 × 6 = 86
  - For "–" setting
    UDL = 55+1.5 × 6 = 64 and LDL = 55 – 1.5 × 6 = 46
- On graph paper draw UDL and LDL for "+" and "–" settings and also draw average of median.
- Join "+" points with different colour and "–" points with different color. As shown in graph 1.

7B. Optimization of Resources

Stage 2: Parameters are important or not

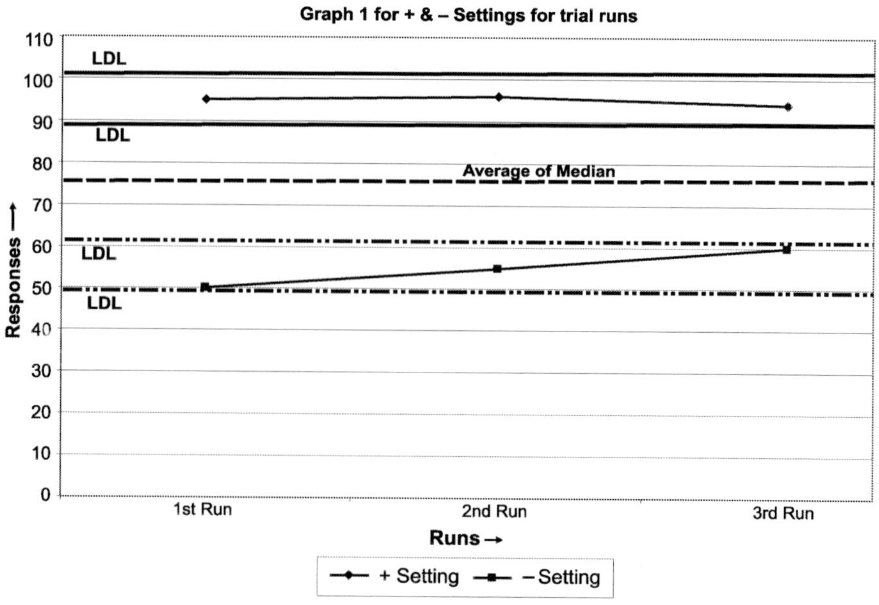

7C. Optimization of Resources

Stage 2: Parameters are important or not

6. Select one parameter (say A) and set the value at "+" setting and Remaining R parameters value at "-" setting and do experiment and get the response. Response is shown in Table 16.1.
7. Select the same parameter (say A) and set the value at "-" setting and Remaining R parameters value at "+" setting and do experiment and get the response. Response is shown in Table 16.1.
8. Repeat above two steps for all other parameters and get the response for each experiment. Response is shown in Table 16.1.
9. Draw all these responses on the same graph.
10. Join "+" points with different colour and "-" points with different colour. As shown in graph 2.

Table 16.1

Experiments	+ Setting	– Setting
A+R–	92	
A–R+		53
B+R–	40	
B–R+		60
C+R–	46	
C–R+		60
D+R–	40	
D–R+		70
E+R–	90	
E–R+		60

7D. Optimization of Resources

Stage 2: Parameters are important or not

Graph 2 for + & – Settings for trial runs and other experiments

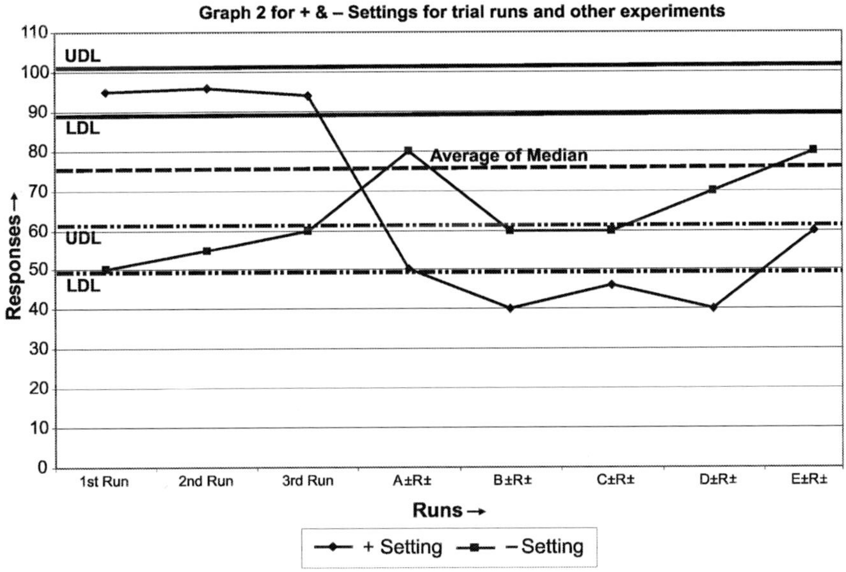

Criteria for Significant /Important Parameter:

1. If both values crosses the center line (average of median), then parameter is significant.
2. If only one value crosses the center line, then parameter is important and effecting the response.
3. If it remains in the band it is, then it is not significant and important also.

7E. Optimization of Resources

Stage 2: Parameters are important or not

Based on the criteria, A is significant and B&D are important parameters:

Remarks:

Stage 3 is to be done only when some of the parameters are significant/important.
If no parameter found significant/ important, some thing wrong has happened during recording the response.

8. Optimization of Resources

Stage 3: Validation of important/significant Parameters

Following the stage 1 rule and see whether D/d ratio is greater than three or not. Following response achieved for parameter A,B, & D when experiment is done for "+" and "–" setting alternatively three times. Response is shown in Table 16.2.

Table 16.2

Resources	+ Setting	– Setting
1st Run	92	54
2nd Run	94	55
3rd Run	90	50
Median	93	54
Range	4	5
D	39	
d	4.5	
D/d	8.67	

9A. Optimization of Resources

Stage 4: Contribution of important/significant Parameters

Rule for calculating contribution of significant/ important parameters:

1. After validating the effect of significant/important parameters, A Factorial table is constructed to carryout the experiment for the combinations as per factorial table. Factorial table is constructed as per following guidelines.

No. of rows = 2^n where n = no.of parameters
No. of Column = 2^n-1
No. of Interaction Column = 2^n-1-n

2. The first parameter is assigned "–" & "+" sign alternatively for all rows. For second parameter, first sign (– sign) of first parameter is assigned two times and then second sign (+ sign) of first parameter is also assigned two times. This is repeated for other rows alternatively. For third parameter, first sign (– sign) of second parameter is assigned two times of first parameter and then second sign (+ sign) of first parameter is also assigned two times of second parameter. This is repeated for other rows alternatively.

   For the interaction of two parameters and three parameters, the sign assigned to each row is the product of sign assigned to each individual parameter. The table so constructed is shown below.

9B. Optimization of Resources

Stage 4: Contribution of important/significant Parameters

Factorial Table 16.3

Trials	A	B	D	AB	AD	BD	ABD
1	–	–	–	+	+	+	–
2	+	–	–	–	–	+	+
3	–	+	–	–	+	–	+
4	+	+	–	+	–	–	–
5	–	–	+	+	–	–	+
6	+	–	+	–	+	–	–
7	–	+	+	–	–	+	–
8	+	+	+	+	+	+	+

Remarks:

Here "–" & "+" sign relate to "–" & "+" settings of the parameter while conducting experiment.

3. The response for each trial (experiment) is recorded. The response for all eight trials is shown below in Tables 16.4 and 16.5

9C. Optimization of Resources

Stage 4: Contribution of important/significant Parameters

Table 16.4

Parameters	+ Setting	- Setting
1st Run	95	50
2nd Run	96	55
3rd Run	94	60
A+R–	50	
A–R+		80
B+R–	40	
B–R+		60
D+R–	40	
D+R–		70

Table 16.5

Trials	A	B	D	Response	Median	AB	AD	BD	ABD
1	–	–	–	50, 55, 60	55	+	+	+	–
2	+	–	–	50	50	–	–	+	+
3	–	+	–	40	40	–	+	–	+
4	+	+	–	70	70	+	–	–	–
5	–	–	+	40	40	+	–	–	+
6	+	–	+	60	60	–	+	–	–
7	–	+	+	80	80	–	–	+	–
8	+	+	+	95, 96, 94	94	+	+	+	+

4. After this median of responses are calculated and recorded. This is shown in Table 16.6.
5. The sum of "+" sign and "–" sign is calculated for each row based on the median value against the sign. This is recorded in rows as Total + & Total –. Refer row 9 & 10 in Table 16.6.
6. Subtract the value of row 10 from row 9. Record the value in row 11 with sign. If "+" value is greater, sign is "+" and if "–" value is greater then sign is "–". *See* Table 16.6.
7. For calculating the contribution of each parameter, subtract the value of row 10 from row 9 for each column and record the value in row 12 in Table 16.6.

9D. Optimization of Resources

Stage 4: Contribution of important/significant Parameters

Table 16.6

Rows	Trials	A	B	D	Response	Median	AB	AD	BD	ABD
1	1	–	–	–	50,55,60	55	+	+	+	–
2	2	+	–	–	50	50	–	–	+	+
3	3	–	+	–	40	40	–	+	–	+
4	4	+	+	–	70	70	+	–	–	–
5	5	–	–	+	40	40	+	–	–	+
6	6	+	–	+	60	60	–	+	–	–
7	7	–	+	+	80	80	–	–	+	–
8	8	+	+	+	95,96,94	94	+	+	+	+
9	**Total +**	274	284	274	**Average of**	**61.13**	259	249	279	224
10	**Total –**	215	205	215	**Median**		230	240	210	265
11	**Total**	59	79	59			29	9	69	–41
12	***Cntb.**	+14.8	+19.8	+15			+7.25	+2.25	+17.3	–10.3

* **(Cntb. = Contribution).**

Remarks:

1. *Contribution decrease by the amount when setting changed from + to –*
2. *Contribution decrease by the amount when setting changed from - to +*

10. Optimization of Resources

Stage 5: Mathematical Equation based on contribution of parameters General Equation is given as below:

Y = Av. of Medians ± (½ × A's Contribution × A) ± (½ × B's Contribution × B) ± .... ± (½ × AB's interaction contribution ×AB)...

Where, Y is the response needed, from above equation and the contribution as shown in Table 16.6 the equation will be as below:

$$Y = 61.13+7.38A+9.88B+7.38D+3.63AB+1.13AD+8.63BD-5.13ABD$$

For getting the response 100 and freezing A & D at "+" setting, the equation will be

$$100 = 7496.13 - 27823.62B \qquad B = 0.27$$

This is not the actual value of B parameter at optimal level. It is a coded value. The actual value of parameter B at this coded value is 1.091 ton. This is shown in Table 16.7.

Table 16.7

−1	0	0.1	0.2	0.3	0.4	0.5	0.6	0.7	0.8	0.9	1.0
0.9	1.05	1.065	1.080	1.095	1.110	1.125	1.140	1.155	1.170	1.185	1.200

0.2	0.21	0.22	0.230	0.24	0.25	0.26	**0.27**	0.28	0.29	0.30
1.080	1.0815	1.0830	1.085	1.0860	1.088	1.0890	**1.091**	1.0920	1.094	1.0950

11. Optimization of Resources

Optimum setting values for all significant/important parameters are

Code	Parameters	Optimal setting
A	Human	80
B	Material Consumption	1.09
D	Working Capital Utilization	70

Parameter C&E may be kept at any value between the design value *i.e.,*
Parameter C, Machine Utilization may be kept from 80-90%
Parameter E, Energy consumption may be kept from 6500-7000.

12. Conclusions

1. Only one optimum level is shown based on the mathematical equation derived from experiment design.
2. Total Experiment is based on perception and intelligent guestimates and no real value based experiment is done. Hence the responses are not real responses. Student may find different response while conducting this optimization experiment.
3. This is an illustrative example for optimization. An expert on the Shianin Design of Experiment is to be consulted while doing this experiment and deriving the equation for optimum level of various parameters effecting the response.
4. Variable Search DOE tool used in this example does not cover complete use of this tool. However, major steps are covered to make student clear about this tool.

Note: *In carrying out the above resource optimization exercise, the author gratefully acknowledges the active contributions made by Shri B. Kumar, SDGM (BHEL, Hardwar).*

❍❍❍

Annexure-1

1. Forecast for World Population, Primary Energy and Power Consumption

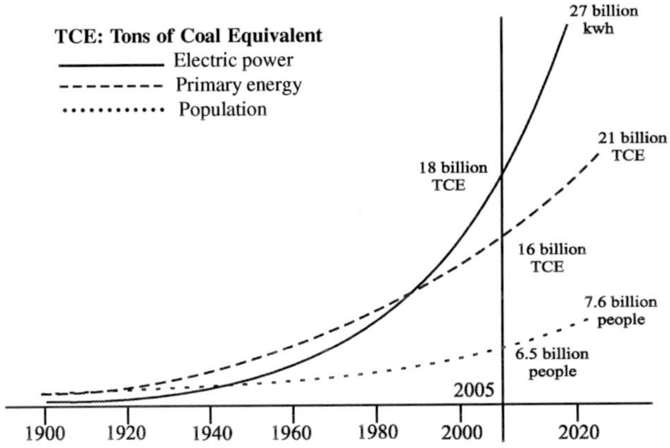

Electricity demand grows at staggering rate: By the year 2020 the global demand for electricity will increase by more than 50%.

2. Development of Primary Energy Consumption for Generation of Power and Heat

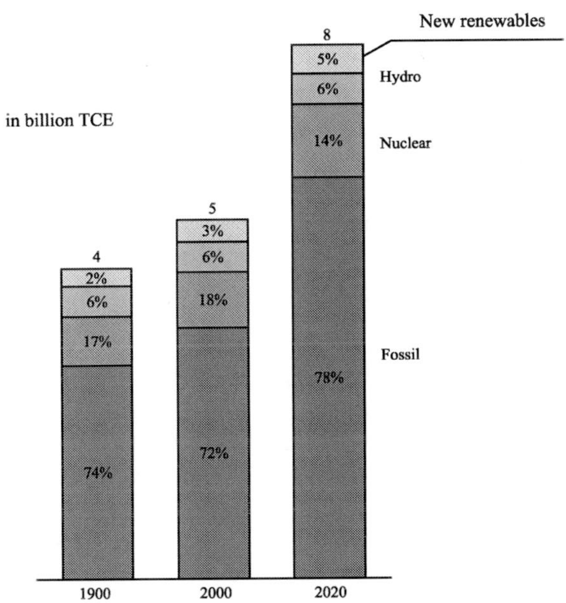

3. Power Generation Forecast

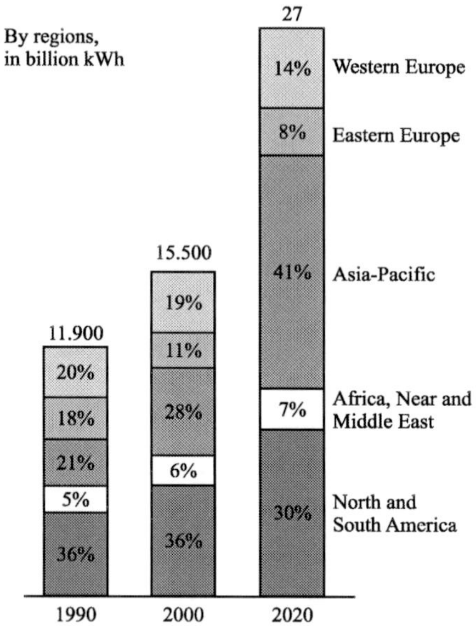

Source: Siemens PG 2005

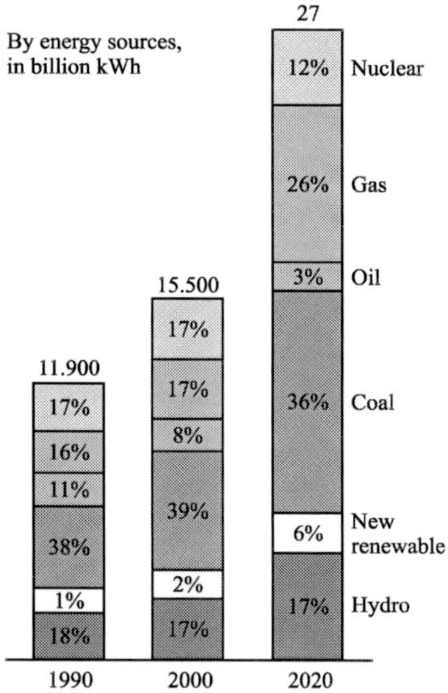

Source: Siemens PG 2005

4. Installed Power Plant Capacity Forecast

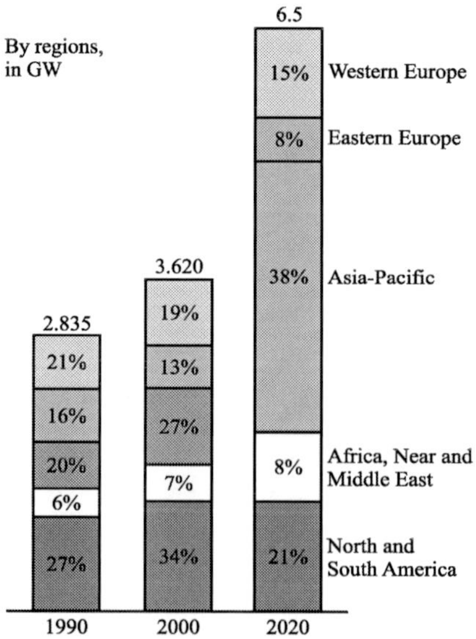

Source: Siemens PG 2005

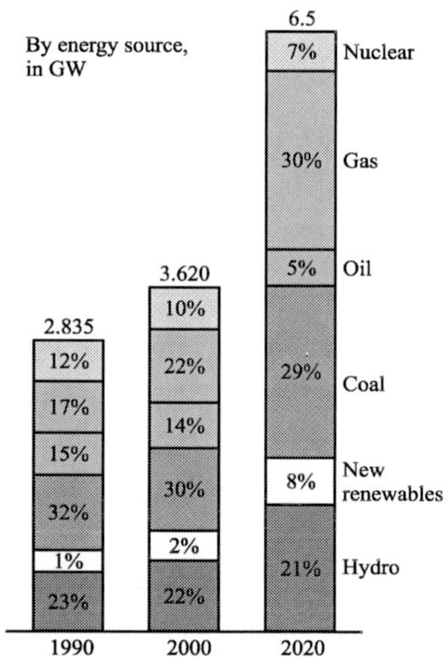

Source: Siemens PG 2005

Fossil Energy sources for generation of heat and power will con tinue to dominate throughout the world in the future.

5. Projected Range of Fossil Energy Sources

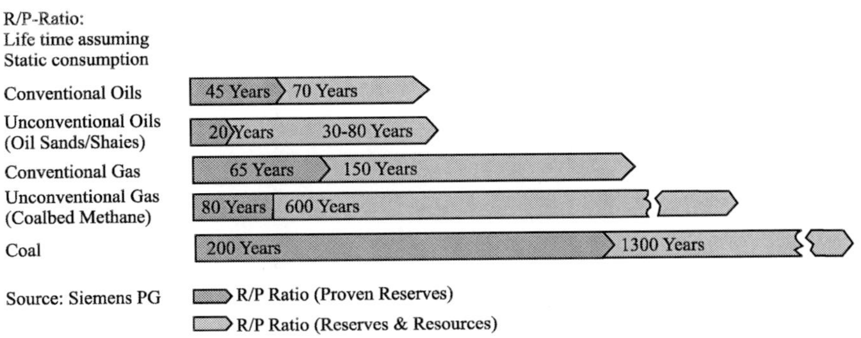

unconventional resources extend the range of fossil energy reserves. New and efficient recovery technologies can contribute to securing fuel availability and continued supply.

6. Trends in the Energy Market

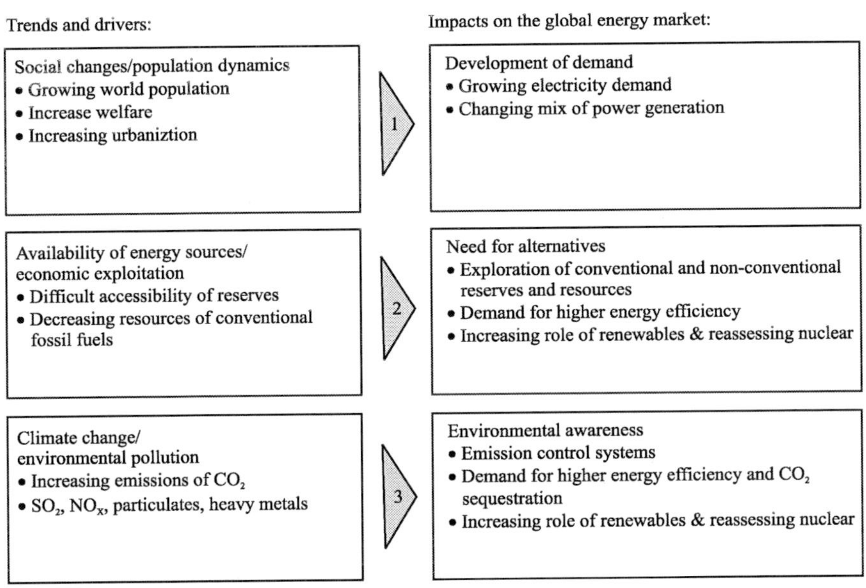

Source: Siemens AG Pocket Diary-2007.

Annexure-2

Area, Population Density, Installed Power Plant Capacity and Power Generation of Selected Countries and Regions

Region	Area in 1000 km²	Population Density		Installed capacity Gross		Power Generation Gross	
		Pop. in millions	Inhabitants Sq. Km	Absolute GW	Per capita KW	Absolute TWh	Per capita KWh
World total	**13,563**	**6450**	**48**	**4310**	**0.67**	**18130**	**2810**
Africa	**30,305**	**905**	**32**	**125**	**0.14**	**530**	**590**
-Algeria	2,382	30	14.0	8.6	0.26	32	960
-Egypt	1,001	74	74	22	0.30	99	1340
-Ethiopia	1,127	77	69	0.9	0.01	2.6	30
-Kenya	583	34	59	1.5	0.05	5.4	160
-Libya	1,760	5.9	3.2	6.4	1.14	22.0	3620
-Morocco	447	32	70	6.5	0.20	21	660
-Nigeria	924	132	142	11.0	0.08	22	170
-South Africa	1,220	47	39.0	4.1	0.87	237	5000
-Sudan	2,506	36	14	1.7	0.05	3.7	100
-Tanzania	945	38	41	1.1	0.03	2.9	80
-Uganda	236	29	12.2	0.50	0.02	2.0	70
-Zaire	2,345	54	23.0	2.9	0.06	6.0	115
-Tunisia	164	10.0	62	3.6	0.35	14	1370
America	**42,060**	**890**	**21**	**1520**	**1.71**	**6060**	**6810**
-Argentina	2,787	39	14.0	28.0	0.75	98	2530
-Brazil	8,512	186	22	98	0.54	402	2160
-Canada	9,976	32	3.2	124	3.85	627	19410
-Chile	757	16	22	12.2	0.74	55	3370
-Colombo	1,139	46	40	16	0.35	52	1140
-Ecuador	284	13.0	46.0	4.0	0.31	13.0	980
-EI Salvador	21	6.9	328	1.6	0.25	4.9	710
-Mexico	1,973	107	54	59	0.55	240	2240
-Peru	1,285	28	22	6.4	0.24	24.0	860
-USA	9,629	298.0	31.0	1112.0	3.73	4290	14400
-Venezuela	912	27.0	29.0	23.0	0.90	100.0	3740
Asia	**26,803**	**3760**	**140**	**1385**	**0.37**	**6195**	**1650**
-Bangladesh	144	142.0	998	.5.6	0.04	23.0	160
-China	9,597	1316.0	137.0	524	0.40	2475	1880
-India	3,288	1103.0	335	139.0	0.13	716	650
-Indonesia	1,919	223.0	116.0	41.1	0.19	165	740
-Iran	1,648	70.0	42.0	43.0	0.62	176.0	2530
-Iraq	438	25.2	58.0	9.0	40.0	36.0	1400
-Japan	378	128.0	339.0	273	2.14	1080	8440
-Korea, South	98	48	488.0	67.0	1.39	355.0	7430
-Malaysia	330	25.0	77.0	22.1	0.88	96.0	3790
-Myanmar	679	51.0	74.0	1.80	0.04	8.80	170
-Pakistan	804	158.0	197.0	22.0	0.14	89.0	560
-Philippines	300	83.0	277.0	19.0	0.23	56.0	670

Region	Area in 1000 km²	Population Density		Installed capacity Gross		Power Generation Gross	
		Pop. in millions	Inhabi-tants Sq. Km	absolute GW	Per capita KW	Absolute TWh	Per capita KWh
-Saudi Arabia	1,961	25.0	13.0	42.0	1.72	166.0	6750
-Singapore	0.7	4.3	6143.0	10.2	2.36	40.0	9300
-Syria	185	19.0	103.0	8.7	0.49	33.0	1740
-Thailand	514	64.0	125.0	31.0	0.48	128.0	1990
-UAE	84	4.0	54.0	18.0	4.09	51.0	11390.0
Australia/ Oceania	**8,536**	**33.0**	**4**	**62**	**1.88**	**285**	**8640**
-Australia	7,687	20.0	3.0	51.0	2.53	235	11663
-New Zeeland	269	4.0	15.0	9.2	2.27	42.0	10422
CIS	**22,260**	**280**	**13**	**345**	**1.25**	**1330**	**4750**
-Kazakistan	2,717	15.4	5.0	18.4	1.23	67	4527
-Russia	17,075	143.2	8.4	222.9	1.56	921	6432
-Ukraine	604	47.0	77.0	55.0	1.18	180.0	3871.0
Europe	**5,666**	**590**	**104**	**865.0**	**1.47**	**3735**	**6330**
-Austria	84	8.2	98.0	19.0	2.31	63.0	7690
-Belgium	31	10.3	335.0	17.0	1.60	86.0	8270
-Bosnia-Herzegovina	51	3.90	77.0	3.90	0.99	12.0	3070
-Bulgaria	111	7.7	70.0	12.4	1.57	43.0	5560
-Croatia	57	4.60	80.0	4.1	0.89	12.0	3080
-Czech Republic	79	10.2	129.0	17	1.67	79.0	7750
-Denmark	43	5.4	126.0	14.0	2.62	42.0	7730
-Finland	337	5.2	16.0	17.0	3.23	87.0	16600
-France	547	60.1	110.0	116.7	1.94	575.0	9520
-Germany	367	83.0	225.0	135.0	1.63	598.0	7230
Great Britain	245	60.0	244.0	81.0	1.35	402.0	6740
-Greece	132	11.0	84.0	14.0	1.25	60.0	5410
-Hungary	93	10.0	109.0	8.5	0.86	39.0	3860
-Ireland	70	4.10	59.0	6.1	1.48	26.0	6280
-Italy	301	58.0	193.0	84.0	1.44	319.0	5490
-Netherlands	42	16.1	338.0	21.0	1.32	102.0'	6260
-Norway	324	4.6	14.0	32.0	6.86	127.0	27490
-Poland	313	39.0	123.0	35.0	0.93	153.0	3970
-Portugal	92	10.1	114.0	13.0	1.23	57.0	4860
-Romania	238	22.3	91.0	18.0	0.82	59.0	2720
-Serbia and -Montenegro	102	11.0	103.0	11.0	1.04	36.0	3430
-Slovakia	49	5.0	110.0	8.5	1.58	33.0	6110
-Spain	505	43.0	85.0	70.0	1.64	279.0	6480
-Sweden	450	8.9	20.0	33.0	3.65	157.0	16700
-Switzerland	41	7.30	177.0	18.0	2.54	70.0	9660
-Turkey	781	73.0	94.0	39.0	0.54	156.0	2130

Source: Siemens AG-Power Generation Information Booklet-2007. Status-2006

Annexure-3

Energy Resources of India

1. Electrical Power Generation Installed Capacity

(As on 31.07.2008): = 1,45,588 MWs; ($)

		Fuel		MWs	%age
(*i*)	Thermal:	Coal	=	77,199;	53.5
		Gas	=	14,716;	10.5
		Oil	=	1,200;	0.9
		Total	=	93,115;	64.9
(*ii*)	Hydro:		=	36,159 MWs	24.7;
(*iii*)	Nuclear:		=	4,120 MWs	2.9;
@ (*iv*)	Renewable:		=	12,194 MWs	7.7;
		G. Total	=	1,45,588 MWs *	

@ Renewable energy sources include Small Hydro Plants, bio-gas, solar, wind and urban and industrial water power.

(*v*) Total Electricity Generation (energy) (2006-07) = 748 Billion KWhrs.

Note: *$It is estimated that the Peak-load Demand at present (2008) is around 1,80,000 MWs, leaving a gap of around 34,000 MWs between demand and availability. The demand is likely to go up to 2,45,000 MWs by 2020, i.e. addition of around 1,00,000 MWs over and above the present installed capacity. At the present average cost of Rs 4.5 crore per MW, a capital investment of around Rs 4,50,000 crore is required during the next 13 years (average Rs 35,000 crore per year).*

["ENERGY SAVED IS ENERGY PRODUCED"]

2. Fossil Fuel Resources: (as in 2007) : ($)

2.1 Coal and Lignite

(*i*) Estimated reserves in the country:

Proven	=	100 Billion Tonnes;
Indicated and inferred	=	160 Billion Tonnes;
Total	=	260 Billion Tonnes;

(*ii*) Present production/extraction (2006-07) = 437 Million Tonnes,

(*iii*) Present consumption level (for energy generation (2006-07) = 316 Million Tonnes,

(*iv*) It is estimated that at the present rate of consumption, India's coal reserves (proven) may last for about 250 years.

(*v*) Indian coal is generally of poorer quality with around 24% Ash and Shale contents, and the rate of energy yield (thermal) ranges from 1600 Kilo-calorie/Kg to around 2400 Kilo-calorie/Kg, as compared to high-grade coal from Australia having an energy yield of around 4000 Kilo calorie/Kg.

(*vi*) Around 20 million tonnes of high grade coal are being imported every year from Australia and some other countries, being partly utilized in Thermal Power Plants and the rest for Steel Plants (mainly coking coal for steel plants).

2.2 Oil (Petroleum) : ($)

	MT= Million Tonnes
(*i*) Estimated reserves (crude) (2007)	= 756 MT;
(*ii*) Present consumption level (2006-07)	
(*a*) Crude oil (in terms of refinery throughput)	= 147 MT;
(*b*) Petroleum Products	= 120 MT;
(*iii*) Production (2006-07)	
(*a*) Crude oil	= 34 MT;
(*b*) Petroleum Products	= 135 MT;
(*iv*) Imports and Exports (2006-07):	
(*a*) Gross Imports (crude and other Petro-products)	= (111 + 17) = 128 MT;
(*b*) Exports (petro-products other than crude) (Processed products)	= 32 MT;
(*c*) Net Imports: (2006-07)	
Crude	= 111 MT;
Other processed petro-products	= (–) 15 MT;
	Net = 95 MT;
Net value of Imports (Crude + others)	= Rs 1802 Billions;

2.3 Natural Gas: ($)

(*i*) Estimated reserves in the country (2006-07) = 1090 Billion Cu. Mtr.;

(*ii*) Gross Production (2006-07) = 32.2 Billion Cu. Mtr.;
(*iii*) Total Annual utilization (2006-07) = 31.00 Million Cu. Mtr;

Notes: ($)(*i*) *To meet increasing demands for Electrical Energy, a substantial quantity of Natural gas is being planned for import from Iran and some other countries in tire next decade.*

(*ii*) *The above Data have been taken from tire Websites of CEA, Ministry of Power, Ministry of Coal, Ministry of Petroleum, Government of India.*

3. Hydro-Power Potential

As per latest estimates (2007), potential for hydro-power generation is around 1,50,000 MWs and of which so far (31.07.08) only around 36,000 MWs could be harnessed (24%).

4. Nuclear

The present status is indicated at para 1 above; the constraints are both technological and lack of availability of usable fissile materials (mainly uranium at present). With NSG-clearance recently granted and with the prospect of Indo-US Civilian Nuclear Agreement coming to operation by end of 2008, the prospect of large expansion in Nuclear Power generation capacity in the next decade or so may become a reality (plans are in hand to add 40,000 MWs in next 10yrs.).

5. Renewables

The present status is indicated in para 1 above. Plans and efforts are in hand to harness these alternative sources as much as possible in the next 15–20 years.

Annexure-4

1. Major Petroleum Exporting Countries	2. Nuclear Supplier Group Countries
Algeria	Argentina, Australia
Angola	Austria, Belarus
Bahrain	Belgium, Brazil
Brunei Darussalam	Bulgaria, Croatia
Congo	Cyprus, Czeeh Rep.
Ecuador	Canada, China
Gabon	Denmark, Estonia
Indonesia	Finland, France
Iran	Germany, Greece
Iraq	Hungary, Ireland
Kuwait	Italy, Japan
Libyan Arab Jamahiriya	Kazakstan, Rep. of Korea
Nigeria	Latvia, Lithuania
Oman	Luxembourg, Malta
Qatar	Netherlands, New Zealand
Saudi Arabia	Norway, Poland
Syrian Arab Republic	Portugal, Romania
Trinidad and Tobago	Russian Fed., Slovakia
United Arab Emirates	Slovenia, South Africa
Venezuela	Spain, Sweden
	Switzerland, Turkey
	Ukrain, UK
	USA

Annexure-5

National Currencies of Various Countries of the World

Country	Currency	Country	Currency
Afghanistan	Afghani	Dominica	E. Carribbean Dollar
Albania	Lek	Dominician Rep.	Peso
Algeria	Dinar	Ecuador	Sucre
Antigua & Barbuda	Dollar	Egypt	Pound
Argentina	Peso	EI Salvador	Co lone
Armenia	Dram	Equatorial Guinea	Bipkwele
Aruba	Aruban Florin	Estonia	Krooni
Australia	Aus. Dollar	Ethiopia	Birr
Austria	Euro	Fiji	Fiji Dollar
Azerbaijan	Manat	Finland	Euro
Bahamas, The	Bahamian Dollar	France	Euro
Bahrain	Dinar	Gambia, The	Delasi
Bangladesh	Taka	Guinea-Bissau	Franc
Barbados	Barbados Dollar	Germany	Euro
Belarus	Euro	Ghana	Cedi
Belgium	Euro	Greece	Euro
Belize	Belize Dollar	Grenada	E. Carribbean Dollar
Benin	Franc	Guatemala	Quetzale
Bhutan	Ngultrum	Guinea	Franc
Bolivia	Boliviano	Guyana	Guyana Dollar
Botswana	Pula	Haiti	Goarde
Brazil	Reai	Honduras	Lempira
Burkina Faso	Franc	Hungary	Euro
Burundi	Franc	Iceland	Euro
Bulgaria	Euro		
Bosnia	Euro		
Cambodia	Riel	India	Rupee
Cameroon	Franc	Indonesia	Rupiah
Canada	Canadian Dollar	Iran I.R.	Rial
Cape Verde	Escudo	Iraq	Dinar
Central African Republic	Franc	Ireland	Euro
Chad	Franc	Israel	New Sheqalim
Chile	Franc	Italy	Euro
China P.R.	Yuan	Jamaica	Jamaica Dollar
China - Hong Kong	HK-Dollar	Japan	Yen
Colombia	Peso	Jordan	Dinar
Comoros	Franc	Kazakhstan	Tenge
Congo D.R.	New Zaire	Kenya	Shilling
Congo, Rep. of	Franc	Korea	Won

Country	Currency	Country	Currency
Costa Rica	Colone	Kuwait	Dinar
Cote d'Ivoire	Franc	Laos PDR	Kip
Croatia	Euro	Latvia	Lats
Cyprus	Euro	Lebanon	Pound
Czech Republic	Euro	Lesotho	Loti
Denmark	Euro	Liberia	Liberian Dollar
Djibouti	Franc	Libya	Dinar
Lithuania	Litai	St Kitts & Nevis	E Carribbean Dollar
Luxembourg	Euro	St Lucia	E Carribbean Dollar
Madagascar	Franc	St Vencent & Grens	E Carribbean Dollar
Malawi	Kwacha	Samoa	Tala
Malaysia	Ringgit	Saudi Arabia	Riyal
Maldives	Rufiyaa	Senegal	Franc
Mali	Franc	Seychelles	Rupee
Malta	Lira	Sirra Leone	Leone
Mauritania	Ouguiya	Singapore	Singapore Dollar
Mauritius	Rupee	Slovak Republic	Euro
Mexico	New Peso	Slovenia	Euro
Moldova	Lei	Solomon Island	Solomon island Dollar
Mongolia	Tugrik	South Africa	Rand
Morocco	Dirham	Spain	Euro
Mozambique	Meticai	Sri Lanka	Rupee
Myanmar	Kyat	Servia	Euro
Sudan	Pound		
Namibia	Namibia Dollar	Surinam	Guilder
Nepal	Rupee	Swaziland	Emalangeni
Netherlands	Euro	Sweden	Euro
Netherlands Antilles	Guilder	Switzerland	Euro
New Zealand	New Zealand Dollar	Syria Arab Rep.	Pound
Nicaragua	Gold Cordoba	Tanzania	Shilling
Niger	Franc	Thailand	Baht
Noigeria	Naira	Togo	Franc
Norway	Kroner	Tonga	Panne
Oman	Omani Rial	Trinidad & Tobago	T Dollar
Pakistan	Rupee	Tunisia	Dinar
Panama	Balboa	Turkey	Euro
Papua New Guinea	Kina	Uganda	Shilling
Paraguay	Guaranie	Ukraine	Hryunia
		UAE	Dirham
Peru	Nuevos Sole	UK	Pound

Country	Currency	Country	Currency
Philippines	Peso	USA	US Dollar
Poland	Euro	Uruguay	Peso
Portugal	Euro	Vanuatu	Vatu
Qatar	Riyal	Vnezuela	Bolivares
Romania	Euro	yemen Republic	Rial
Russia	Rouble	Zambia	Kwacha
Rwanda	Franc	Zimbabwe	Zimbabwe Dollar

Annexure-6A

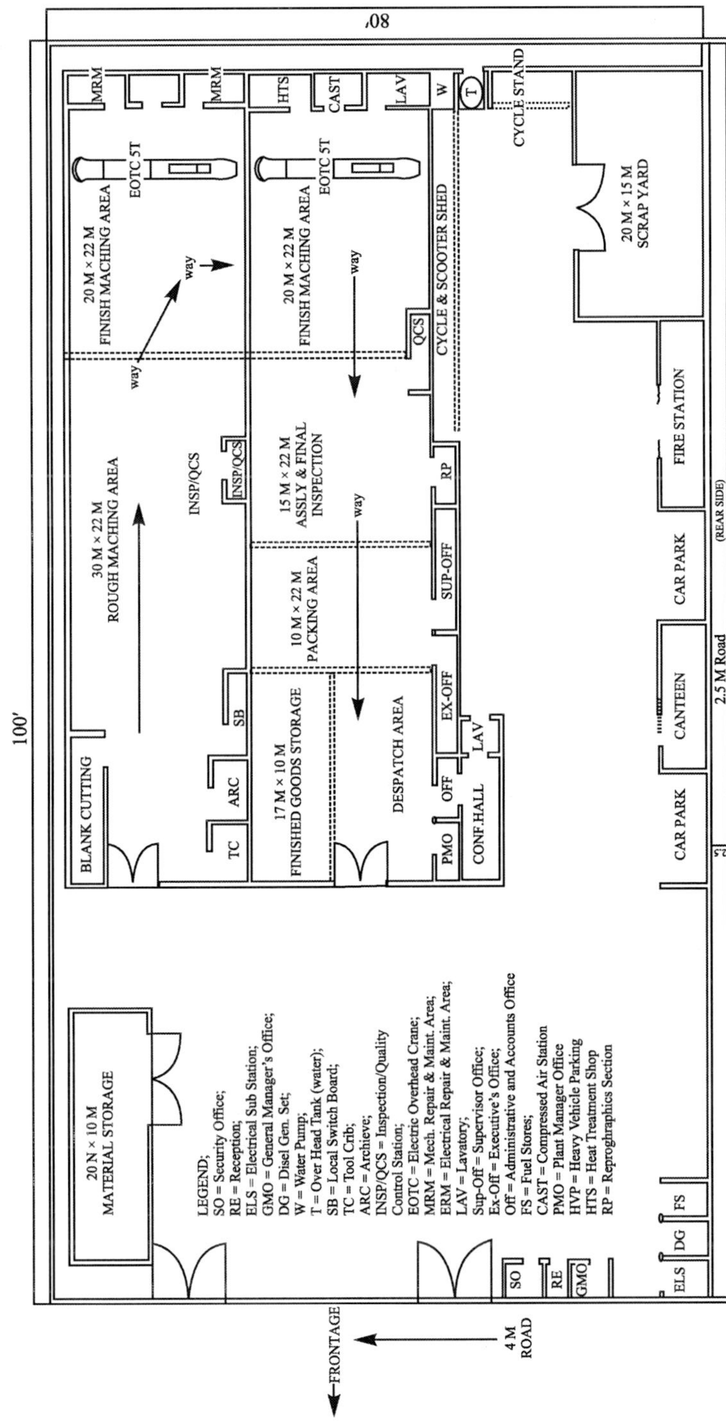

LAYOUT OF DIE SHOP (SCALE: 1 CM = 5 M)

Annexure-6(B)

FACILITIES INSTALLED
(Capital Investment made)

Sl. No.	Description	(Rs Lakh (GB)*
1	Developed industrial Plot: 100 mtr × 80 mtr = 8000 sq. Mtr @ Rs 3000 per sq mtr	240.00
2	Building 1 Shed (Main Production shop (65 m × 45 m) = 2925 sq. m @ Rs 12000 per sq mtr (with 5-T cranage structure); with services like power supply distribution system, water supply/plumbing system, telecom and computer network);	360.00
3	Incoming material stores with 5-T cranage (20 m × 10 m) = 200 sq M; @ Rs 15000 per sq mtr;	30.00
4	Other buildings (offices, canteen, lavatories, conference rooms etc.) (Approx—700 sq mtr) @ Rs 5500 sq mtr	38.00
	Sub-Total (A)	668.00
5	Plant & Machinery for Production (Machine-tools, other equipment & devices: detailed listing in Annexure 6(C)	748.00
6	Power supply system (receiving sub-station and internal distribution network (500 KVA system) (Transformer, Switchgears, Cables, etc.)	6.00
7	Diesel genset for emergency power supply (125 KVA, 416 Volts; related switch gears) (LS)	3.00
8	Overhead Water Tank (10,000 ltrs) with water pumping set, pipe-lines, pump house, etc. (LS)	6.00
9	Compresed Air supply system (Air compressor, piping, etc.) (LS)	5.00
10*	Vehicles (1 car, 1 van, 1 Truck-5-T, 1 Mini Truck-1.5-T)	33.00
11	Computers and reprographic devices	5.00
12	Fire-fighting Equipment and shed	7.00
	*GB = Gross Block	

Sl. No.	Description	(Rs Lakh (GB)
*13	Material Handling Equipment	
	2 Nos EOT cranes (5-T) (22.5 m span)	30.00
	2 Nos (2-T) Battery Operated Fortk-lifters	8.00
	3 Nos Hydraulic Load Lifters (0.5 T, 0.3 T)	1.50
	1—Jib crane (in Assembly area (2-T)	2.00
	1—Suspension crane (3-T) (8-M span) in incoming material store	3.00
14	Canteen facility (LS) (excluding building cost)**	2.00
15	Emergency Medical aid center (excluding building cost)**	1.50
16	Assorted shop accessories (LS)	3.00
17	Equipment and devices for Mechanical and Electrical/Electronic Repair Maintenance Centre (including tools, tackles etc.) (excluding building cost)**	5.00
18	Assorted tools, tackles, jigs, fixtures, etc. to start with manufacturing activities ....(LS)	5.00
	Sub-Total (B) =	877.00
	Grand total (A+B) =	1545.00

Notes: *(i) *Additional vehicles, as required, can be hired from Transport Agencies,*

**(ii) *Only furniture, and furnishing items, utencils and power supply installations; canteen service run through External Agency who brings their own equipment and utensils, cooking gas etc. Medical center (emergency medical aid) is also run through an External Agency who brings their own equipment/devices and staff.*

Annexure-6(C)

List of Machine Tools and Other Equipment for Production Shops of the Die Manufacturing Unit (including those required for inspection/QC)

Sl. No.	Description	Quantity Nos.Sets	Installed Cost (GB) Rs Lakh
	Group-A: Metal Cutting and Forming		
1	CNC Jig Boring machine	1...........	190.00
2	Optical profile grinding machine	1...........	50.00
3	Single Column Vertical boring and milling machine (table dia = 1200 mm)	1...........	80.00
4	CNC Universal Milling M/cs	2...........	120.00
5	Centre lathe (CD-1000 mm, SOB = 500 mm)	1...........	20.00
6	General purpose Milling M/cs (Horizontal)	2...........	30.00
7	General purpose Milling M/c (Vertical)	2...........	30.00
8	Surface grinding M/c, (Magnetic chuck, horizontal Bed: 1000 mm × 750 mm)	1...........	15.00
9	Surface grinding M/c (magnetic chuck, 750 mm × 550 mm)	1...........	10.00
10	Circular grinding machine	1...........	10.00
11	Lapping machine	1...........	3.00
12	Vertical slotting machine	1...........	5.00
13	Column drilling machine (19 mm) ..	1...........	2.5
14	Portable drilling machine (12 mm) ..	1...........	0.5
15	Plano-Milling machine (table size, 1000 mm × 1500 mm)	1...........	150.00
16	Tool & cutter grinding machine	1...........	1.00
17	Universal tool cutter grinding M/c	2...........	4.00
18	Bar cutting Band saw machine	2...........	8.00
19	Power hack saw machines	2...........	3.00
20	General purpose pedestal grinding machine (300 mm dia, and	2...........	1.00
	150 mm dia)	2...........	1.00
21	Abrasive cut off machine	1...........	0.50

Sl. No.	Description	Quantity Nos/Sets	Installed Cost (GB) Rs Lakh
	Group-B; Miscellaneous Equipment		
22	Optical profile projector	1...........	3.00
23	General Purpose Are Welding M/c (300 Amps)	1...........	0.50
24	Salt-bath Hardening Furnace	1...........	3.00
25	Hydraulic Straightening Press (63 T)	1...........	2.00
26	Quality control stations with necessary devices, gauges, etc.	1...........	5.00
		Total =	748.00

Annexure-6(D)

Organization Chart for the Die Manufacturing Unit

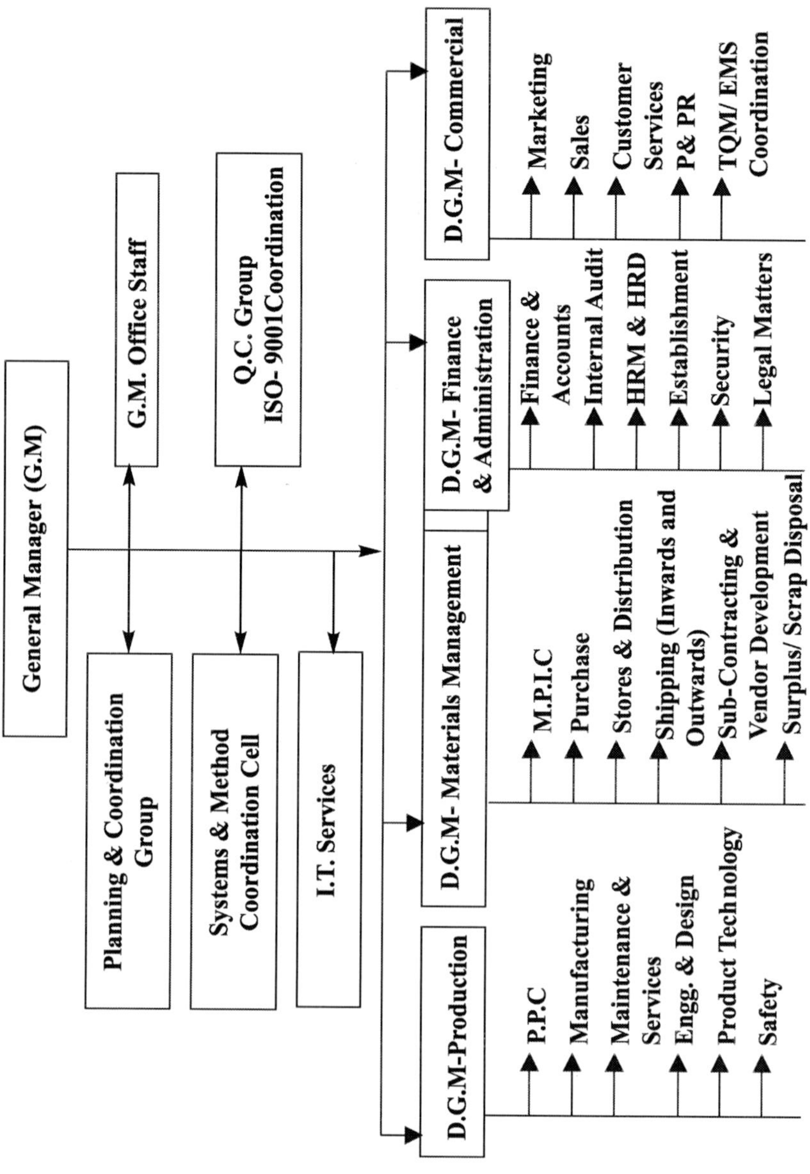

Annexure-7

Some Important Industrial Directories and Handbooks

1. Indian Industries Directory.
2. The Indian Business Directory.
3. Directory of 15000 Indian Manufacturers, Exporters and Suppliers.
4. CII (Confederation of Indian Industry) Directory.
5. World Industry and Trade Organizations in 200 Countries.
6. Handbook of Research Institutions in India.
7. The Gujarat Directory of Manufacturers.
8. Kothari's Industrial Directory of India.
9. World Importers' Directory.
10. Kompass India.
11. Directory of Useful Addresses.
12. Indian Pharmaceutical Guide.
13. Hotel and Restaurant Guide of India.
14. Dairy India.
15. Indian Poultry Industry Yearbook.
16. Indian Electronics Directory.
17. Drugs Directory.
18. All India Textiles Directory.
19. Gujarat Dyestuffs Manufacturers Association: Souvenir and Directory.
20. Gujarat State Plastic Manufacturers Association (Gspma).
21. Directory of Indian Processed Food and Allied Industries.
22. Chemical Weekly Buyers Guide.
23. All India Ready-Made Garments Exporters Directory.
24. Rubber and Rubber Goods Industry in India.
25. All India Directory of Woollen, Silk and Textile Industries.
26. Textile Directory of Ahemdabad.
27. Commercial and Industrial Guide.
28. The Indian Businessman's Guide to America.
29. The Indian Businessman's Guide to Africa.
30. The Indian Businessman's Guide to the Gulf.
31. The Indian Businessman's Guide to South America.
32. The Indian Businessman's Guide to Japan.
33. The Indian Businessman's Guide to South East Asia.
34. The Indian Businessman's Guide to Cis Countries.
35. Apeda Export Statistics for Agro & Food Products - India.
36. Indian Exporters Directory.
37. Apeda Exporters Directory.

38. Indian Export Directory.
39. Natural Resource Links.

Notes: (*i*) *In addition to the above listing, one may always refer to telephone directories, the yellow pages and other ready reference source.*

(*ii*) *The above directories and handbooks are available in large book stalls in most metropolitan cities.*

Annexure-8

National Laboratories and Institutes

(A selected listing)

The following Laboratories and Institutes in India are doing fundamental and applied research on the subject mentioned against each. Industry, trade, other research organizations, and even educational institutions can benefit from their research and application of scientific knowledge.

S. No.	Name	Location	Functions performed
1.	**National Physical Laboratory**	New Delhi	Research in problems relating to physics, both fundamental and applied. Maintenance of Standards. Testing facilities are also available.
2.	**National Chemical Laboratory**	Pune	Fundamental and applied research covering the whole field of Chemistry for which other specialized institutes have not been set up. The National Collection of Type Cultures is housed in the Laboratory.
3.	**National Metallurgical Institute**	Jamshedpur	Fundamental and applied metallurgical research. It also maintains Regional Laboratory of Foundry Research Stations.
4.	**Central Drug Research Institute**	Lucknow	All aspects of drug research including evaluation and standardization of crude drugs, Discovery of substitutes for pharmacological drugs and plants, Pharmaceutical and synthetic chemical bio-chemistry and bio-physics, infection immunization Pharmacology, Chemotherapy and experimental medicine.

S. No.	Name	Location	Functions performed
5.	**Central Food Techno-logical Research Institute**	Mysore	Food processing and conservation of food, food engineering and all aspects of fruit technology. Regional fruit and vegetable preservation stations at Trichur Nagar, Mumbai, Simla and Lucknow have been established.
6.	**Central Fuel Research Institute**	Dhanbad (Bihar)	Fundamental and applied research on fuels - solid, liquid and gaseous; Physical and Chemical surveys of Indian coals are conducted through seven coal survey stations under the institute.
7.	**Central Glass and Ceramic Research Institute**	Jadavpur (Kolkata)	Research on different aspects of glass and ceramics, pottery, porcelain, refractories and enamels; development of processes for manufacture of glass and ceramic articles; standardization of raw materials' used in the ceramic industry.
8.	**Central Building Research Institute**	Roorkee	Engineering and structural aspects of building and human comforts in relation to buildings.
9.	**Central Electr-onics Engine-ering Laboratory**	Pilani (Rajasthan)	Design and construction of electronic equipment and components and testing equipment.

S. No.	Name	Location	Functions performed
10.	**Central Electro Chemical Research Institute**	Karaikudi (Tamilnadu)	Research on different aspects of electro-chemistry, including electro-metallurgy, electro-deposition and allied problems.
11.	**Central Leather Research Institute**	Chennai	Fundamental and applied aspects of leather technology. It has regional extension centers at Mumbai, Kolkata, Kanpur, Rajkot and Jalandhar.
12.	**Central Mining Research Station**	Dhanbad (Bihar)	Research in methods of mining, research on safety in mining and mine machinery.
13.	**Regional Research Labora-tory**	Hyderabad	Research on problems relating to the industries and raw materials of the region.
14.	**Indian Institute of Bio-Chemistry**	Kolkata	Research in various aspects of bio-chemistry, as applied to Medicine, bacteriology, etc.
15.	**Central Salt and Marine Research Centre**	Bhavnagar (Gujarat)	Investigation on production of pure salts; reduction in cost of production, economic by-products of salt manufacture; of new methods and techniques for the recovery, production and utilization of marine and allied chemicals.
16.	**Earth-quake Research Institute**	Roorkee	Research on seismic zones and development of technology for earthquake damage control systems, etc.

S. No.	Name	Location	Functions performed
17.	**Hydrology Research Institute**	Roorkee	Hydrological research, river research, water shed research, etc.
18.	**Regional Research Laboratory**	Jammu Tawi (J&K)	Research in problems relating to the industries and raw materials of the region and research specially directed to medicinal plants of the Himalayas (Kashmir Region).
19.	**Central Mechanical Engineering Institute**	Durgapur (West Bengal)	Research in mechanical engineering in all aspects.
20.	**National Environ-ment Engineering Research Institute**	Nagpur (Maharashtra)	Research in all aspects of public health and environmental engineering, co-ordination of work of all interested agencies in this field in the country.
21.	**National Aeronau-tical Laboratory**	Bangalore	Scientific Investigation of the flight problems with a view to their practical application to the design, construction and operation of Aircrafts in India.
22.	**Indian Institute of Petroleum**	Dehradun (Uttarakhand)	Research in Petroleum refining and processing of natural gas, petro-chemicals; providing facilities for the training of personnel for petroleum industry.
23.	**National Geophysical Research Institute**	Hyderabad	Correlation of the field data in all fundamental aspects of geology and geo-physics with laboratory investigations and theoretical studies.

S. No.	Name	Location	Functions performed
24.	**National Institute of Oceano-graphy**	Panaji (Goa)	Research on various aspects of physical, biological and chemical oceanography including prospecting for petroleum and minerals in sea bed.
25.	**Regional Research Labora-tory**	Jorhat (Assam)	Research in problems relating to more efficient utilization and better conservation of important natural resources of Assam and other regional needs posing special problems.
26.	**Central Indian Medicinal Plants Organi-zation**	Lucknow	Co-ordination of activities in the development and cultivation and utilization of medicinal plants on organized basis.
27.	**Central Scientific Instru-ments Organi-zation**	Chandigarh	Functions performed Promotion and development of indigenous manufacture of scientific instruments for teaching, research and industry.
28.	**Indian National Scientific Documen-tation Centre**	New Dehi	Provides full range of documentation services.
29.	**National Register Unit**	New Delhi	Maintenance of information pertaining to Indian scientific and technical personnel in the country and abroad.

S. No.	Name	Location	Functions performed
30.	**Central Design and Engine-ering Research Institute**	New Delhi	Provides assistance in the translation of laboratory results into industrial practice and designing of plants based on process developed.
31.	**Regional Research Laboratory**	Bhubaneshwar	Research in problems relating to the industries and raw materials of the region.
32.	**National Biological Laboratory**	New Delhi	Fundamental and applied research in modern biological sciences.
33.	**Structural Engine-ering Research Centre**	Roorkee	Research in specialized design and development work in structural problems connected with buildings, bridges and other structures.
34.	**Industrial Toxicolo-gical Research Centre**	Lucknow	Studies in harmful effects of industrial toxins on skin, blood, Gastro-intestinal tract, central nervous system, bones, etc.
35.	**Bhava Atomic Research Centre (Barc)**	Trombay (Mumbai)	Atomic and Nuclear energy research centre.
36.	**Tata Institute of Fundame-netal Research**	Mumbai	Scientific research institute (fundamental research in all branches of science).
37.	**Institute of Plasma Research**	Gandhinagar (Gujarat)	Scientific research on plasma physics and controlled nuclear fusion technology.

Annexure-9

List of Books for Suggested Reading

(A selected listing only)

S. No.	Title of the book/reference		Author/Source
	(A) ORGANIZATION AND GENERAL MANAGEMENT		
1.	Natural Resource Management: An Introduction	-	Edited by Azmal Hussain (ICFAI Univ. Press)
2.	Business Organization and Management	-	by M.C. Shukla
3.	Factory Organization and Management	-	by NFT Saunders
4.	Production and Operations Management	-	by Chunawalla Patel
5.	Fundamentals of Industrial Administration	-	by Edward Tregaskiss
6.	Production Planning and Inventory Control	-	by John E. Magee
7.	Principles of Management	-	by M.C Shukla
8.	Training and Development Hand Book	-	Published by McGraw Hill Book Co.
9.	Business Incubation: An Introduction	-	Edited by V.V. Ramani, A.V. Balakrishna
10.	Management Ideas that Work	-	by Nasreen Taher, Swapna Gopalan
11.	Management and Organization	-	by Loui A. Allen
12.	Industrial Organization and Management	-	Published by McGraw Hill Book Co.
13.	Story telling in Management	-	by Nasreen Taher Swapna Gopalan
14.	Lean Management: Concepts and Industry Perspectives	-	E. Mrudula
15.	New Concepts in Management	-	by Iswar Dayal
16.	The Ethics of Corporate Conduct	-	Edited by Clarence Walton (Prentice Hall)
17.	E-Governance in Developing Nations	-	by S.S. Misra, Amrita Mukherjee
18.	HRM in the Knowledge Economy	-	by G.B.K. Murthy
19.	Empowering Teams: An Introduction	-	by Swapna Gopalan, Nasreen Taher

S. No.	Title of the book/reference		Author/Source
20.	Management Training in Organizations	-	by Iswar Dayal
21.	Human Capital Measurement: An Introduction	-	by K. Sangeetha
22.	Visions and Mission Statements: Concepts and Cases	-	by Anitha Arunsimha
23.	Research and Development Management	-	by Daniel D. Roman
24.	Management Insights: Perspective from Experts	-	Edited by K.B.S. Kumar
25.	Case Studies on Growth Strategies: Vol-I	-	Edited by Souvik Dhar
26.	Knowledge Sharing: An Introduction	-	Keka Lahiri
27.	Management Guide for Engineers and Technical Administrators	-	Published by McGraw Hill Book Co.
28.	Engineered Materials Hand Book International	-	Published by ASM
29.	Leadership-A 360-Degree Appraisal	-	K.B.S. Kumar
	(B) FINANCIAL MANAGEMENT		
1.	Financial Management NPC Management Guide	-	by Shahid Pravin
2.	Finance for Non-Finance Executives (Vision Books New Delhi)	-	by N.J. Yasaswi
3.	Financial Management: Theory and Practice	-	Published by Tata McGraw Hill, New Delhi
4.	Financial Management and Policy	-	Published by Prentice Hall, NJ. USA
5.	Financial Management	-	by M.Y. Khan and P.K. Jain
6.	Performance Budgeting (NPC)	-	by U.K. Kohli
7.	Guide to Company Balance Sheet and Profit & Loss Account	-	by H.P.S. Pahawa
8.	How to use Management Ratios	-	by C.A. Westwick
9.	Financial Management Practices and Theories	-	by Prasanna Chandra

S. No.	Title of the book/reference		Author/Source
10.	Accounting and Finance for Managers	-	by B.K. Chatterjee
11.	Problems of Working Capital	-	by R.K. Misra
12.	Watch your figures	-	by C. Northcote Parkinson and M.K. Rustamji
13.	Cost Estimating for Engineering and Management	-	by Philip F. Ostwald
14	Business Environment Analysis- An Introduction	-	Edited by Sankar Muralidharan
(C)	**PROJECT MANAGEMENT AND CAPITAL BUDGETING**		
1.	Projects: Planning, Analysis, Selection, Implementation & Review.	-	by Prasana Chandra
2.	Project Preparation. Appraisal, Budgeting and Implementation	-	by Prasana Chandra
3.	Capital Budgeting and Company Finance	-	by A.J. Merret and Allen Sykes
4.	Network Analysis for Planning and Scheduling	-	by A. Battersby, (MacMillan, London)
5.	"Capital Budgeting in Indian Industries"	-	Indian Management, March 1973
6.	"Capital Expenditure Analysis in Practice"	-	Indian Management, July 1975
7.	Capital Budgeting Hand Book	-	Published by Dow-Jones-Irwin, Ill, USA
8.	Project Appraisal and Planning for Developing countries	-	Published by Hienemann Educational Book, London
9.	Project Management with CPM and PERT	-	by J.J. Moder and C.R. Philips
10.	Manual of Industrial Project Analysis in Developing Countries	-	Methodology and Case studies (OECD Sponsored)
11.	The Capital Expenditure Decision	-	by Qurin D.G.
12.	Industrial Engineering Hand Book Book Co. (Maynnard and others)	-	Published by McGraw Hill
13.	Hand Book of Project reports	-	by R.K. Garg, published by Bharat Publishing House

S. No.	Title of the book/reference	Author/Source
14.	Management by Network Analysis	- by Dr. A. Bhattacharya, Published by IE (I), Calcutta
15.	Project Management	- by B.B. Goel, Published by Deep and Deep Publications
16.	Capital Investment Projects: Concept to Commissioning	- by D.J. Syam, EMPI-Business School Publishing, New Delhi
	(D) MATERIALS MANAGEMENT	
1.	Material Management	- by A.R. Palit
2.	Inventory Control: Theory and Practice	- by Starr and Miller
3.	Inventory Management in India	- by R.S. Chadda
4.	Purchasing Hand Book	- by Alijian G.W. (Published by McGraw Hill Book Company)
5.	Production and Inventory Management in Computer Age	- by Oliver W. Wight
6.	Stock Control in Manufacturing Industries	- by Adin B. Thomas
7.	Materials Management	- by Dean S. Ammer
8.	Logistics and Supply Chain Management	- by Martin Christopher (Pitman)
9.	Supply Chain Management for Global Competition	- Edited by B.S. Sahay (MacMillan)
	(E) MARKETING/COMMERCIAL MANAGEMENT	
1.	Business Marketing: An Introduction	- Edited by S.N. Mookherjee
2.	Marketing Management- A Finance Emphasis	- by Dr. B.K. Chatterjee
3.	Principles of Marketing Management	- by Philip Kotler
4.	Effective Marketing Management	- Published by Gower Publishing Co. Ltd. England.
5.	Negotiation Hand Book	- by Patrick J. Cleary (Prentice Hall)
6.	Marketing in Unpredictable World	- by Amitabha Ghose

S. No.	Title of the book/reference	Author/Source
7.	Services Marketing: Issues and Cases	- by Keka Lahiri
8.	Customer Retention Management; Concepts	- by S. Jaya Krishna
	(F) QUALITY MANAGEMNT, STANDARDS, ETC.	
1.	Hand Book on Quality Control	- by J.M. Juran
2.	ISO-9000 Quality Management Standards (ISO Standard Compendium)	- Published by ISO-Geneva
3.	CII and EFQM -Model for Business Excellence (TQM)	- Published by TQM-Division, CII India, New Delhi
4.	Hand Book of Statistical Quality Control	- Published by BIS, New Delhi
5.	ISO-9000- What it is and Why is it Important	- by Praful C. Mehta (East Man Kodak, New York)
6.	ISI-Hand Book of Mathematical, Physical, Chemical and Engineering Tables (SP-8-1970: BIS- New Delhi)	- Published by BIS, New Delhi:
7.	Standardization: A New Discipline	- by Lal C. Varman
	(G) MISCELLANEOUS	
1.	Labour Laws-One should know	- by Ajay Garg
2.	Law of Contract	- by Avtar Singh
3.	Various Indian Acts and Regulations (Statutory) Relating to Industrial and Business Establishments as listed out in Chapter-14, Section-7 of this book.	....
4.	Hand Book of Enquiry Officers	- by G.B. Singh
5.	Industrial Safety	- by Ronold P. Blake
6.	Value Engineering for Management	- R.H.V. Lawson
7.	Materials Handling-Traffic and Transportation	- by Elias S. Tyler
8.	Perspective Management	- by V.S. Murthy
9.	Safety Management	- by R.H. Simonds
10.	Evaluation of Management Training	- by Peter Warr

S. No.	Title of the book/reference	Author/Source
11.	Technological Forecasting and Long Range Planning	- by Robert U. Ayers
12.	The Corporate Planning Process	- by Melville C. Branch
13.	Computers and Management in a Changing Society	- by D.H. Sanders
14.	Communication (NPC)	- by Ena Chaudhary
15.	Value Engineering: A Systematic Approach	- by A.E. Mudge
16.	Industrial Security Management	- by S.C. Dey, S.C. Kaushal
17.	Corporate Laws and Secretarial Practices	- by N.D. Kapoor
18.	Dictionary of International Trade	- by Subhash Narula, published by Tax Institute
19.	Mercantile Law	- by P.R. Chadha
20.	Intellectual Property Right	- by Sahid Ali Khan
21.	Intellectual Property-a power Tool for Economic Growth	- by Kamal Idris (WIPRO)
22.	Copyright Act, Patent Act. Patent Rule etc.	- Publishers of Law books
23.	The Essential Guide to Knowledge Management	- by Amrita Tiwana (Pearson Education Asia)
24.	The Commerce of Environment	- by Amandio FCD Silva
25.	Hand Book of Corporate Operations Management	- by D.J. Syam, Cambridge India (Kolkata)
26.	New Decision-Making Tools for Managers	- Dorian Shainin (Harvard University Press) (Co-author)
27.	Statistics in Action	- Dorian Shainin (McGraw-Hill) (Co-author)
28.	Industrial Engineering Hand Book	- Dorian Shainin (Co-author) (McGraw Hill)

INDEX

F

G

H

I

J

K

L

M

N

O

P

Q

R

S

T

V

W

❍❍❍